AROUND CHAUTAUQUA LAKE

Fifty Years of Photographs

1875 - 1925

AROUND CHAUTAUQUA LAKE

Fifty Years of Photographs 1875 - 1925

Paul Leone

Mary Poshka

With the assistance of
Victor Norton, Jr.

Chautauqua Region Press
Westfield, New York
1997

Cover: Mayville dock, 1875. The *Floating Bird*, *Nettie Fox*, *C.J. Hepburn*, and the *Col. Phillips*. The tracks and depot of the Buffalo, Corry and Pittsburgh Railroad, formerly the Buffalo, Oil Creek Crosscut Railroad, are visible in the foreground. *CCHS*

Closing photos, clockwise from upper left:

Art Carpenter, Sr. in rowboat. *VN*
Fishermen in Mayville. *CMN*
Charles M. and Sadie Sweet Nichols. *CMN*
Summer cottage. *RL*

Printed in the United States of America

International Standard Book Number: 0-9658955-0-5

Chautauqua Region Press
19 Spring Street
Westfield, New York 14787

TABLE OF CONTENTS

ACKNOWLEDGMENTS

Chautauqua County is an area rich in history. Our yesterdays have held a fascination for local historians and writers for many years. Thanks to these caretakers and chroniclers of our county's history we have a priceless well of information at our fingertips. Without their many hours of research and meticulous work at preservation, this book would not have been possible. We extend our heartfelt appreciation to Reed Library at the State University College at Fredonia, New York; the Chautauqua County Historical Society, Michelle Henry, Director; Mrs. C. Malcolm Nichols; the Fenton Historical Society, Christin Stein, Director; Victor Norton, Jr.; Roger L. Westley; and Jack T. Ericson for granting permission to make use of their photographic and post card archives.

We would especially pay tribute to Harold J. Ahlstrom and Helen G. Ebersole, authors of *Chautauqua Lake Steamboats* and *Chautauqua Lake Hotels*, respectively, both published by the Fenton Historical Society. Their scholarship has proven invaluable to the authors.

A special thank you to Jack T. Ericson for the many hours he devoted to searching the photographic archives at the Reed Library and the Chautauqua County Historical Society. We are also grateful to Devon Taylor, Village of Mayville Historian, and June Miller-Spann, archivist at Smith Memorial Library at Chautauqua Institution, for their help, and for the cooperation of the Patterson Library in Westfield, Deborah Williams, Director. Finally, the authors thank Lori Crowell of Chautauqua Printing for her expertise and patience during the preparation of the book's final layout.

Credits for the images used in *Around Chautauqua Lake* are given in the captions according to the following code system:

RL - Reed Library

CCHS - Chautauqua County Historical Society

FHS - Fenton Historical Society

CMN - C. Malcolm Nichols

JE - Jack T. Ericson

PL - Patterson Library

VN - Victor Norton, Jr.

RW - Roger Westley

INTRODUCTION

A photographic history of Chautauqua Lake and its surroundings reveals a community blessed with physical beauty and an energetic spirit determined to exploit it. By the mid 1870s, when the earliest of the photographs in *Around Chautauqua Lake* were taken, the area was only just emerging from virtual isolation. Despite its local popularity and obvious attractiveness, the lake had been, until then, merely the most convenient route between the north and south county and between Lake Erie and the Ohio River. Before the arrival of the Crosscut Railroad at Mayville in 1868, the lake was almost unknown outside its immediate vicinity.

The opening of the Methodist summer camp at Fair Point in 1874 and President Ulysses S. Grant's visit there the following summer brought the Chautauqua region national recognition. Commercial interests, specifically the railroads, succeeded through the next quarter century in making Chautauqua Lake one of the mid-Atlantic's premier resort areas. Touting Chautauqua's healthy and bracing climate, as well as its serene beauty, local developers built large and extravagant hotels around the lake to accommodate a growing number of vacationers. Chautauqua County contained more miles of railroad track in 1875 than any other county in New York State. Major lines passed through Mayville on the lake's northern tip and Jamestown to the south. The lake was no more than a few hours journey from most of the major Middle Atlantic cities and only an overnight trip from New York or Chicago. In the days before the automobile, the well-to-do often spent the greater part of the "season" at a resort. The best of Chautauqua's hotels, like the fashionable Kent House at Lakewood and the magnificent Grand Hotel at Point Chautauqua, provided their guests not only with solicitous service but with recreational activities including dancing, sailing, fishing, and billiards. And always, the graceful and majestic steamboats of the "great white fleet" were available to ferry passengers from one lake site to another.

Around Chautauqua Lake ought very well to contribute to the image of romance and simplicity one often holds of the late Victorian and early twentieth century years. Certainly, selecting and preparing these photographs contributed to the longing of one who would like to have experienced those years. Romance aside, however, the photographs also depict the results of an agressive energy and industry among Chautauqua's movers and shakers who understood opportunity. In a region of such natural advantages in a developing country, fortunes might be made. A random selection of turn-of-the-century photographs from around Chautauqua Lake provides ample evidence of a vigorous entrepreneurial spirit and of the work of the area's most notable entrepreneurial family.

William Broadhead from Jamestown made his fortune in textiles. Before the new century was very far along, his two sons controlled the major steamboat lines on the lake as well as the electric railway lines running on either side. The Broadheads had built a hugely popular amusement park at Celoron, and they were engaged in the manufacture of shale brick for the paving of Jamestown's streets. Mr. Almet N. Broadhead held primary responsibility for his family's enterprises. Not all of his endeavors were profitable, but, as the photographs make clear, Almet Broadhead ran a first-rate operation.

It will be useful here to mention the several names of the Chautauqua Lake Railway that for sixty years ran between Jamestown and Mayville on the lake's east side. The local railroad commenced operation in 1887 under the original name, but the constant strugggle involved in turning a profit necessitated four separate reorganizations during its lifetime. After the railroad extended to Barcelona Harbor in 1894, it was called the Jamestown & Lake Erie (J. & L.E.) Railroad. It became the Jamestown & Chautauqua (J. & C.) Railroad in 1898 and the Jamestown, Chautauqua & Lake Erie (J.C. & L.E.) Railroad from about the turn of the century until 1914 when the Broadhead interests purchased and converted it from a steam to an electric line. The Jamestown, Westfield & Northwestern (J.W. & N.W.) Railroad, as it was then known, is well within the memories of Chautauqua County's elders. One may follow its route along much of the lake shore by noting the path of the posts and wires still in place.

Credit for the minute identification of steamboats, buildings, lake sites, and all other lake appurtenances in *Around Chautauqua Lake* belongs to Victor Norton, Jr. of Bemus Point. Vic is Chautauqua Lake's most knowledgable historian. I am indebted to him for the many pleasurable hours we spent together examining photographs and for the pleasant trip we took around the lake following both the Chautauqua Traction and the J.W. & N.W. routes. The text of this volume benefits from his technical expertise as well as his discerning eye. Pointing out the Traction Company's double line in a Sherman's Bay photograph, for example, he told me the wires were made of copper. The double line was expensive, but it reduced the possibility of voltage loss. To my reverential silence, both for the extent of his knowledge and for Almet Broadhead's impressive class, he added, with a smile of approbation, "Broadhead had to have been the best."

Most of these photographs appeared on stereopticon or postal cards, and most were snapped by local photographers. Chief among them are the two Monroes, Charles and George, who had studios in Jamestown; Jamestown photographers Hoard and Upham; and Rufus Beaujean and his successor, H.M. Smith from Mayville. Generally, the stereopticon cards are earlier. It is my fervent hope that *Around Chautauqua Lake* changes the reader's perception of the lake. By all means take this volume with you on your next trip *Around Chautauqua Lake.*

PML
May 25, 1997

Chautauqua Lake has been a center for recreation and amusement since passenger railroad service connected the Chautauqua County communities of Mayville, Westfield and Jamestown with Pittsburgh, Cleveland and Buffalo in the 1860s. From Mayville and Jamestown visitors would travel by steamboat to points around the lake. During their heyday in the late nineteenth and early twentieth centuries, steamers not only provided transportation for pleasure seekers but for local residents as well. Daily trips between Jamestown and Mayville were made with stops at various points along the way. Steamers also offered day excursions and carried freight and the U.S. mail up and down the lake. In 1900 there were six large steamers operating on the lake.

Grand hotels were built along with more modest establishments to accommodate the burgeoning tourist population. Communities began to spring up around the resort areas. Local businesses supplied the needs of summer sojourners and the large hotels. Tourism meant employment for the residents of these new towns.

Who came to Chautauqua Lake? A promotional pamphlet on the lake and its environs written in 1874 said this: "Any one of respectability may come here and spend a few weeks or months at comparatively small cost, not being obliged to follow the dictates of gaudy fashion and costly entertainments in order to be respected. Comfort and pleasure are the ruling passions rather than a desire to display costly trappings, followed by riotous and ruinous dissipation."

Just as advancements in transportation ignited the halcyon days of Chautauqua County, they also signalled the end of the era. The advent of personal automobiles allowed people to travel to other parts of the country at their leisure. Travel to vacation spots all over the United States became feasible for families. Chautauqua Lake's steamers and great hotels became a memory. Fires consumed many of the hotels. Some fell into disuse, were abandoned, and razed.

But there is a saying "What goes around, comes around." And, indeed, we have come full circle. Tourism today is Chautauqua County's biggest industry. Chautauqua Lake is easily accessible by a fine grid of highways. Chautauqua Institution attracts visitors from all over the world. Summer residents come to cottages, summer homes, condominiums, campgrounds, motels and bed and breakfast accommodations.

The lake today offers something for everyone. The white sails of the regatta and the hum of motor boats abound as water skiiers demonstrate their skill. The lake is still renowned for its fishing. The arrival of winter means a quiet time for enjoying skating, ice fishing and snowmobiling.

Chautauqua Lake's natural beauty is enjoyed by thousands each summer. Its intriguing peninsulas and rolling hills still catch the eye and splendid vistas attract many a photographer. At night the water is a reflecting pool for beautiful sunsets and lights glimmering on the shoreline.

And there are gentle reminders of a past gone but not forgotten. The days of the steamboats were recalled in 1976 as the *Chautauqua Belle* was launched on her maiden voyage. The Bemus Point-Stow Ferry continues to make its daily runs at the narrows though shadowed by the Veterans Memorial Bridge spanning the lake. Nineteenth century dwellings around the lake retain their beauty and charm. The sole survivors of the grand hotels, the Hotel Athenaeum at Chautauqua and the Lenhart at Bemus Point are extant reminders of a time of grace and elegance.

We cordially invite you to join us as we take a step back in time to wander *Around Chautauqua Lake.*

MLP
June 4, 1997

About Victor Norton, Jr.

Four generations of Nortons worked the lake out of Bemus Point. Patriarch of the family, Caleb Norton, removed from Dewittville up the lake about 1820 and purchased land along Lakeside Drive. There he opened a blacksmith shop and helped construct Bemus Point's steamboat dock. Caleb was a passenger on the steamer *Chautauqua* when it blew its boiler at Whitney's Bay in 1871. This, the lake's worst accident, claimed eight lives and caused injuries from which Caleb never recovered.

Sons Earl and George ran a boat livery which they sold out to Mep Mason, Chautauqua Lake's fiddler and owner of the Mason House, around the turn of the century. About this time, George bought a small plate camera and began to shoot pictures of the buildings and folk around Bemus Point. Victor, Sr., Earl's son, reacquired the boat livery around 1915. Victor, Sr. delighted in lake history and seriously collected and documented lake photographs. With his son, Victor, Jr., he operated the boat livery and the Bemus Point Cottages until his death in 1975. Victor, Jr., continued the business for ten more years. He and Malcolm Nichols planned the Fenton Museum's first Chautauqua Lake Room. Vic is still in possession of George's original glass plates, and he maintains one of Chautauqua County's finest photographic archives.

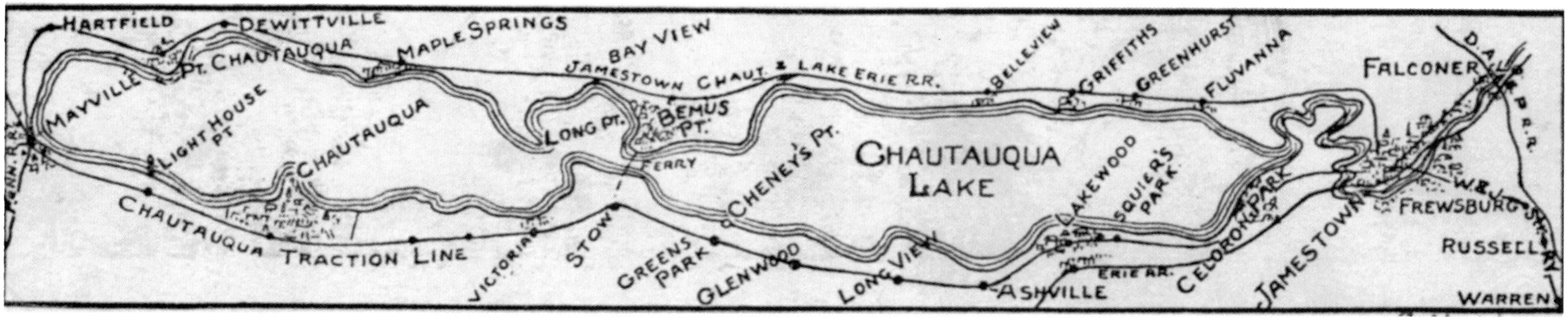

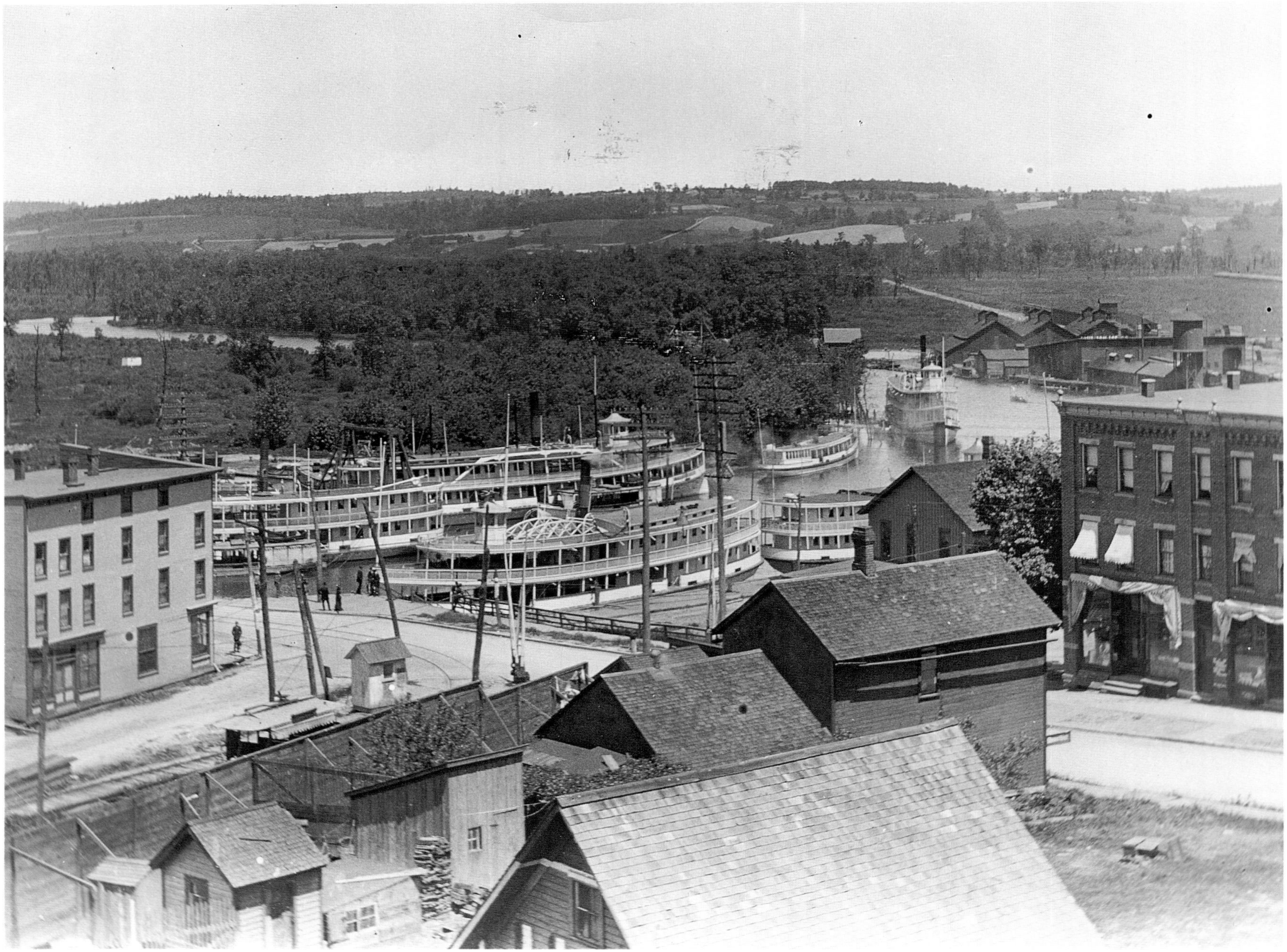

JAMESTOWN BOATLANDING

The boatlanding at Jamestown is located along the curving Chadakoin River, three miles below Chautauqua Lake, at the intersection of Eighth Street and Jones and Gifford Avenue. During the era of the lake resorts and steamboat travel, the boatlanding became a primary terminal of the sophisticated network of transportation facilities servicing the lake. The major steamboats in Chautauqua Lake's fleet docked either here or at Mayville. By the early twentieth century a steam railroad on the east side of the lake and an electric line on the west, each with a station at the boatlanding, connected Jamestown with Mayville. Jamestown and the lake were easily accessible to Cleveland, Pittsburgh, New York, and even Chicago via the Erie Railroad system. The Jamestown Street Railway, a trolley line, ferried passengers from downtown Jamestown to the boatlanding. The lake's popularity and commercial interests working to exploit it made the boatlanding a colorful and active place. Today the site is a city park known as McCrea's Point.

Boatlanding, ca. 1900. Clockwise from the dock: the *City of Cincinnati*, the small steamer *Celoron* moored by the *City of Cleveland*, the small steamer *Greenhurst* by the *City of Chicago*, the *City of Rochester,* the *City of New York*, and the *City of Buffalo* (stern only). The wooden frame building on the dock is the waiting room for both the Jamestown, Chautauqua and Lake Erie Railroad and the steamboats. At the curve of the Chadakoin stand the railroad's engine house and water tower. The track bed leads around the east side of the lake. The large building in three sections beyond is Johnson's Icehouse. The building to the right is today Joyce's Keg Room. *JE*

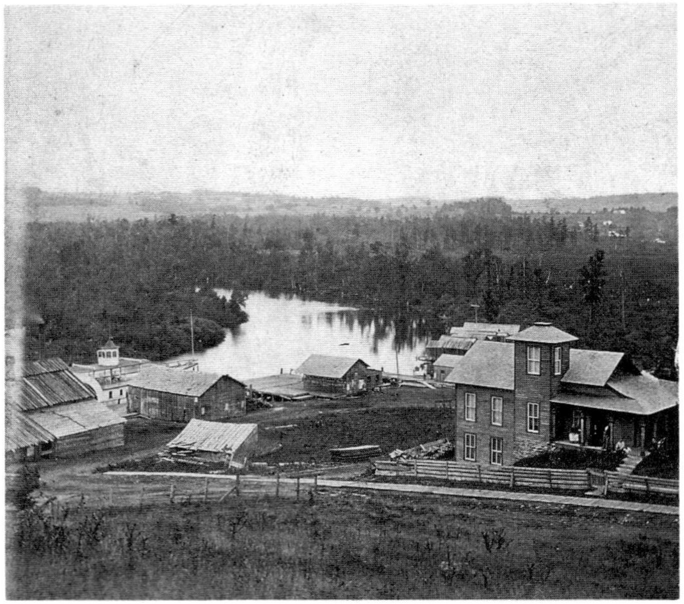

Boatlanding, ca. 1875. This early view shows the boatlanding in its primitive stage. Three large steamships, the *Col. Phillips*, whose pilot house is visible in the photograph, the first *Jamestown*, and the *Nettie Fox* were running the lake at this time. The earliest of the lake resorts had been built and the glory days of Chautauqua Lake were at hand. *CCHS*

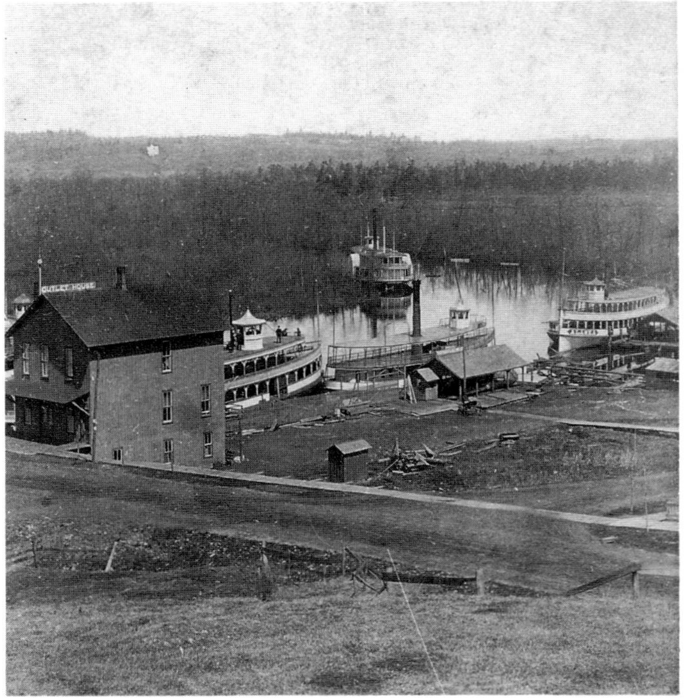

Boatlanding, 1880. Five years later, the second *Jamestown* is just visible behind the building. Shown clockwise are the *Mayville* at the bend, the *Alaska*, the *W.B. Shattuc*, and the *J.A. Burch*. *CCHS*

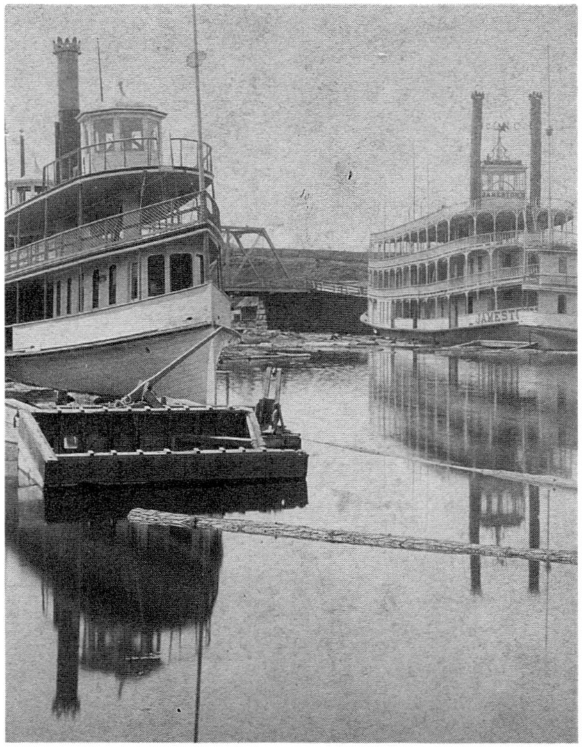

Boatlanding, ca. 1881. The *W.B. Shattuc*, the *Jamestown*, and the stern of the *M.A. Griffith* seen from the north looking toward the Fairmount Avenue bridge. *CCHS*

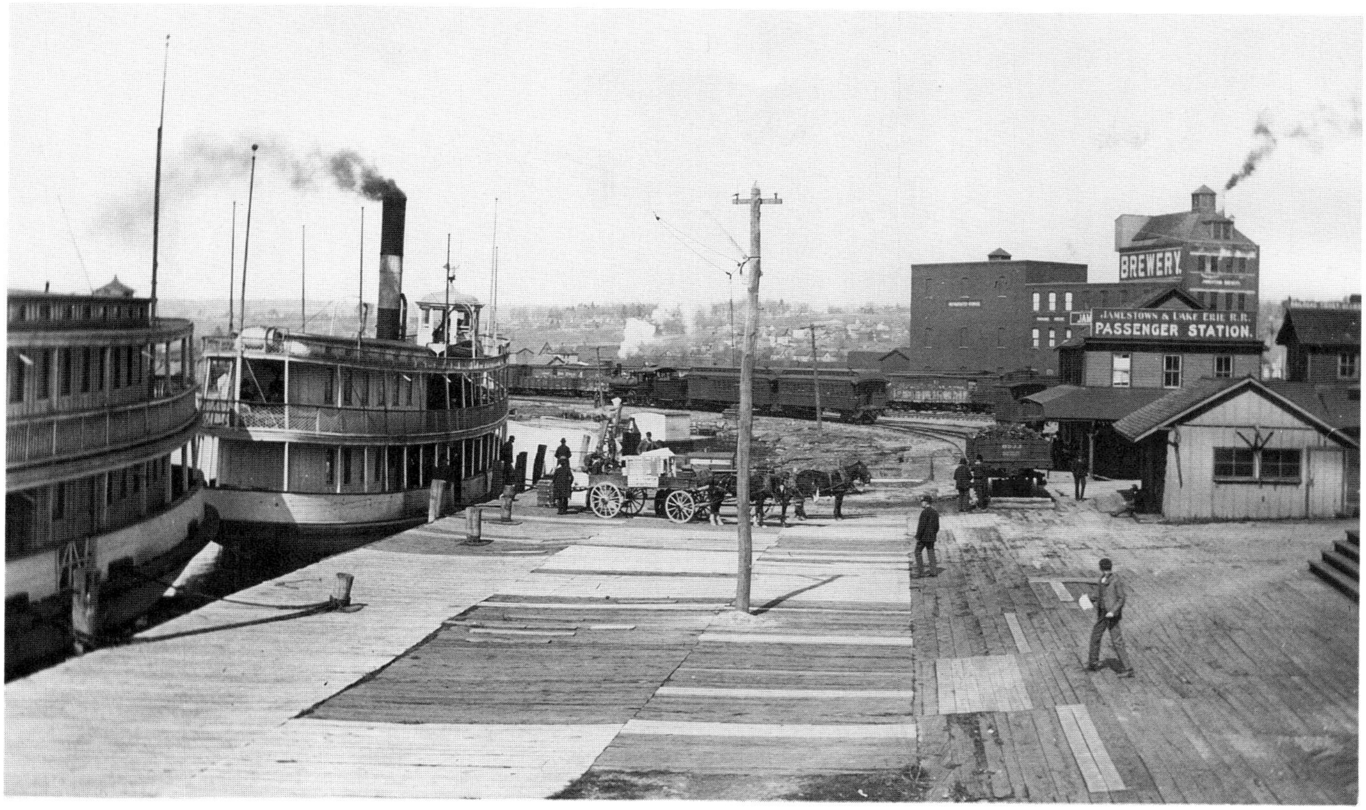

Boatlanding, ca. 1898-1900. The steamers (l-r) *City of Cincinnati* and *City of Pittsburgh* are docked at the boatlanding. The Jamestown and Chautauqua Railroad train heads for Mayville via the east side of Chautauqua Lake. Note that the passenger station still bears the name "Jamestown & Lake Erie R.R." The railroad had been reorganized and the sign had not yet been repainted. The Jamestown Brewing Company building still stands on Eighth Street. *JE*

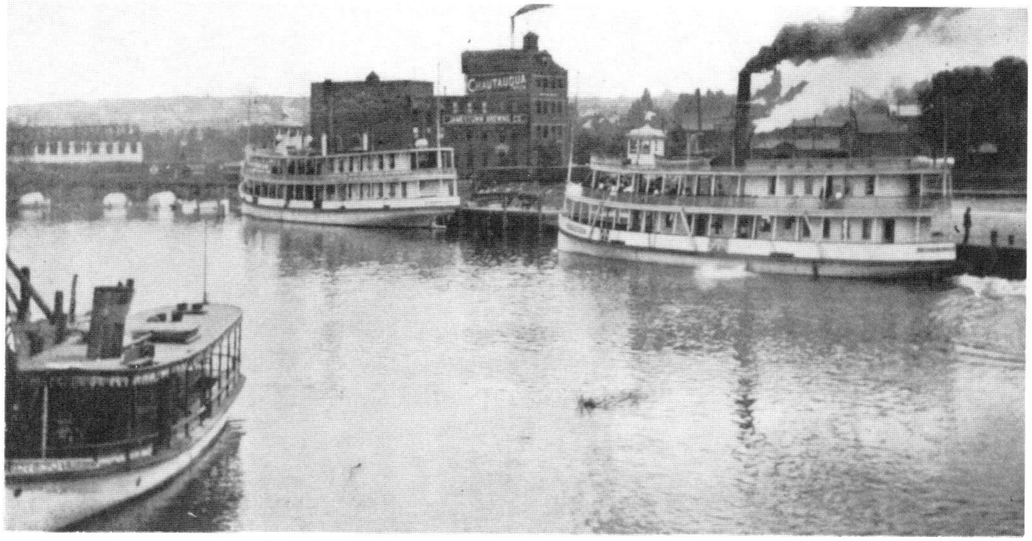

Boatlanding, ca. 1907. A view from the Fairmount Avenue bridge. The little steamer seen in the lower left corner is either the *Celoron* or the *Greenhurst*, two identical ferries that worked the lower lake until 1911. The *City of New York* can be seen in the center and, to the right, the *City of Pittsburgh*. The Jamestown Brewing Company is in the background. *CCHS*

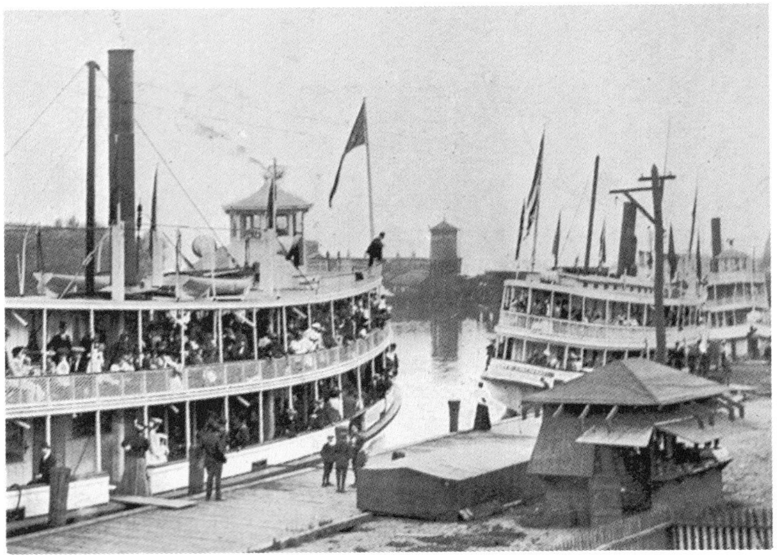

Boatlanding, ca. 1906. An excursion party has boarded the *City of New York* and the *City of Cincinnati* for a day on the lake. The railroad water tower appears in the background. *CCHS*

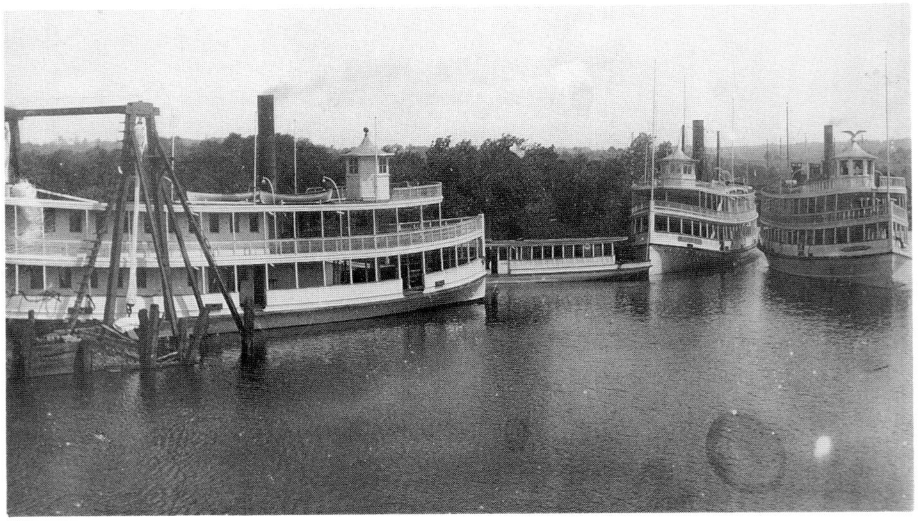

Boatlanding, ca. 1900. The *City of Cleveland* in a sling. The frame hoist lifted the stern of a steamboat to repair or replace the propeller or rudder. Note the stern of the small steamer *City of Rochester*, the *City of Chicago*, and the *City of Buffalo*. The view is from the dock across the Chadakoin. *RL*

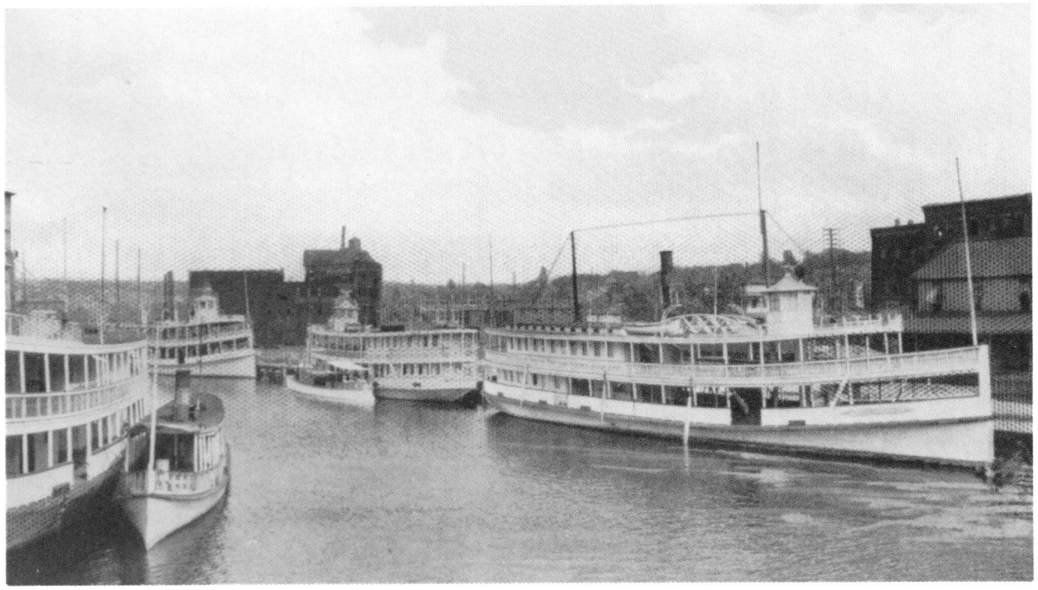

Boatlanding, ca. 1908. Frank Gifford's little *Onosee* is dwarfed by the large commercial steamers. Gifford was a prominent Jamestown banker and industrialist and the son-in-law of the late Governor Reuben E. Fenton. Mr. Gifford commuted in the *Onosee* from his summer home at Long Point. The small steamer to the lower left is the *Mayville*. Next to it are the *City of Cleveland*, the *City of New York*, the *City of Buffalo*, and the *City of Cincinnati*. *CCHS*

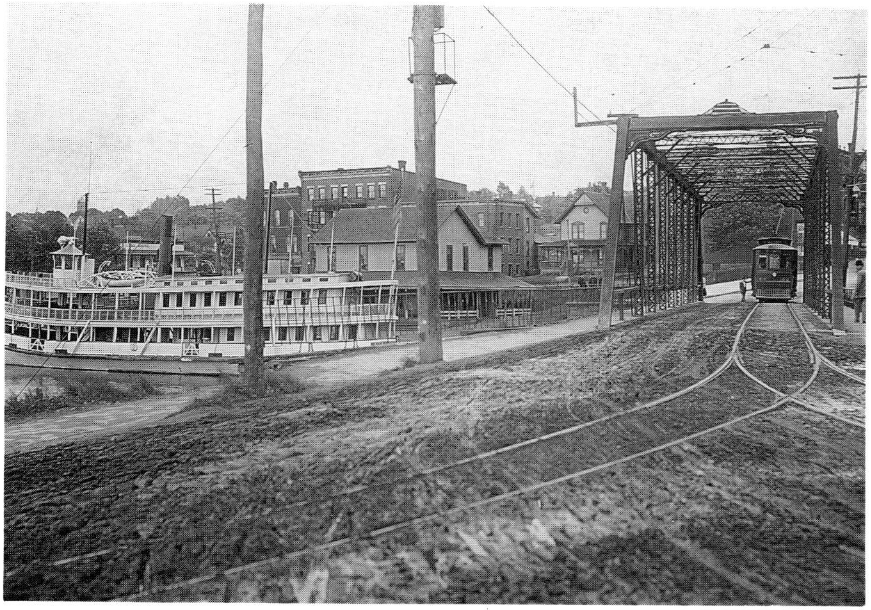

Fairmount Avenue bridge, ca. 1908. This photograph was taken from Jones and Gifford Avenue just west of the bridge. The steamer *City of Cincinnati* is docked. The offices and waiting room for the Jamestown, Chautauqua and Lake Erie Railroad are in the center. The trolley tracks to the left lead to Celoron, those to the right to Lakewood. *RL*

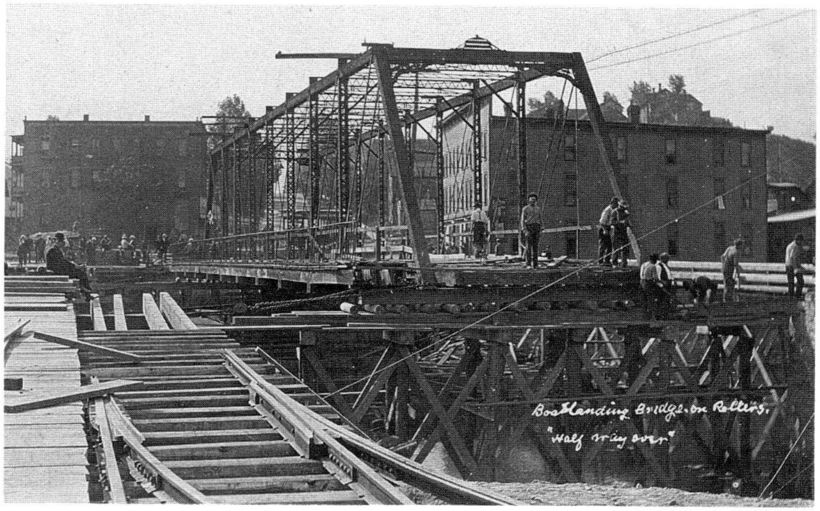

Fairmount Avenue bridge, ca. 1910. The current bridge, made of cement, was built in 1910. Before construction began, the iron span was moved on rollers to the left so that trolley service would not be interrupted. Workmen are shown here undertaking that job. *RL*

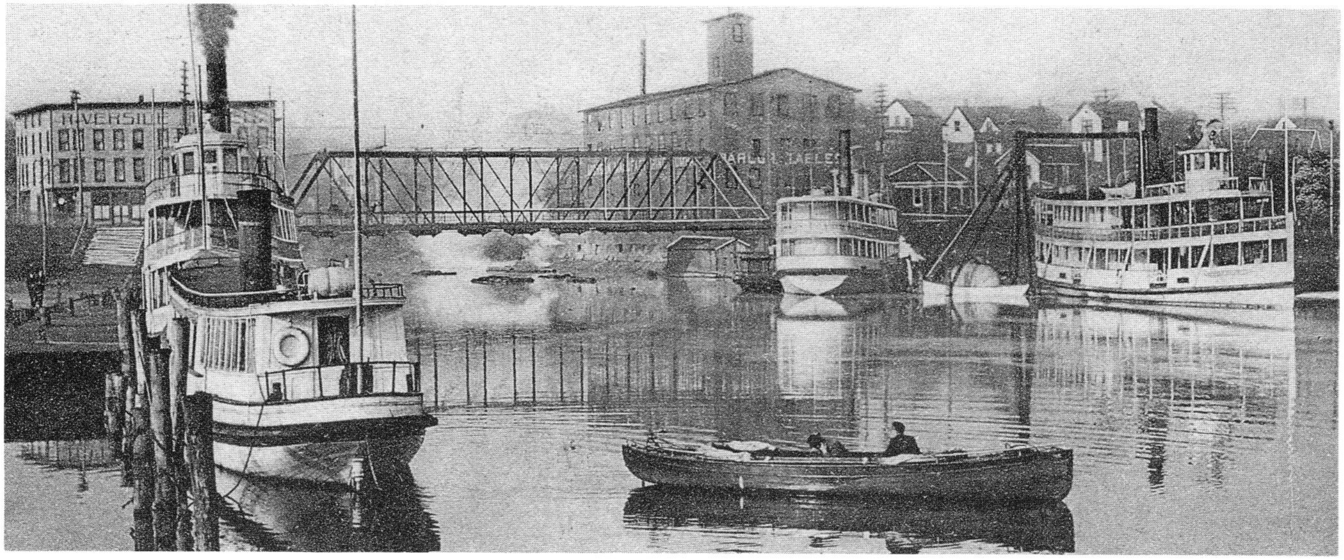

Boatlanding, ca. 1906. A look back at the boatlanding from the Chadakoin River. The river continues below the Fairmount Avenue bridge through Jamestown. Celoron is to the right along Jones and Gifford Avenue. The Riverside Hotel stands to the left of the bridge and the Jamestown Table Company opposite. Clockwise from the lower left are the *City of Rochester, City of Pittsburgh, City of Buffalo*, and the *City of Cleveland*. *RL*

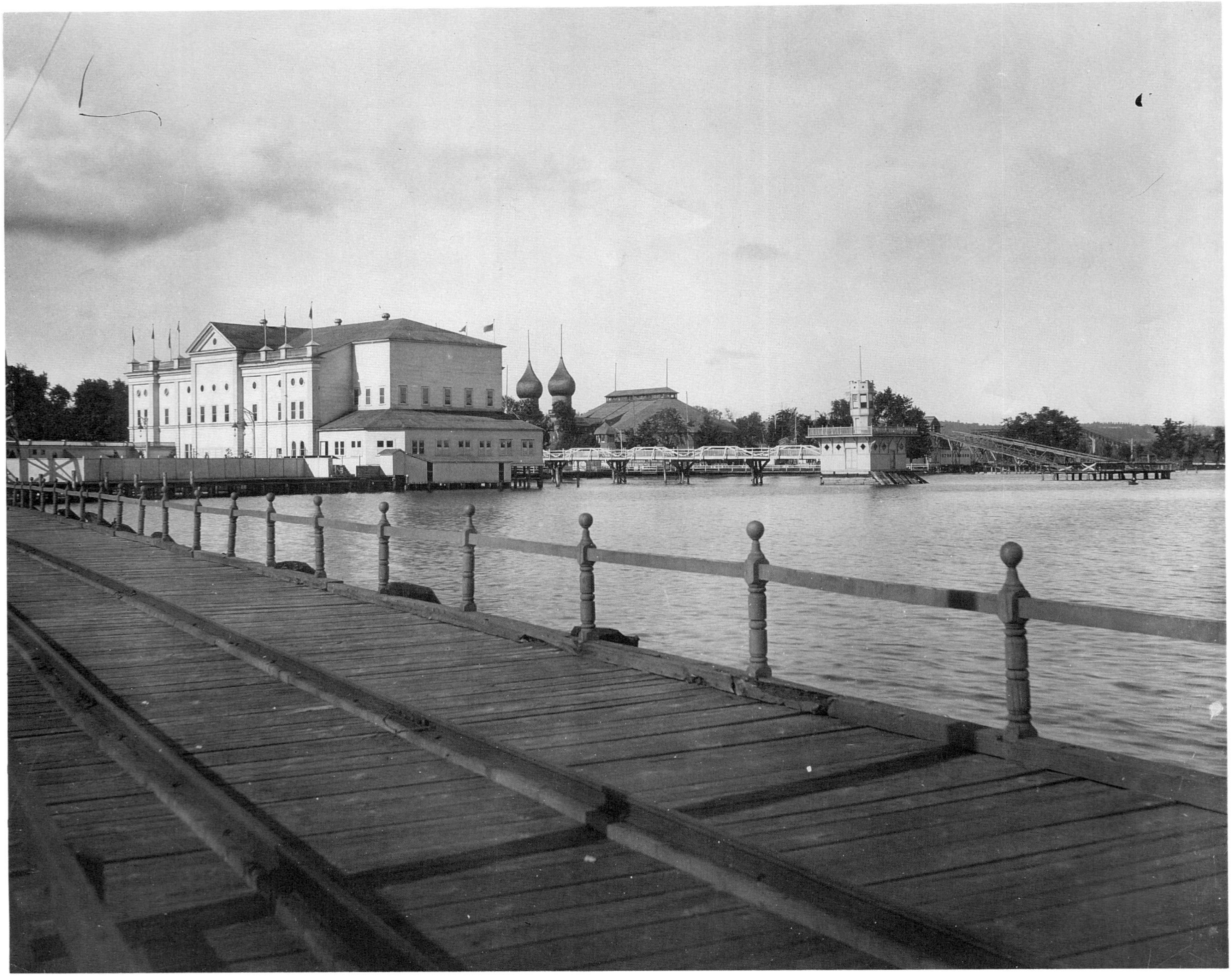

CELORON

The tiny, unprepossessing village of Celoron was for almost seventy years the site of one of the country's most notable amusement parks. The village lies at the foot of the lake's west side, a mile and a half by road above the boatlanding. Celoron Park, remembered fondly today by Chautauqua's elders, opened with much fanfare on May 18, 1894. Almet Broadhead, the energetic president of the Celoron Amusement Company, modelled Celoron after the famous amusement parks at Coney Island and Atlantic City.

By 1894, the Broadhead family owned both the Jamestown Street Railway and the Chautauqua Steamboat Company which operated most of the major steamboats working the lake. Celoron was built as a destination for the locals on the streetcar line and for the summer trade from the lake resorts. From the beginning Mr. Broadhead insisted that Celoron remain free from the "objectionable" features common to most amusement parks. Each year he added new and delightful attractions. In addition to the rides, the park boasted in its early years a bathing beach, dance hall, zoological gardens, and a summer theater. The photographs that follow are from the park's glory days through the first quarter of the twentieth century. Celoron began to be dismantled in the late 1950s and closed forever in the summer of 1962.

Waterfront, Celoron, ca. 1901. Looking over the steamboat dock. The summer theater, auditorium, search light tower, and toboggan slides. *FHS*

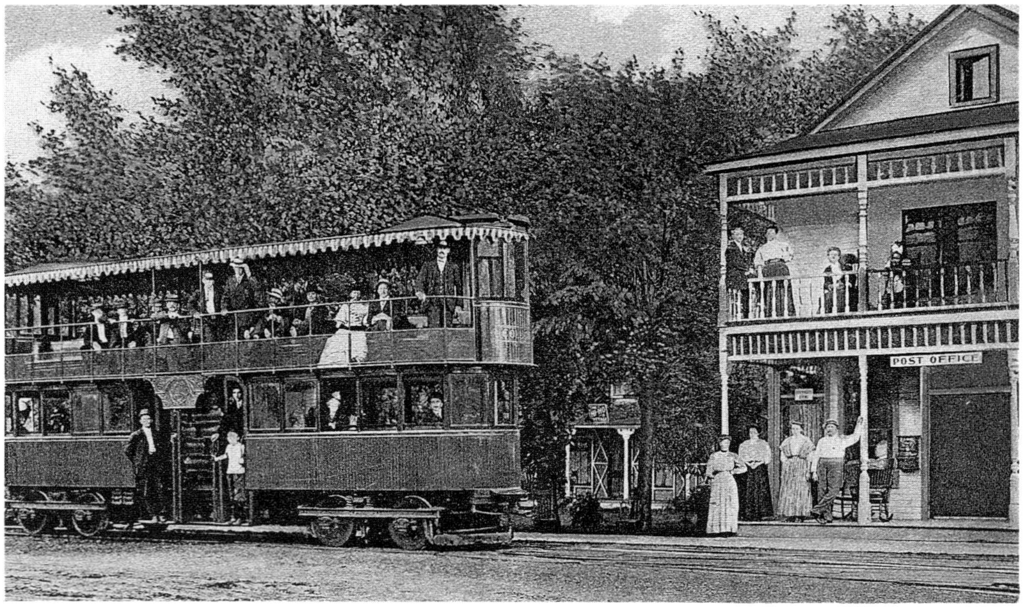

Celoron, ca. 1900. The "Columbia," a double-decker trolley, was purchased in 1893 by Almet Broadhead for the Jamestown Street Railway. The car was built by the Pullman Company and exhibited at the Columbian Exposition held in Chicago that year. The interior of the lower deck, containing "ladies" and "smoking" compartments, was extravagantly decorated. The upper deck swayed when the car was in motion. The "Columbia" was operated by coachmen at either end of the upper deck and by a conductor. It made regular runs between Jamestown and Celoron until 1913. This photograph shows the "Columbia" at rest outside the Celoron Post Office on Boulevard Street. *RL*

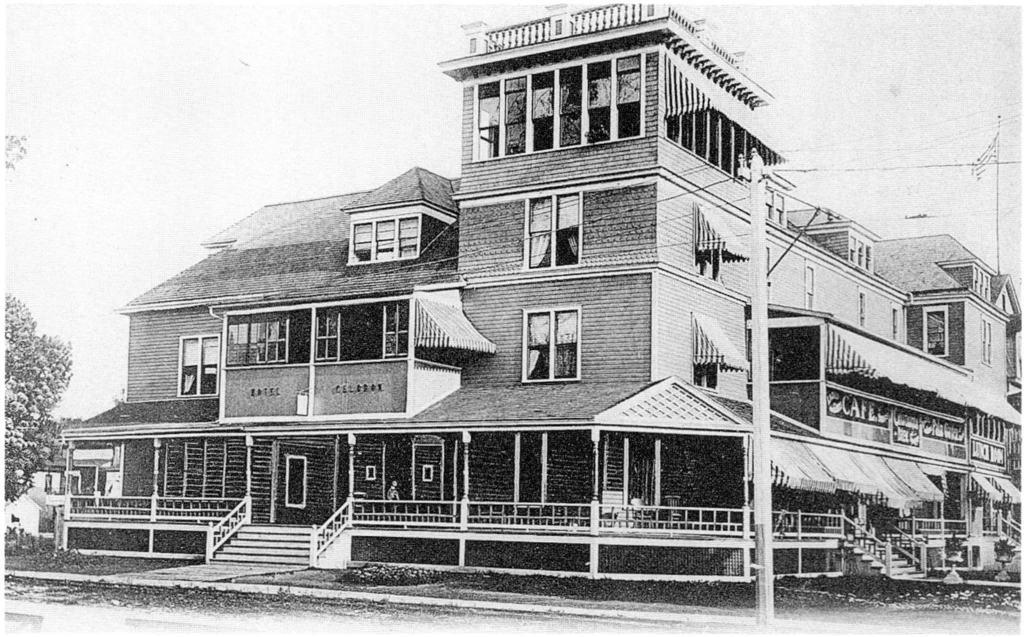

Hotel DeCeloron, ca. 1908. The DeCeloron, built in 1893, was owned by the Jamestown Brewing Company. It contained thirty-six rooms. This view was taken from the lake side. A second hotel known as the Imperial was erected next to the DeCeloron a few years later. The two hotels stood directly behind the band shell. A fire in 1914 severely damaged the Imperial and completely destroyed the DeCeloron and all its furnishings. *RL*

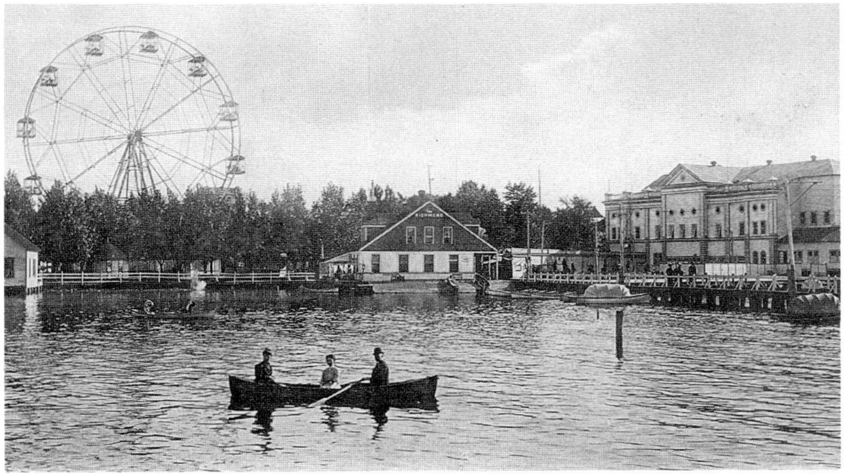

Celoron Park, ca. 1904. A view of the park at dusk looking across the lake from Fluvanna. The lake narrows here to form the Chadakoin River, or outlet, which flows east (left in the photograph) through Jamestown. The white railings of the steamboat dock are visible between the theater and the Richmond Hotel. *RL*

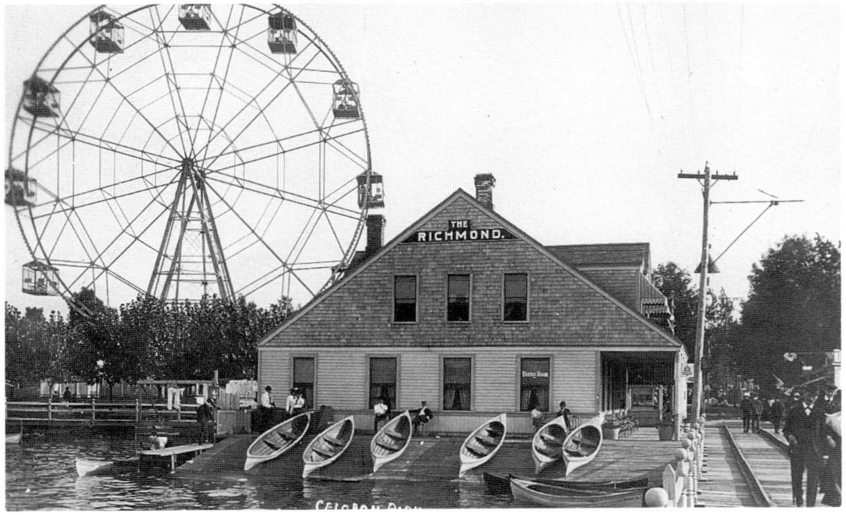

Richmond Hotel, ca. 1905. Rowboats could be hired at the Richmond which stood on the shoreline at the base of the dock. The hotel provided food and drink to park patrons. The spectacular Phoenix Wheel began operating on Memorial Day in 1896. Note the trolley tracks on the dock. Cars were available to carry disembarking passengers from the steamboats. *RL*

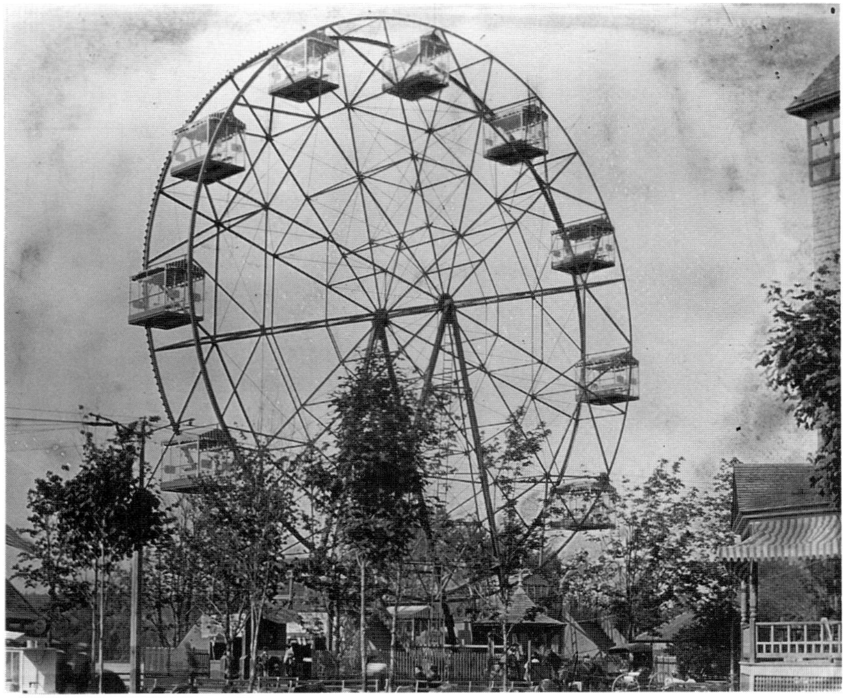

Phoenix Wheel, ca. 1898. This impressive attraction was purchased by Almet Broadhead at the Cotton States and International Exposition held in Atlanta in 1895. Its name derived from its manufacturer, the Phoenix Iron Company, located in Phoenixville, Pennsylvania. Each of the wheel's twelve wire cages carried fifteen or more riders either standing or sitting on benches. The Phoenix Wheel remained one of Celoron's most popular attractions until 1952 when it was dismantled and removed to the Los Angeles Fairgrounds in Pomona, California. *FHS*

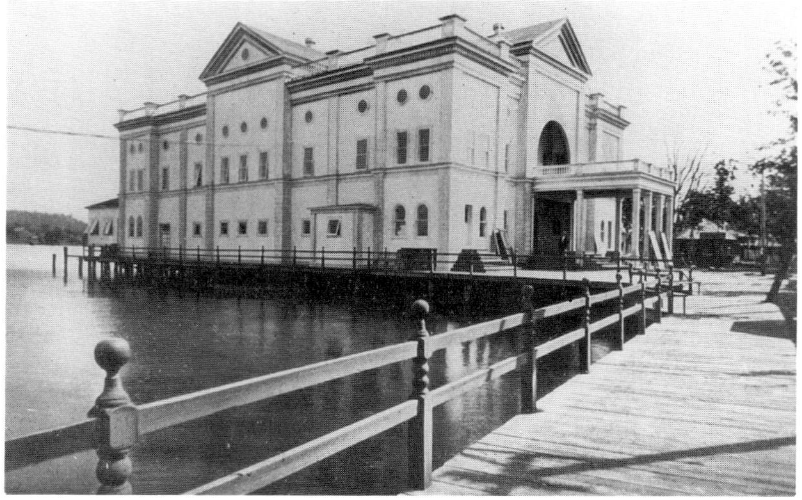

Summer theater, ca. 1910. The Summer Theater, adjacent to the steamboat dock, opened in 1897, the fourth season of Celoron's operation. It was built on pilings driven into the lake bottom. Initially, the theater booked vaudeville acts. Travelling companies and stock shows performed here until 1924 when the theater was converted into a dance hall. Known as the Pier Ballroom, it featured the best of big band entertainment. The Pier Ballroom was destroyed by fire in 1930 and replaced the same season with a new dance hall, Castle Gardens. *FHS*

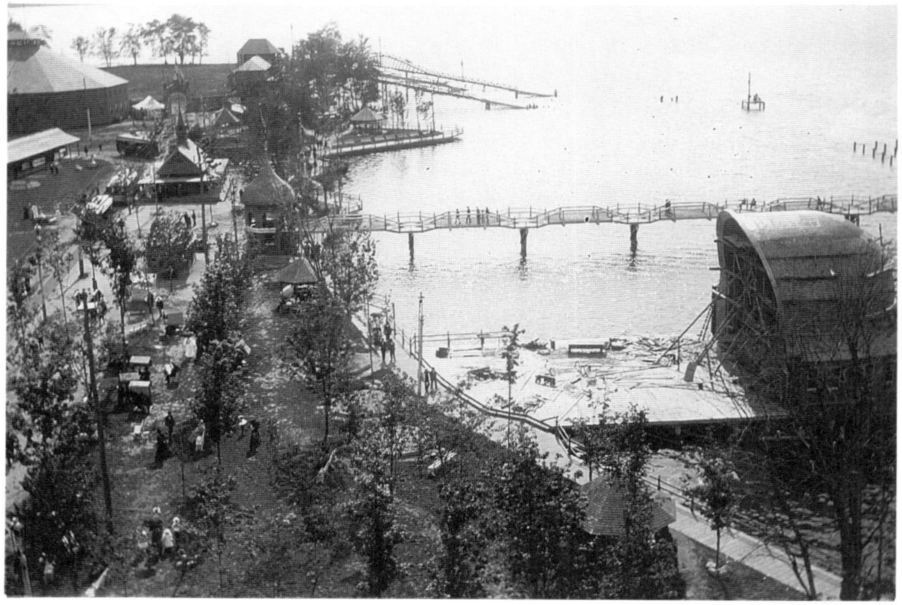

Bandstand, ca. 1894. Construction of the bandstand at its first location on the platform that three years later held the summer theater. The bridge to the searchlight tower is just beyond. *FHS*

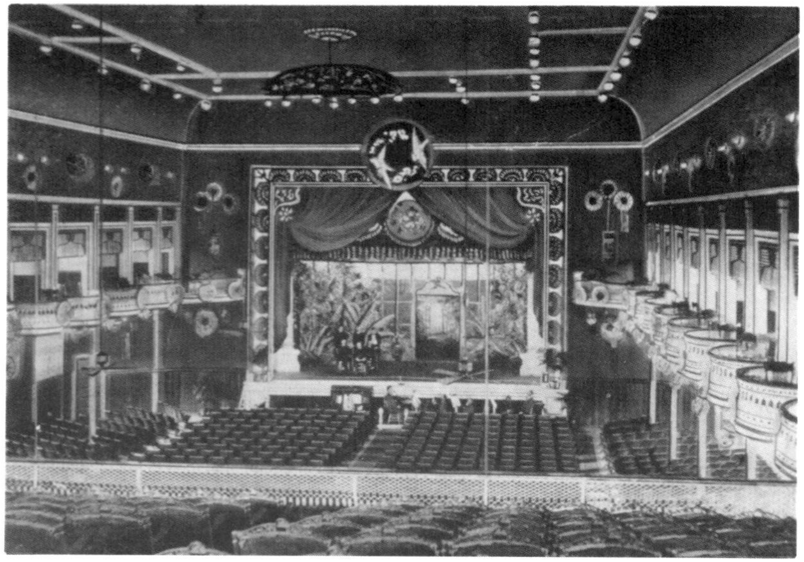

Theater interior, ca. 1912. The theater was elegant, its seats and curtain plush red. General admission to events and performances was ten cents. The boxes held four at one dollar per box. *RL*

Celoron Park, ca. 1900. Trapeze and daredevil acts were regularly featured at Celoron. The scaffold from which the high diver is preparing to dive rose above the fourth story of the Hotel DeCeloron. This photograph was taken before the erection of the vaudeville stage. The peaked roof of the Hotel DeCeloron was damaged by fire in 1902 and replaced with a flat roof. The trolley from Jamestown approached the park from the right rear of the bandstand, circled the foreground in the photograph, and exited between the Phoenix Wheel and the DeCeloron. The road behind the bandstand is an extension of Dunham Avenue. *RL*

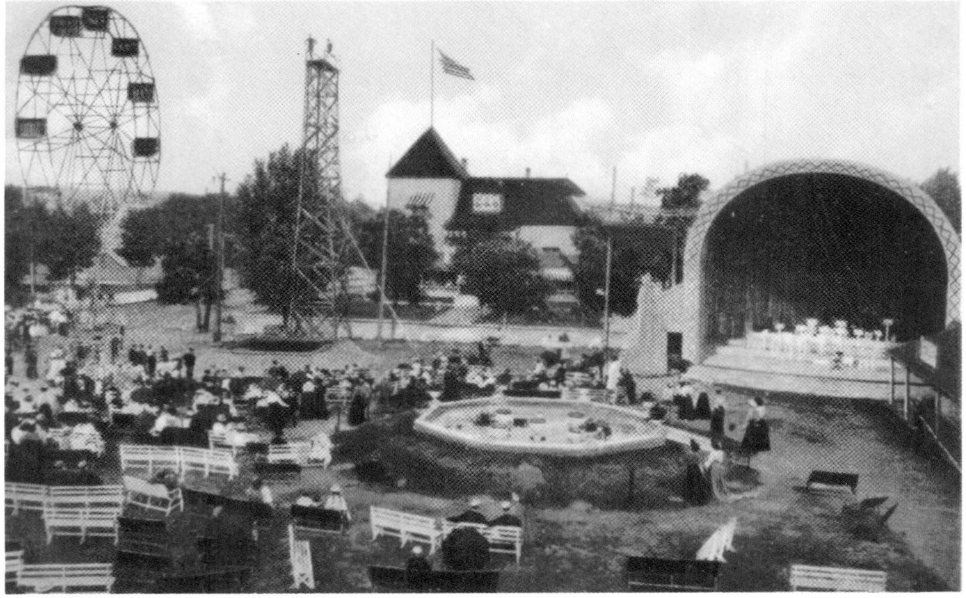

Bandstand, ca. 1909. Flags in the bandstand signify, perhaps, the Fourth of July. The bandstand was removed from its original site on the lake shore to make room for the theater. The view is down the lake and the Chadakoin towards Jamestown. The lake is to the left, the village of Celoron to the right. Dunham Avenue, the main street entrance to the park, ran behind the bandstand and connected with the dock. The open building next to the bandstand was a stage for vaudeville acts. It contained a screen for motion pictures projected from the tower in the foreground. Benches surrounded an electric fountain that featured colored lights and music. *PL*

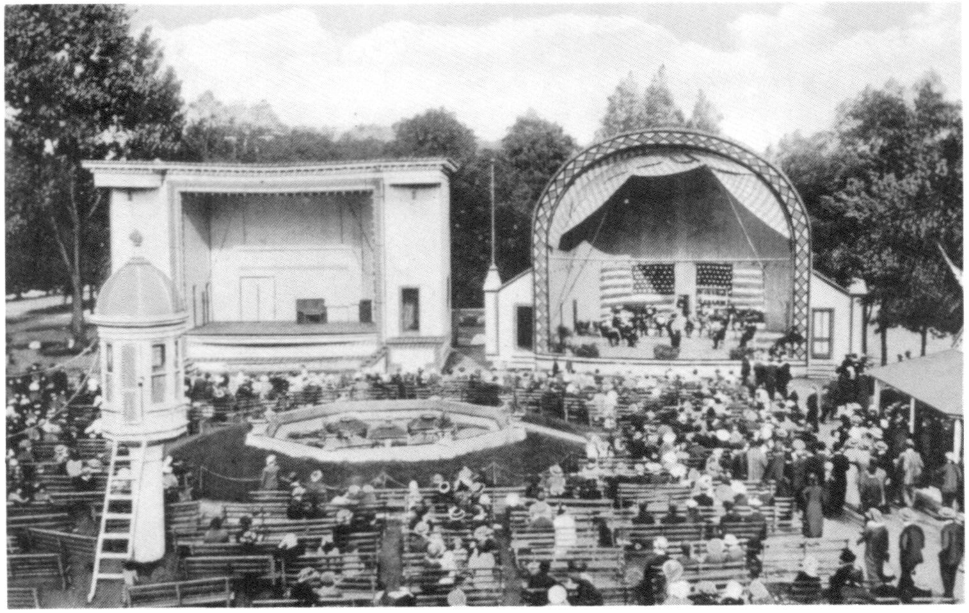

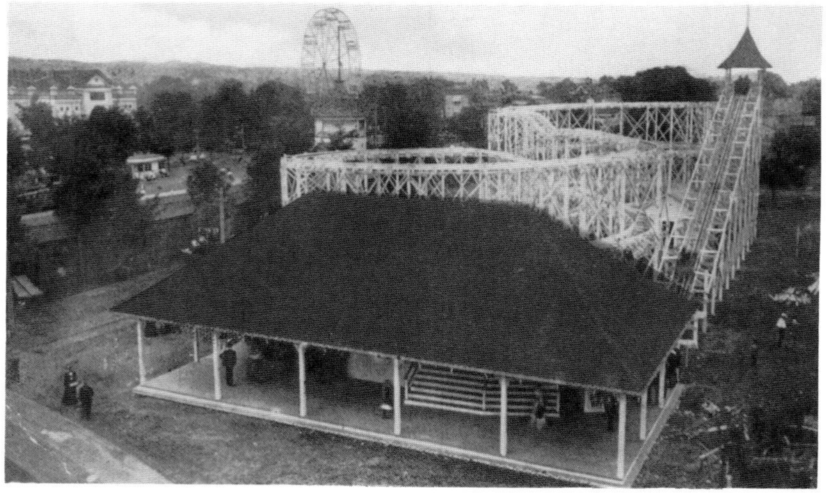

The "Figure Eight," ca. 1911. This roller coaster ride stood across the street and trolley tracks from the auditorium. Notice the car approaching the summit of the incline and a second car following. The conspicuous lack of crowds in this photograph perhaps indicates inclement weather. The theater is at the upper left. The "Figure Eight" was dismantled in 1933. *RL*

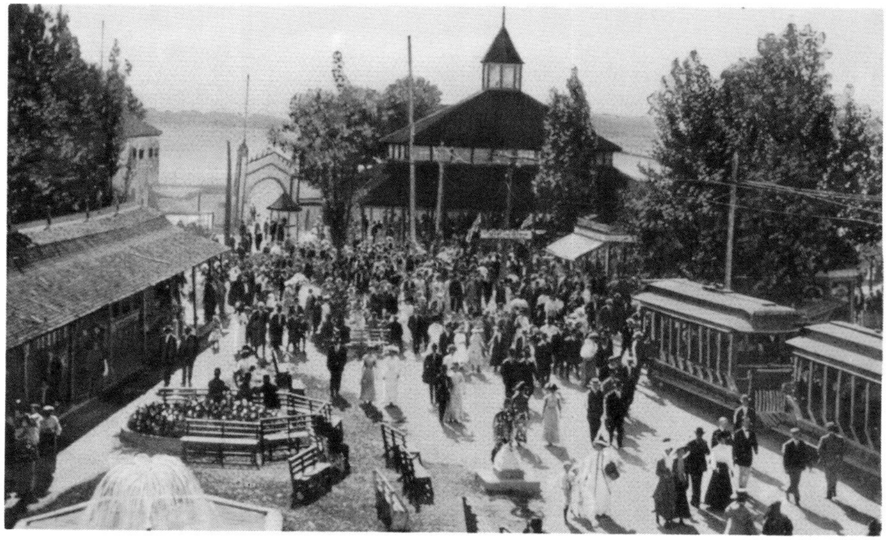

Celoron Park, ca. 1911. A view from the west. The auditorium and merry-go-round are visible in the background. The summer or open trolley cars allowed for a cool ride back to Jamestown after a fun-filled day at the park. *RL*

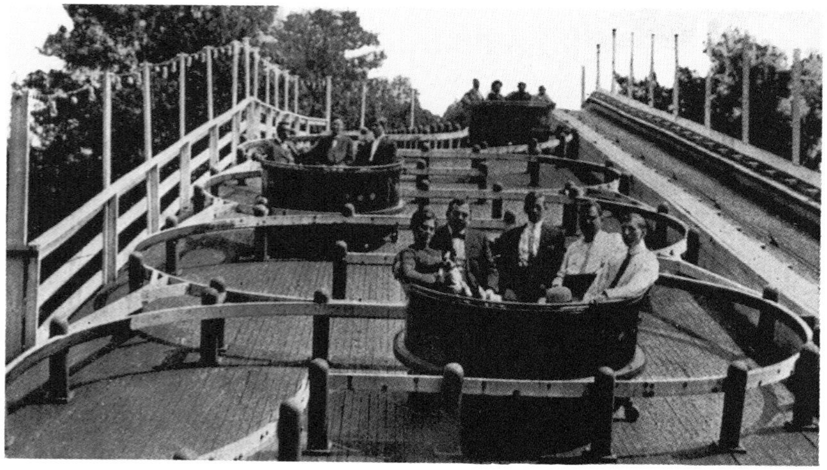

Coney Island Tickler, ca. 1910. Left to right: Mrs. Ed Connelly and dog, Ed Connelly, Caya Johnson, "Poodle" Frank, unidentified. Ed Connelly was a popular singer at Celoron. It was said of the Tickler that if you didn't know your ride companions at the top of the incline, you would at the bottom. *FHS*

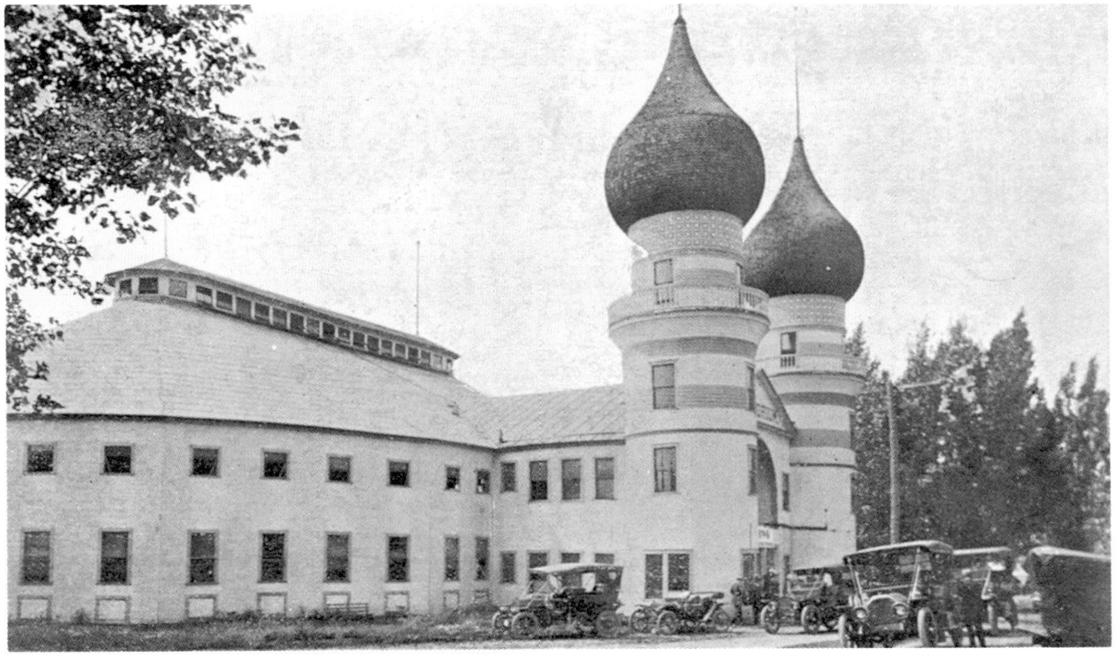

Celoron Auditorium, ca. 1915. This imposing structure was built in 1895. It had a seating capacity of 6,000. In 1896, William Jennings Bryan, who ran unsuccessfully for president against William McKinley, addressed a capacity crowd here. The building's extensive interior was used for roller skating in the summer and ice skating in the winter. A long single-story wooden annex, through which skaters could test their speed, ran from the rear of the auditorium almost to the lake. *RL*

Baseball diamond, ca. 1905. Several of baseball's immortals, including Babe Ruth, Cy Young, and Christy Mathewson, brought exhibition teams to play at Celoron. In 1902 the mighty Boston Red Sox defeated the locals 3-2 in ten innings. The auditorium annex, which passed through the grandstand, is visible on either side of the structure. The annex was torn down in 1909. *RL*

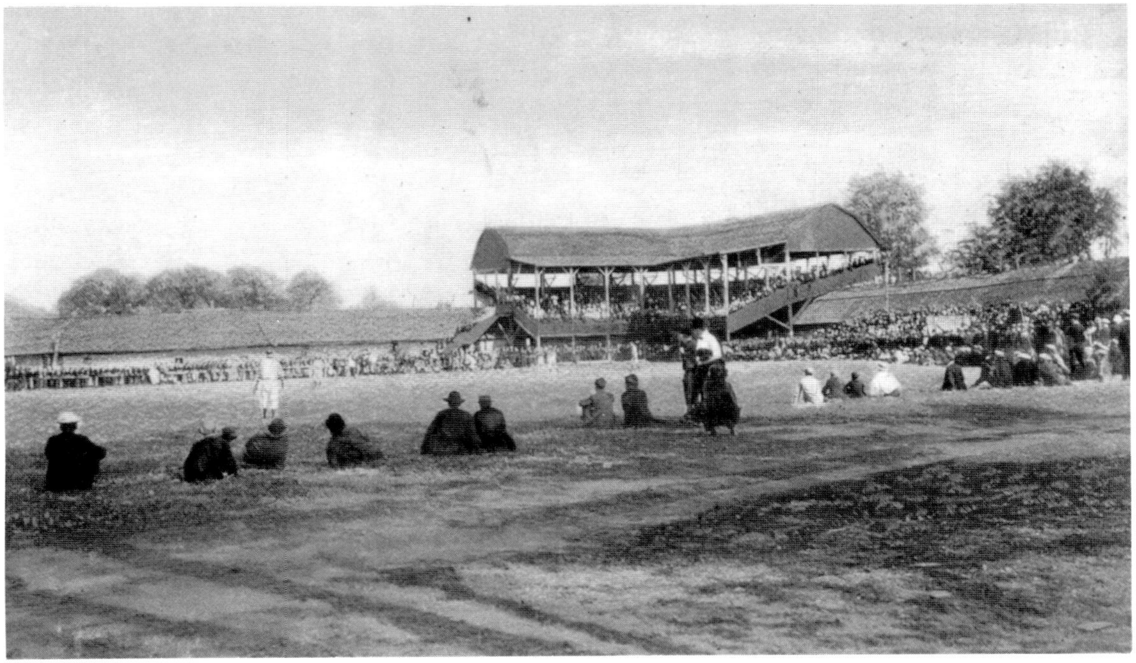

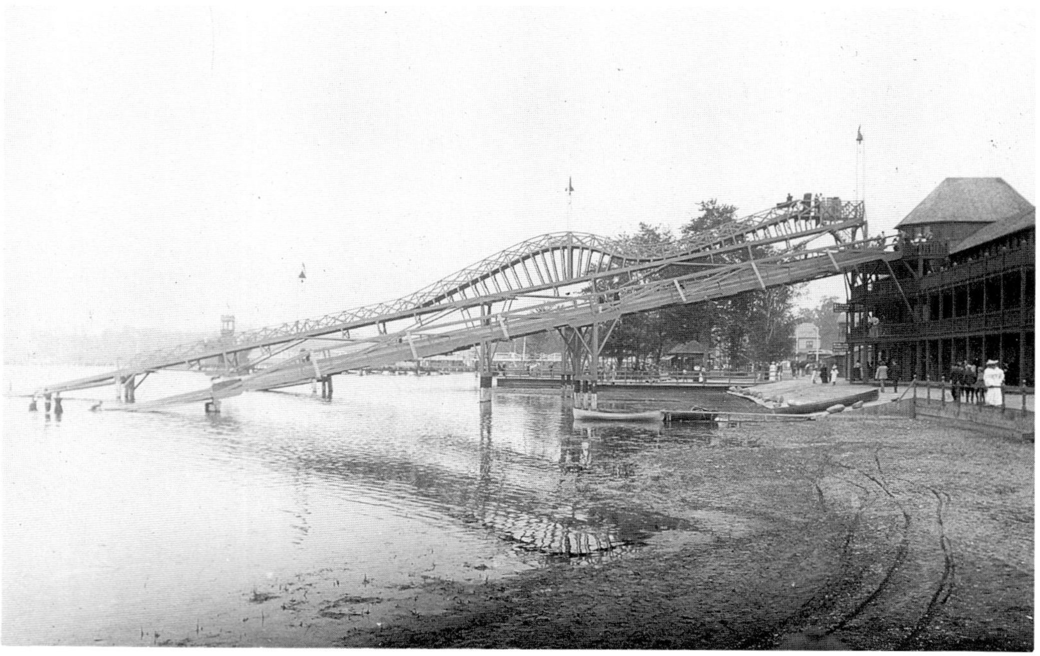

Toboggan Slides, ca. 1908. Celoron's second bath house and the toboggan slides, including the camel back. The toboggans ran on rollers over a track depositing riders into the lake. *CCHS*

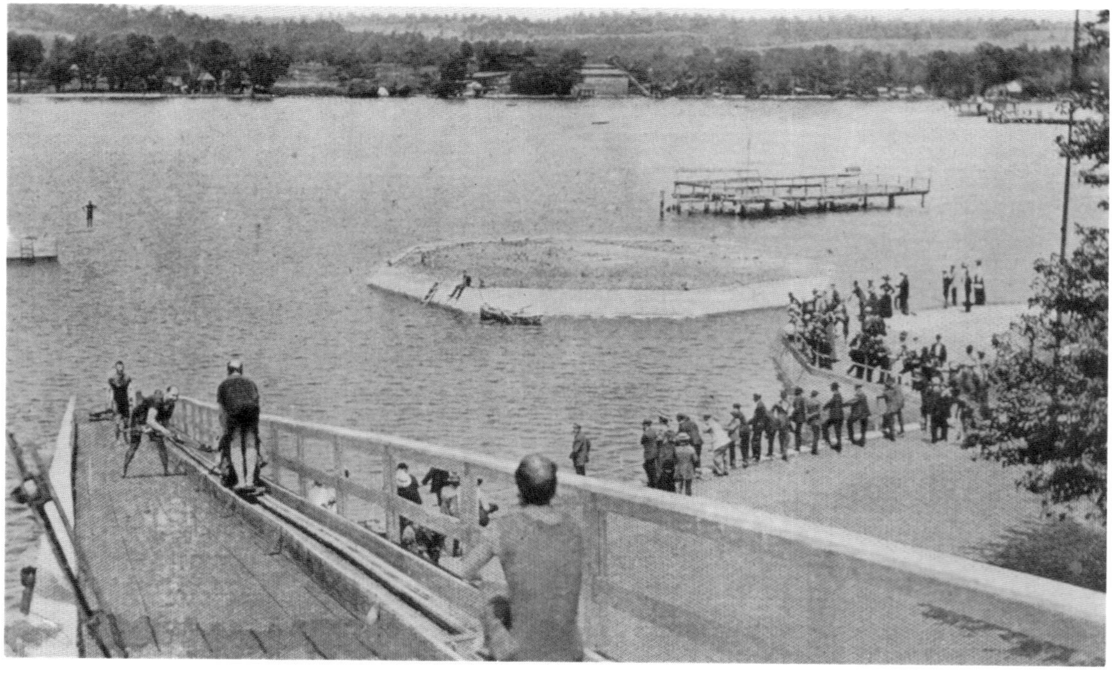

Toboggan Slide, ca. 1915. Originally three toboggan slides extended from the roof of the bath house into the lake. The beach and bath house were located in the baseball diamond's deep right field. The island was intended for a bandshell that never materialized. Later it held the Circle Swing, an airplane ride illuminated by colored lights. The wooden platform beyond the island was used to launch fireworks. An ice house with ramp is visible across the lake at Fluvanna. *RL*

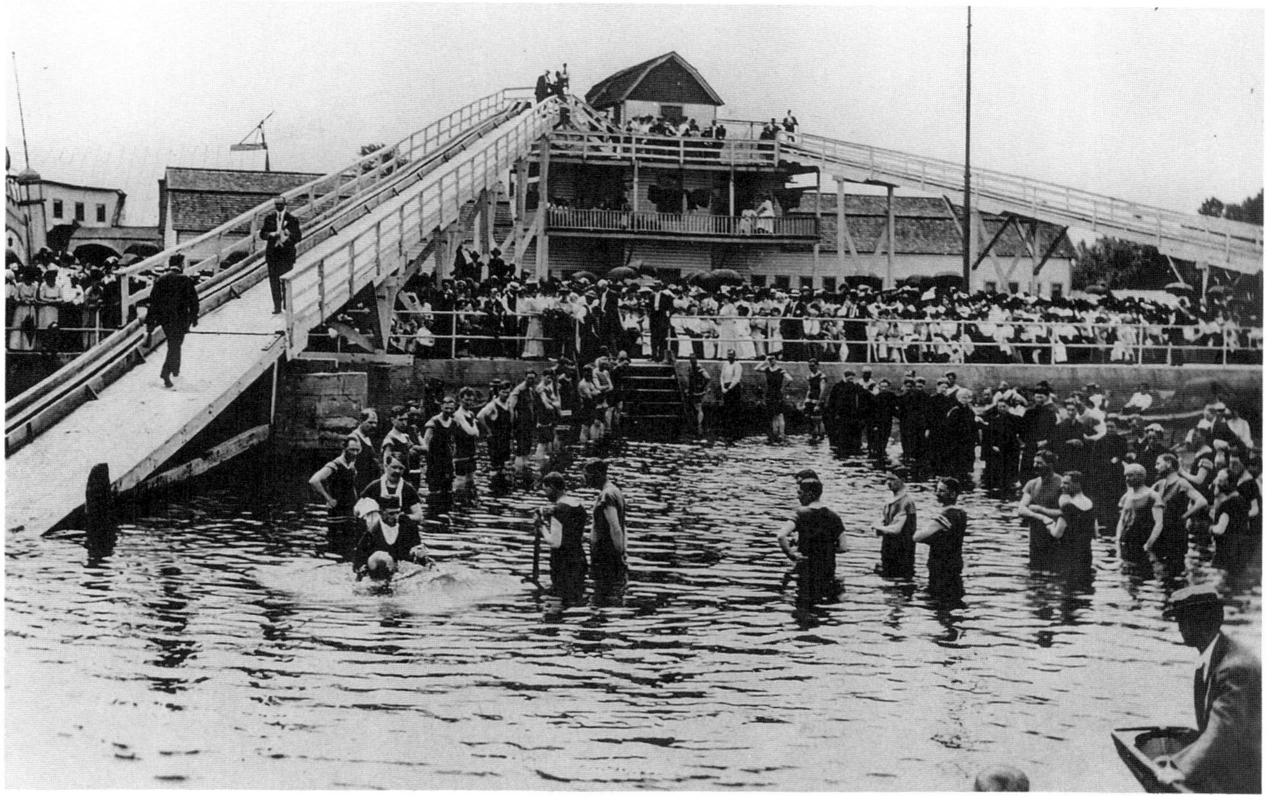

Bath house and twin toboggan slides, 1910. A Bible students' convention enjoys the facilities for a public baptism. *VN*

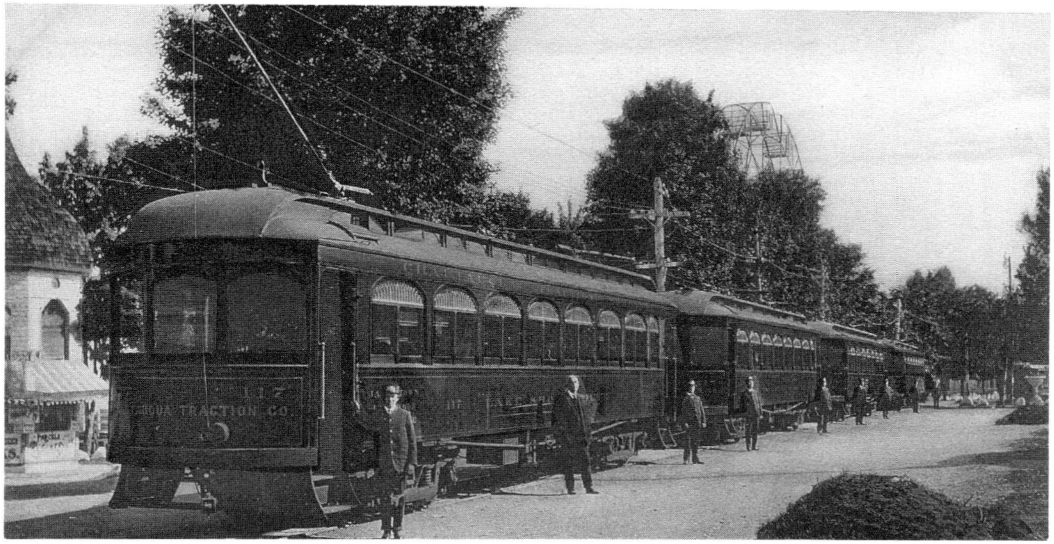

Celoron, ca. 1909. Chautauqua Traction Company cars and motormen pose in Celoron at the trolley stop. The track was laid from Jamestown in 1893 in preparation for the park's opening. The cars face Jamestown for the return trip. The theater and lake are to the left. *RL*

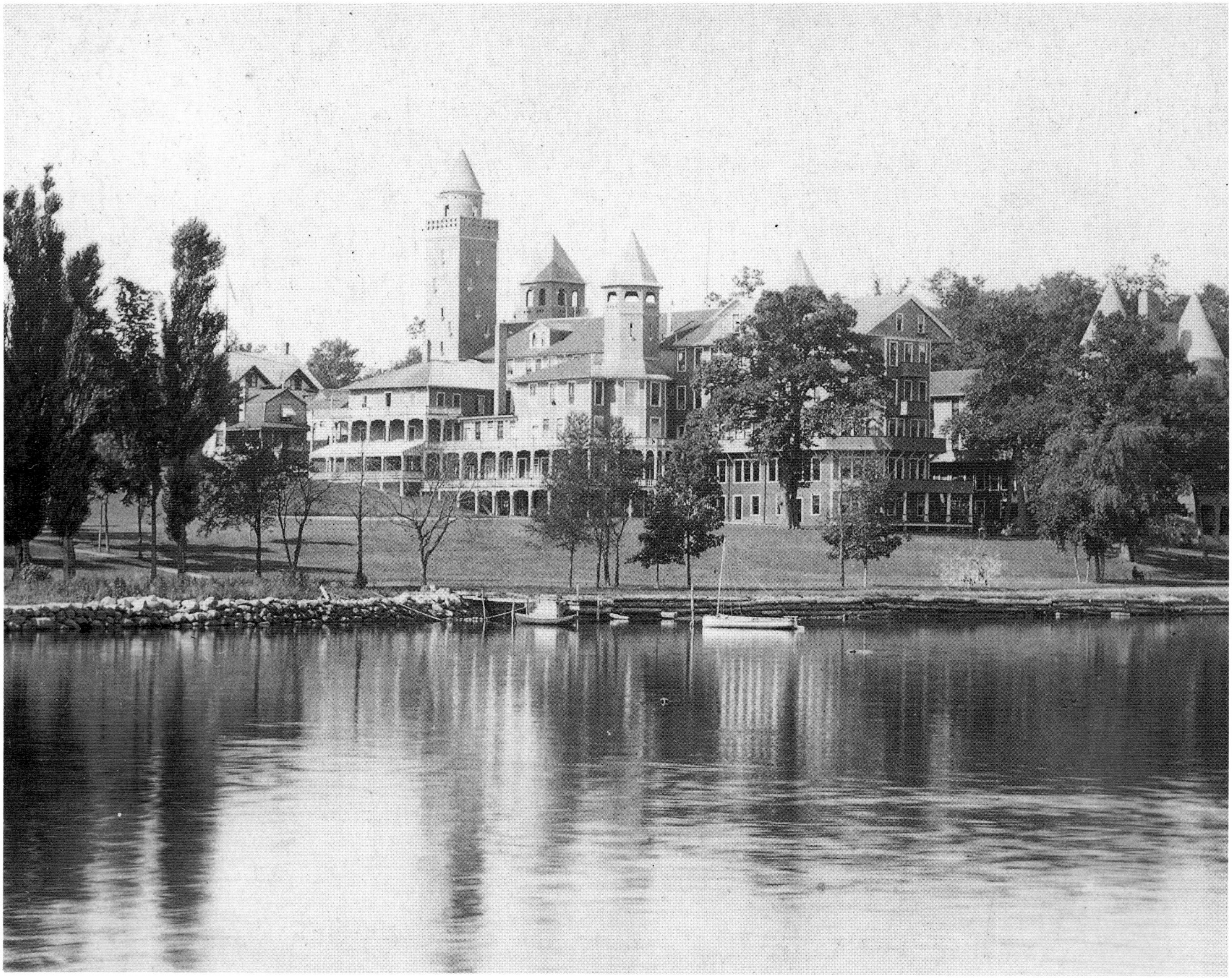

LAKEWOOD

BEECHWOOD SHERMAN'S BAY

John Cowing's Lakeview House, built in 1870, began the development of Chautauqua Lake's most fashionable resort area. Cowing's family owned the tract of land called "Lakeview" on the lake's lower west side. Following the construction of the hotel, a town began to grow. In 1874 a group of developers, including Warren and John Packard of Warren, Ohio, purchased the "Lakeview Tract," and the land was subdivided into individual lots for summer cottages. Another subdivision, the Howard Park Association, was located to the west. The cottages were of frame construction, two and three stories in height, usually with porches and dormers. The homes reflected the architectural styles of the times with ornate wood carvings and embellishments. Many of these cottages remain today and are called "home" by Lakewood families. Renamed "Lakewood" in 1880, it was a village of shaded avenues, beautiful lawns, and elegant cottages. The dock was a busy place as lake steamers transported visitors to and from its two fabulous resort hotels. Now a residential community, Lakewood was once known as the "Saratoga" of Chautauqua Lake. The season extended from June into October and attracted "the wealth and fashion from leading American cities." Famous visitors included John Philip Sousa, Grover Cleveland, Ethel Barrymore and Theodore Roosevelt.

Beechwood, located just east of Lakewood near the present Lakewood Rod and Gun Club, was the second stop from Jamestown along the Chautauqua Traction Line. Sherman's Bay lies west of Lakewood in the vicinity of what is now Big Tree Road.

Sterlingworth Hotel, ca. 1890, Lake View. One of two extravagant Lakewood resort hotels. The Sterlingworth faced Terrace Avenue at the foot of Chautauqua Avenue on today's Lakewood village park. One tall tower above the main entrance and six smaller rounded towers gave the imposing structure a castle-like appearance. The Sterlingworth was built by Ernest Frisbee in 1889. Its relatively short life coincided with the best years of Chautauqua Lake's resort era. *CCHS*

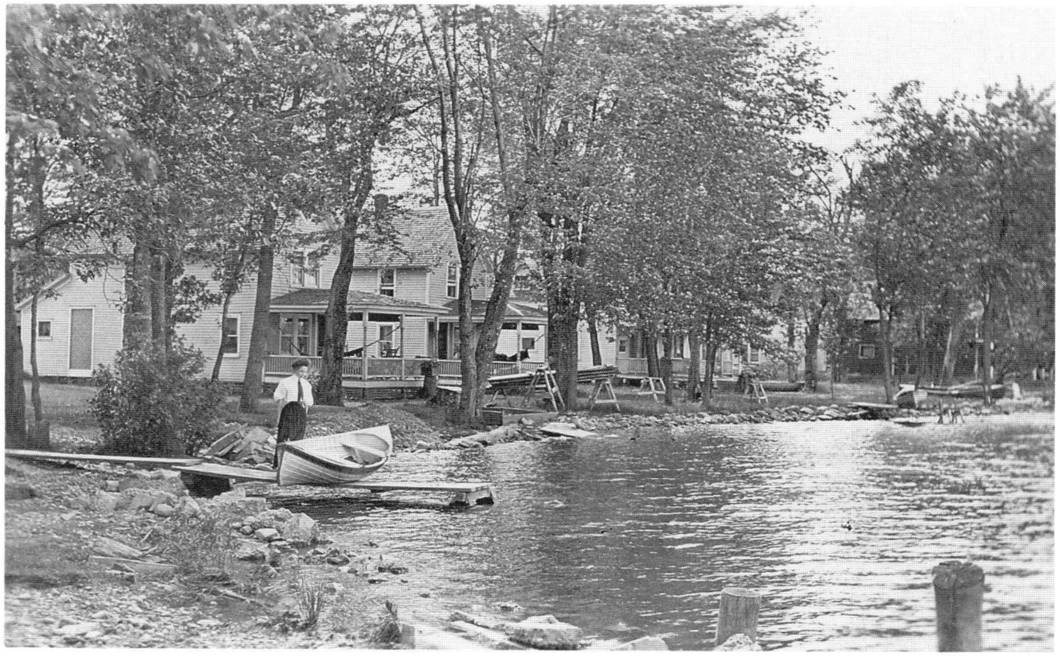

Beechwood, ca. 1910. Cottages at Beechwood near today's Beechwood Restaurant. Everyone wanted a summer home on the lake. Beechwood remains a community of modest cottages and year-round homes. A popular joke had it that the flimsy buildings were made with whatever material was available, including telephone pole crossarms. *RL*

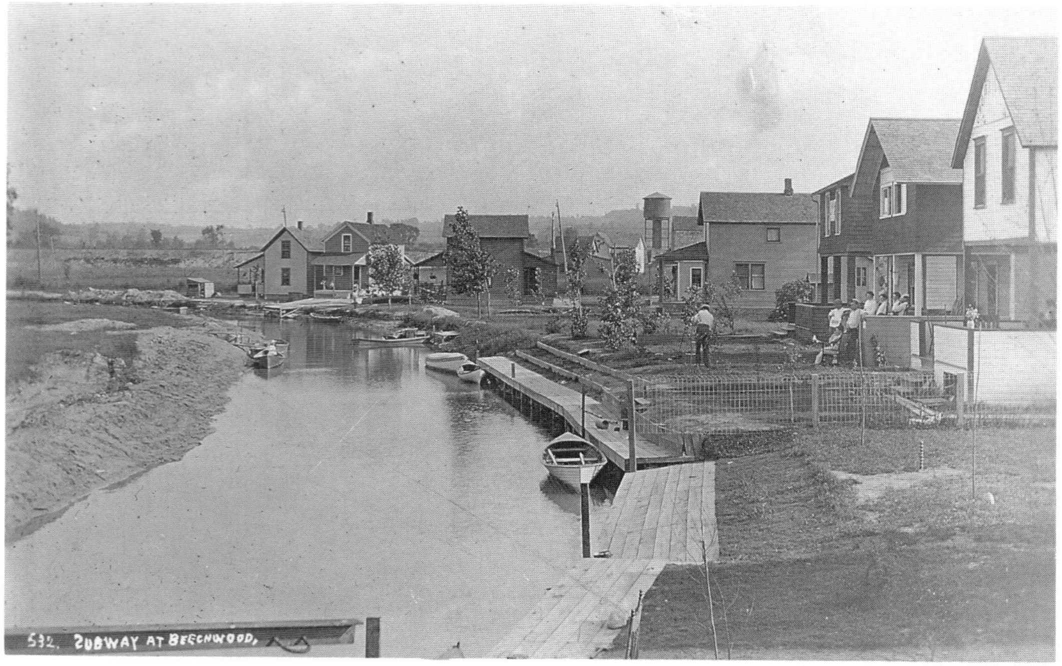

Beechwood, ca. 1910. Ziba Squier, former mayor of Celoron, dug the "Subway," a horseshoe-shaped canal which led into and out of the lake. The canal began just west of the Beechwood Restaurant where Canal Street is today. It circled below Summit Street and entered the lake between Olive and Gerald Streets. Mr. Squier intended to lay out the property between in building lots. The lots, however, were never developed. Streets in the vicinity are named for Ziba Squier's children. The canal was impossible to maintain and was eventually filled in. *RL*

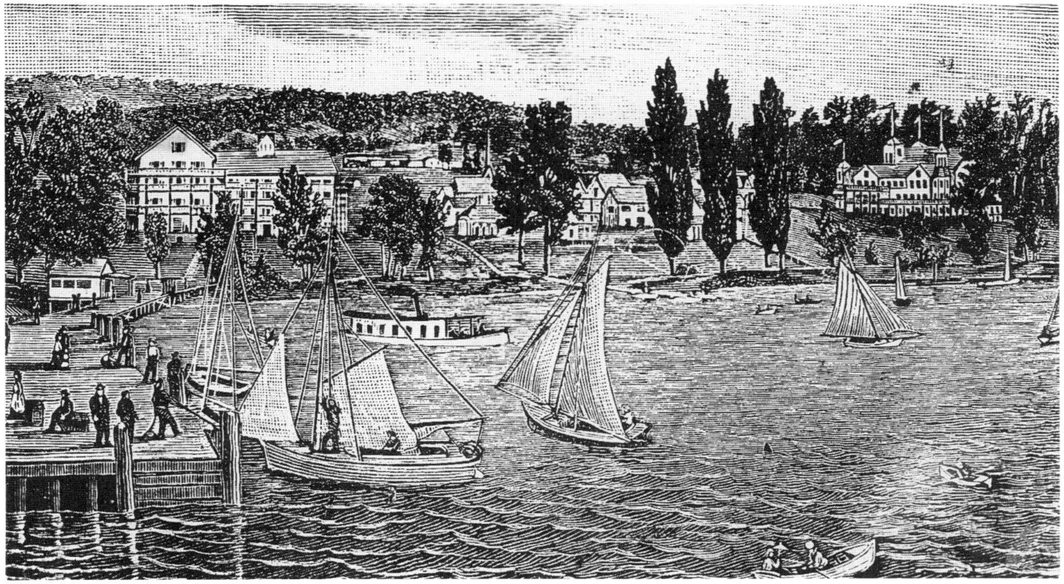

Woodcut, Lakewood shoreline, ca. 1885. Fashionable Lakewood in the midst of its popularity. The first Kent House to the left was built in 1875 by Alba Kent. The Lakeview House to the right stood just up the lake at the foot of Chautauqua Avenue. The pretty village grew around the two hotels. Note the impressive dock before the Kent House. *CCHS*

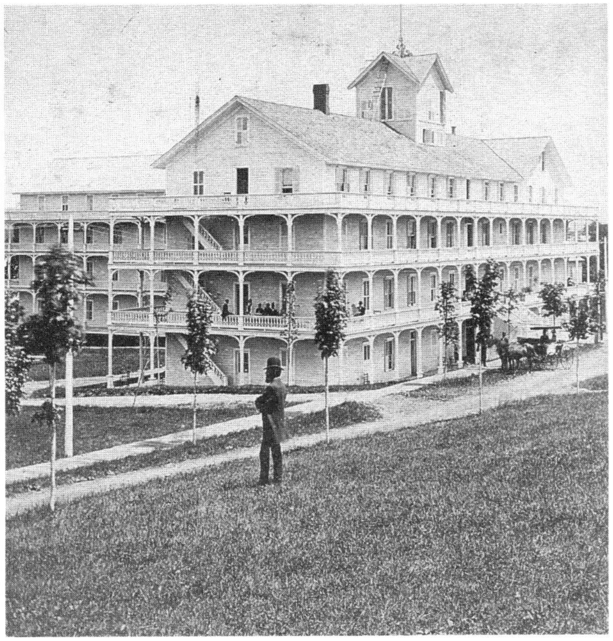

Kent House, ca. 1876. Built in 1875, enlarged in 1876, the "new and complete" Kent House could accommodate 500 guests. Cottages for vacationers were also available. The hotel enjoyed enormous popularity throughout its lifetime. Alba Kent's steamboat *Waukeegan* transported guests to the busy hotel from the boatlanding in Jamestown. A fire in 1887 destroyed the Kent House. *CCHS*

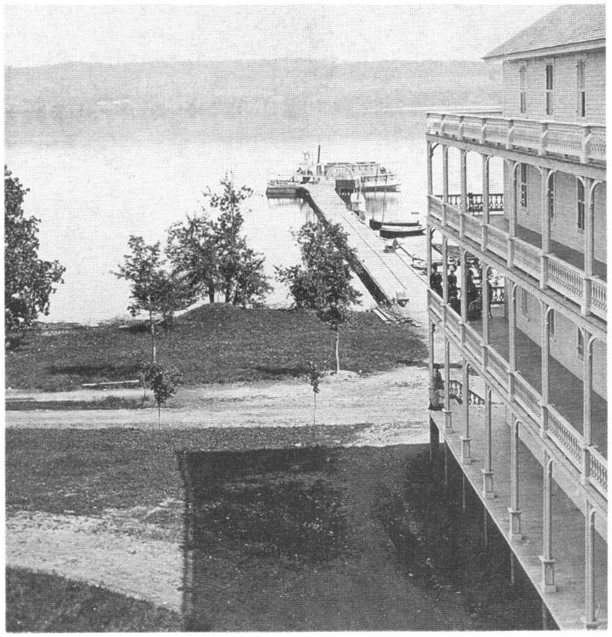

Lakewood, ca. 1876. A scenic view of the eastern shoreline of Chautauqua Lake from the piazza of the first Kent House. Lake steamers conveyed guests to the hotel's dock which was 100 feet wide and 400 feet long. The steamer in this view is the *May Martin*, a short-lived steamer which ran on the lake from 1876 to 1878. *CCHS*

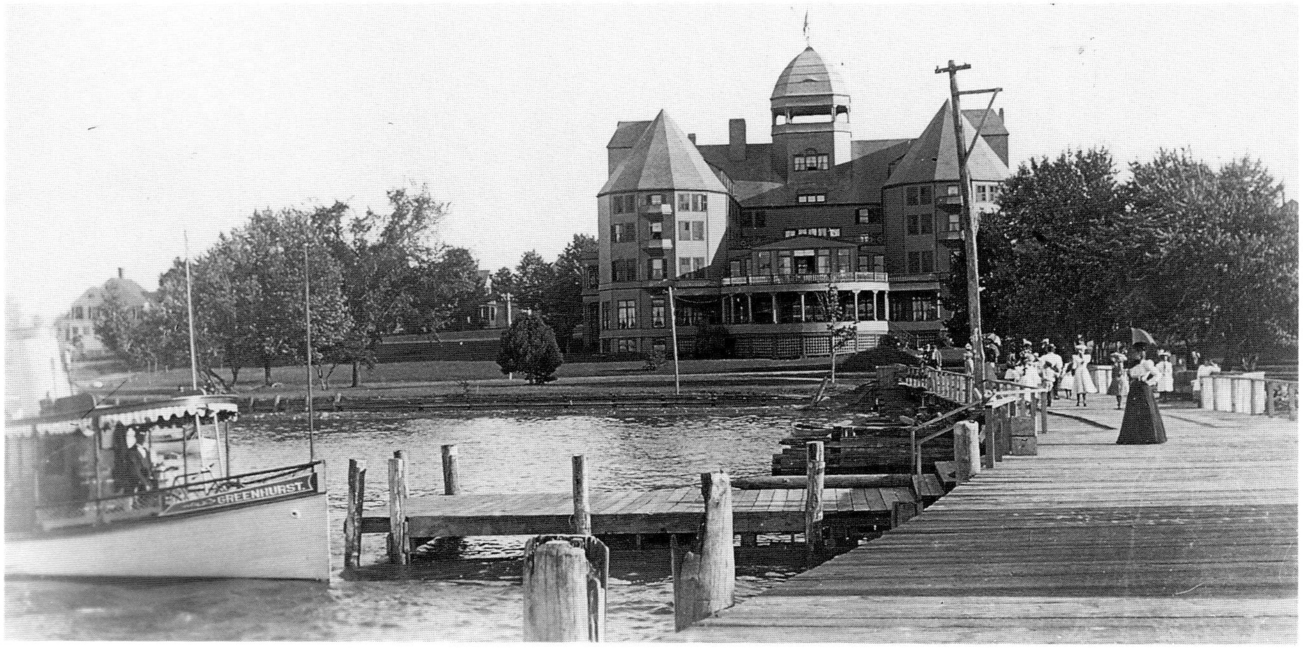

Kent House, ca. 1890. The second Kent House replaced its predecessor in 1888. Five stories of elegance, complete with observatory and verandahs, faced Chautauqua Lake. The second Kent House ceased operation in 1903 and its contents were auctioned in 1909. The decaying building was finally demolished in 1916 signalling the end of an era for Lakewood. Much of the salvaged materials were used in the building of new Lakewood homes. The ferry *Greenhurst* is at the dock. *JE*

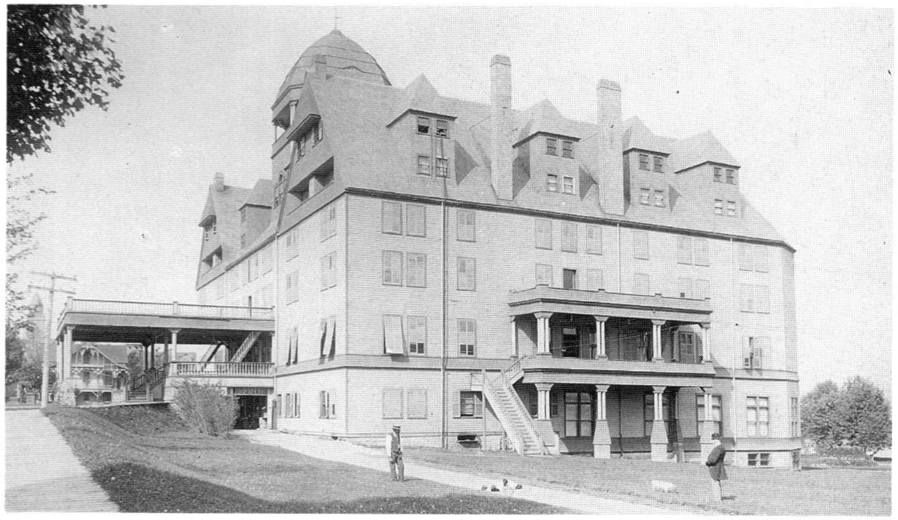

Kent House, 1891. Looking west up Terrace Avenue. The two Kent Houses stood at the present site of the Chautauqua Lake Yacht Club. *FHS*

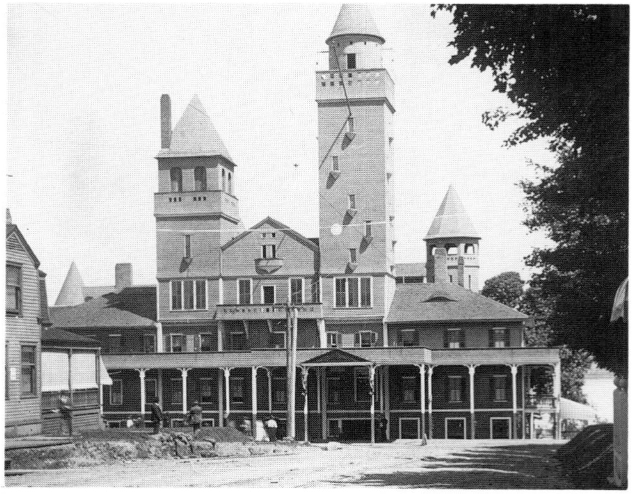

Sterlingworth Hotel, ca. 1895. Ernest Frisbee's major reconstruction of the earlier Lakeview House at the intersection of Chautauqua and Terrace Avenues. The Sterlingworth opened successfully in 1889, but maintenance costs proved prohibitive and it was sold at a judgment sale in 1895. It operated as the Waldmere until 1903 when it was destroyed by fire. *FHS*

Chautauqua Hotel, ca. 1910. The Chautauqua Hotel stood at the intersection of Chautauqua and Summit Avenues. A block away toward the lake at Terrace Avenue stands the Lakewood Country Club on the former site of the Sterlingworth Hotel. The Erie Railroad depot was located two blocks above the Chautauqua Hotel on Chautauqua Avenue. The hotel provided a trolley waiting room and postal service. *RL*

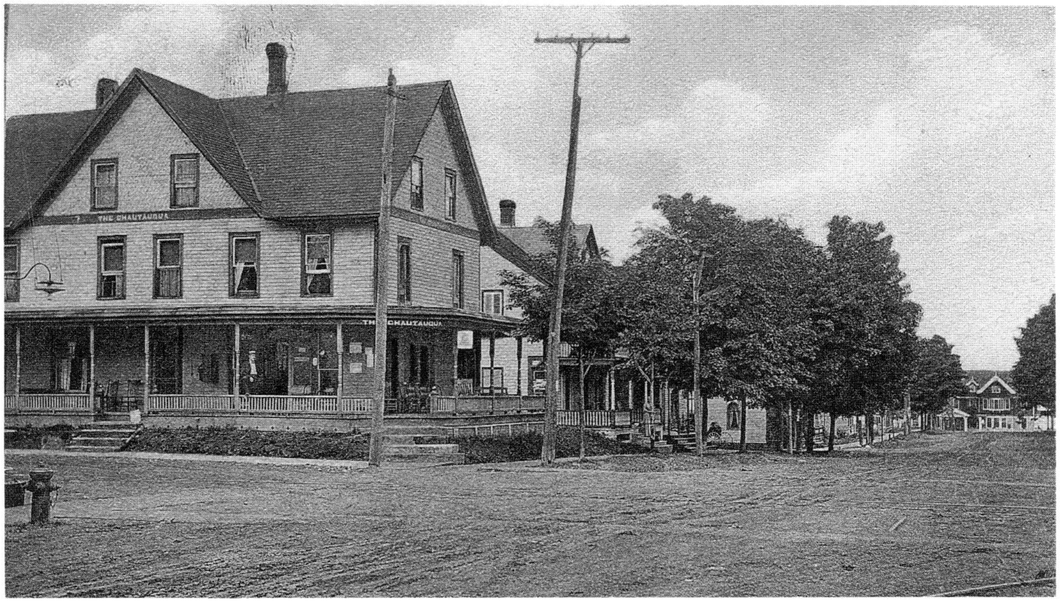

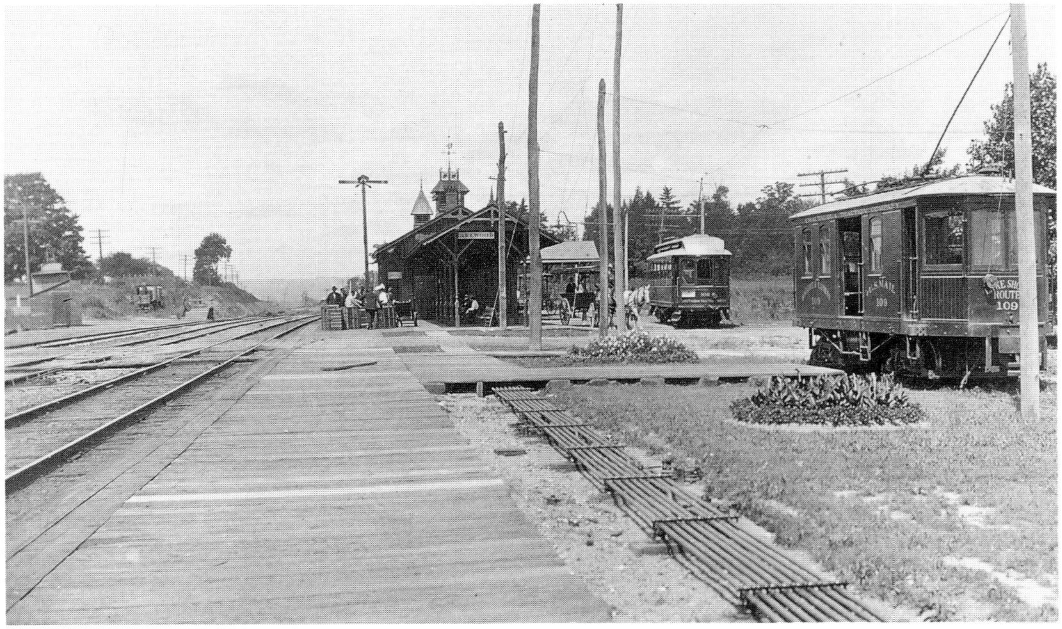

Erie depot and Chautauqua Traction cars, ca. 1908. Looking west. Chautauqua Avenue crosses the Erie tracks just below the depot. The car in the rear faces up the lake. The car in the foreground is a baggage car. Passengers on the Erie trains had a short walk to the lake hotels. *FHS*

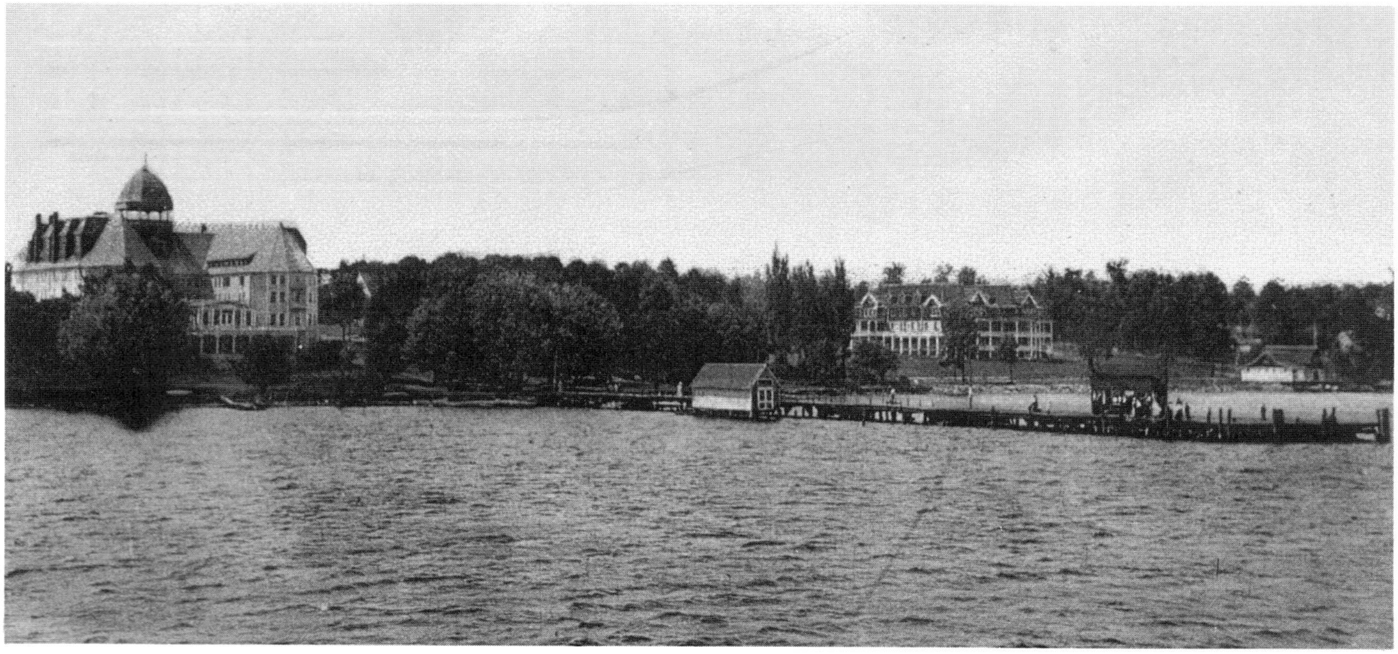

Lakewood shoreline, ca. 1910. The second Kent House to the left and the Lakewood Country Club to the right. The Chadakoin Rowing Club, which removed from Greenhurst across the lake, stands just below the Country Club. *RL*

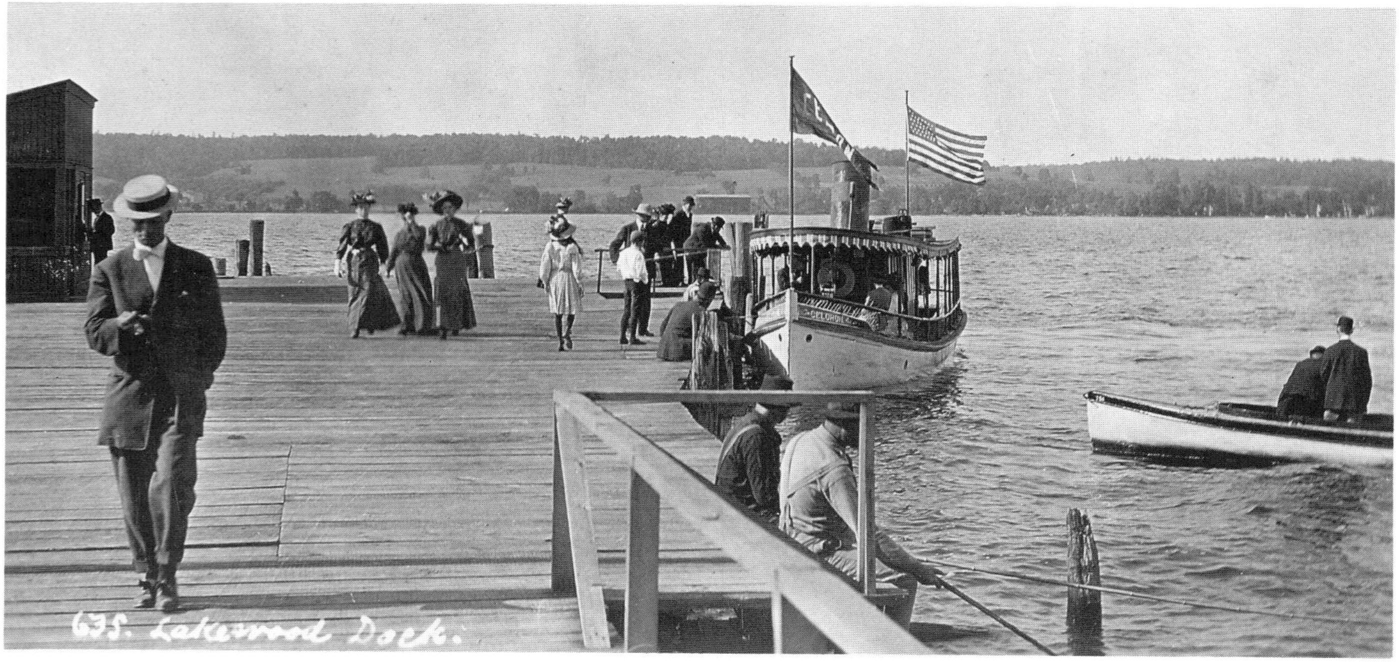

Lakewood dock, ca. 1909. The ferry *Greenhurst* at the wide Lakewood dock. The Kent House had been closed for several years before this photograph was taken. It remained on shore in a steadily deteriorating state until it was finally demolished in 1916. *RL*

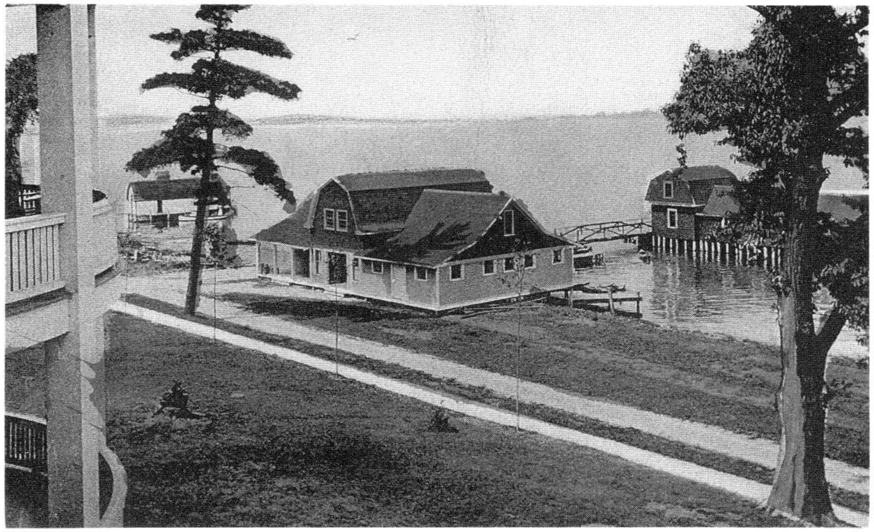

Chadakoin Rowing Club, ca. 1908. The second home of the Chadakoin Rowing Club, purchased from the Lakewood Country Club in 1908. The building burned in 1928, and a new boat club was built in 1930 on the site of the Kent House. This club is now the Chautauqua Lake Yacht Club. *RL*

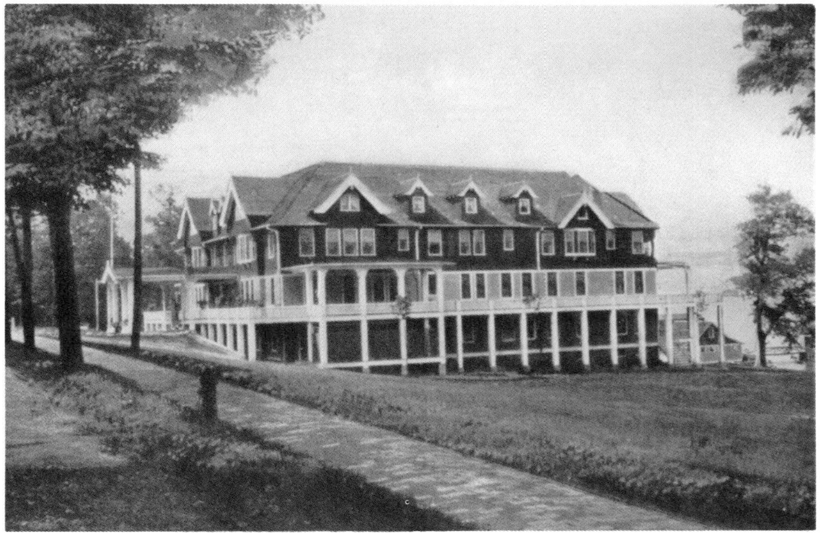

Lakewood Country Club, ca. 1908. Organized in 1900 by a group of summer residents, the clubhouse was completed in 1906 at the site of the Waldmere-Sterlingworth Hotel. The vast building housed a fine dining area, meeting rooms and recreational facilities. The grounds sloped to the lake where members could enjoy bathing on the beach. The clubhouse closed during World War I and was sold in 1919 becoming the Lakewood Inn, which prospered throughout the 1920s. The Village of Lakewood purchased the property in 1929 and demolished the building to make way for Lakewood Park which opened in 1935. *RL*

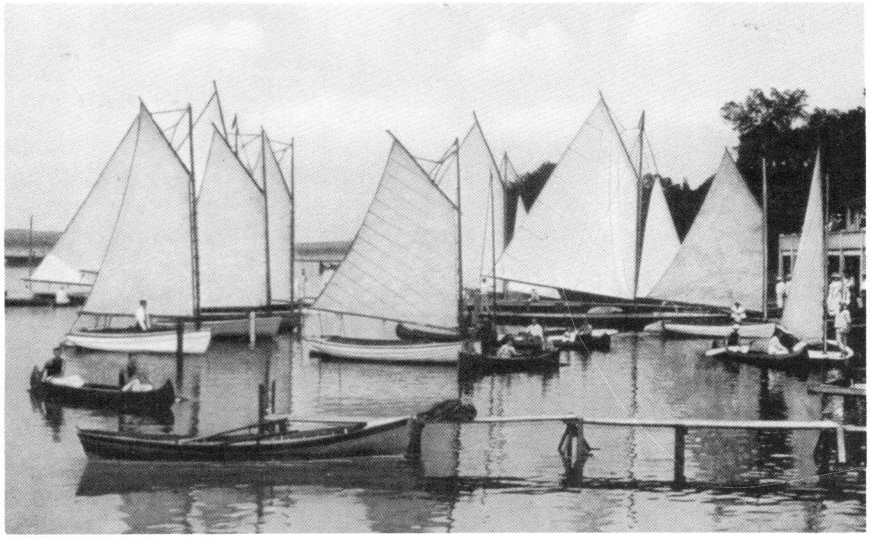

Chadakoin Rowing Club, ca. 1910. Sailing regatta at the Chadakoin Rowing Club. Sailing continues to be a popular sport on Chautauqua Lake. *RL*

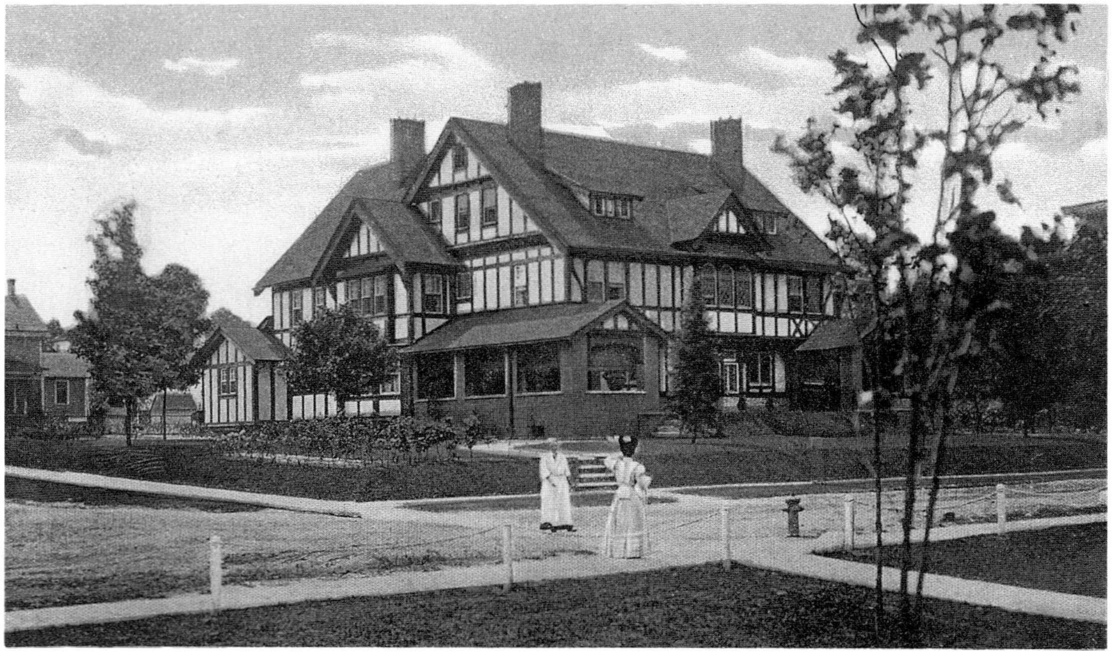

Sorg Manor, ca. 1910. This lovely Tudor style home was built by Paul Arthur Sorg of the American Tobacco Company in 1906 as a summer residence. It was known as "Bide-a-Bit." Mr. Sorg had a stable of fine horses and several rigs. The Sorg house stood across the street from the Lakewood Country Club. It remains today "The Green Farm," a fine gift and clothing shop. *RL*

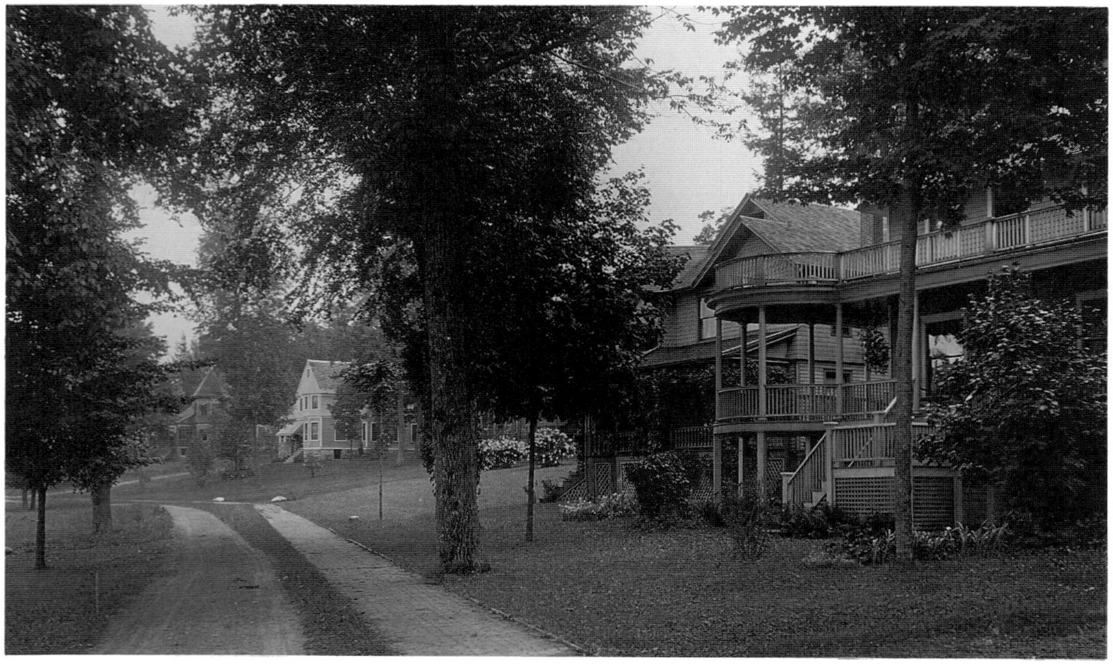

Shore Drive, Lakewood, ca. 1908. View eastward at Atlantic Avenue. The two homes to the left were removed along with two others to make room for the Packard estate, built in 1912. The two homes to the right are still standing, fine examples of Lakewood's Victorian-era architecture. *FHS*

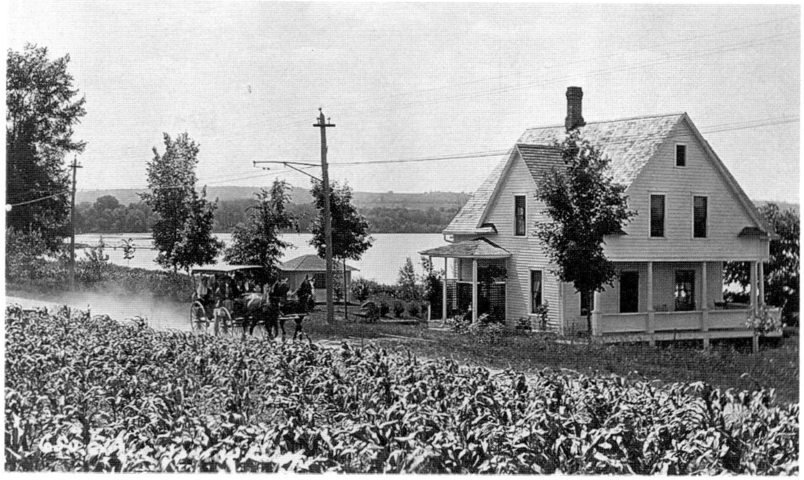

Sherman's Bay, ca. 1906. A carriage heads toward Lakewood along Summit Avenue. The Chautauqua Traction Line ran very close to the lake at this point. The tracks lay between the street and the house. *RL*

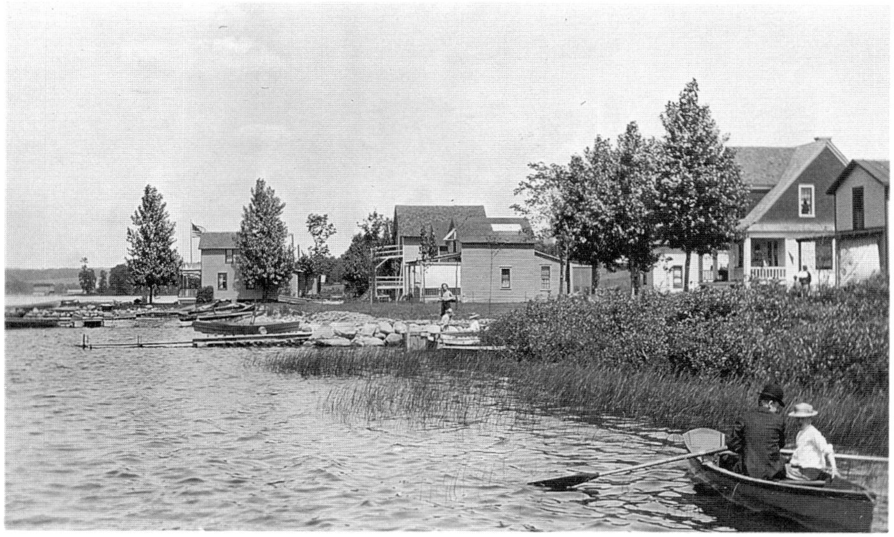

Sherman's Bay, ca. 1910. The lakeshore at Sherman's Bay looking toward Lakewood. Daniel Sherman, town supervisor and sheriff, settled on the lakeshore in 1816. The Sherman name, spelled with or without a second "a," has been prominent in Chautauqua County throughout its history. Many of the summer cottages at Sherman's Bay have been converted to year-round homes. *RL*

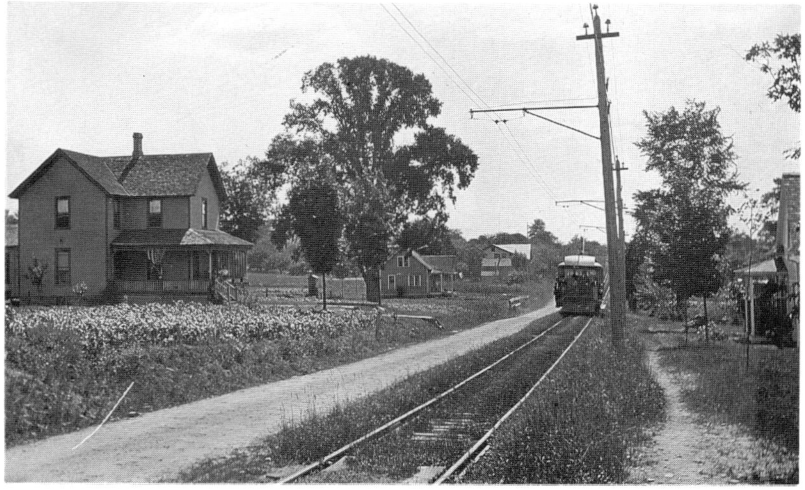

Sherman's Bay, ca. 1906. Looking west on Summit Avenue. Chautauqua Lake is to the right. The double copper line of Almet Broadhead's Traction Company was expensive, but it maintained necessary voltage. The farmhouse in the photograph is still standing. *RL*

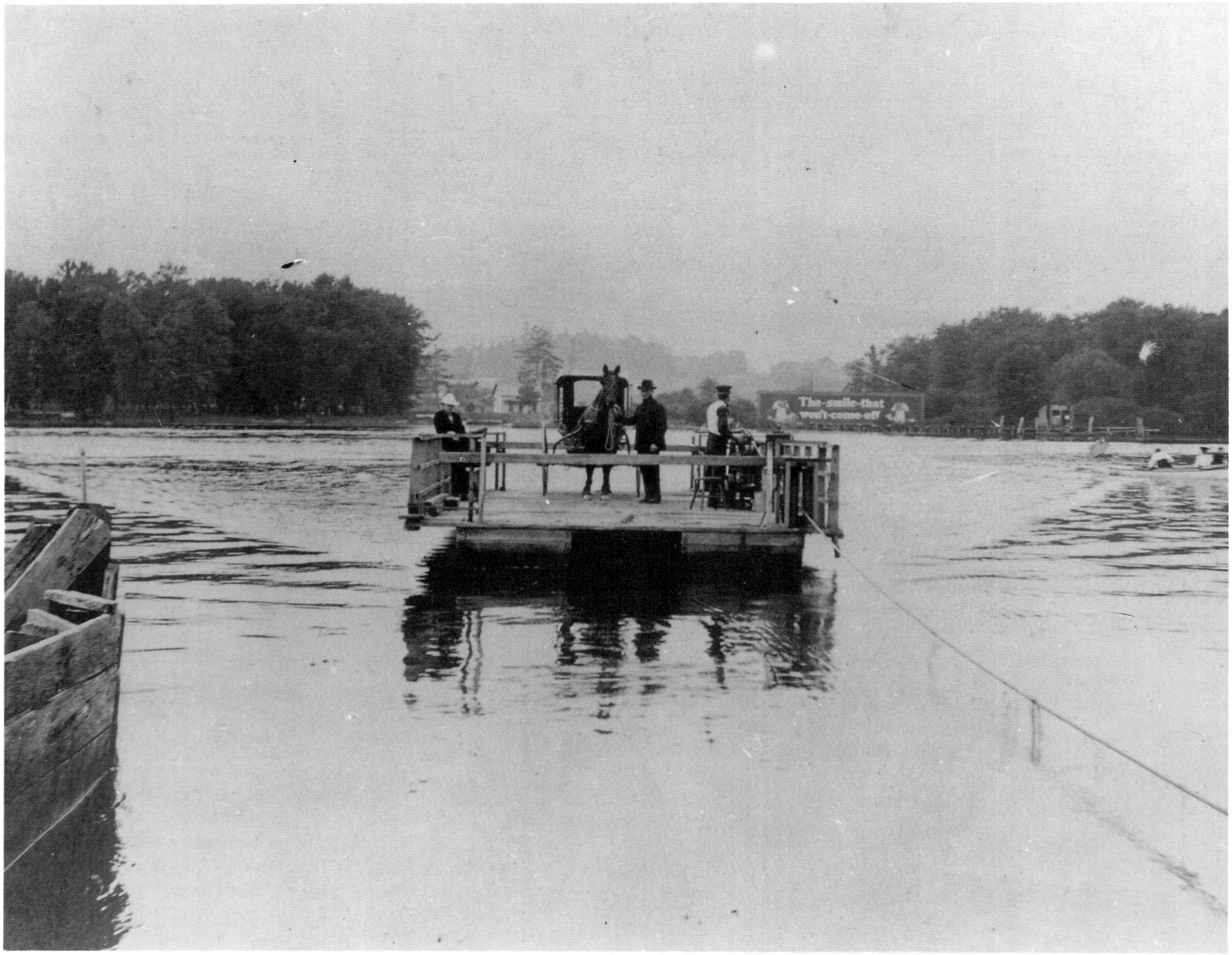
The-smile-that
won't-come-off

MIDLAKE WEST

STOW TOM'S POINT VICTORIA WOODLAWN SYLVAN PARK

Hogan's Hut is the most distinguishable landmark in the little village of Stow. In 1811, Thomas Bemus, a substantial landowner on the Stow side of the lake, was granted a license by the *County of Chautauque* to begin operation of a ferry across the 1,000 foot "narrows." The Bemus Point - Stow Ferry has been carrying passengers and cargo between the two villages ever since. Completion of the Chautauqua County Veterans' Memorial Bridge in 1982 destroyed the ferry's commercial value, but its operation continues today through the help of volunteers. "Tom's Point," location of the Sportsman's Club, is named for Thomas Bemus. Victoria, about midway between Jamestown and Mayville, is named for the wife of William Marcy who built a successful hotel there in 1890. Both Stow and the Victoria Hotel were serviced by the Chautauqua Traction Company after 1904. Woodlawn is a pretty, secluded area still occupied by seasonal cottages. Sylvan Park, on the site of the present Camp Chautauqua, was a picnic area developed by the Chautauqua Traction Company. The Traction Company opened its picnic grounds in 1907, the year the Long Point picnic area closed.

Bemus Point-Stow Ferry, ca. 1906. "The smile that won't come off." A Quaker Oats billboard to the left of the dock at Stow. Ferry operator Alton Ball and passengers approach the Bemus Point landing. *RW*

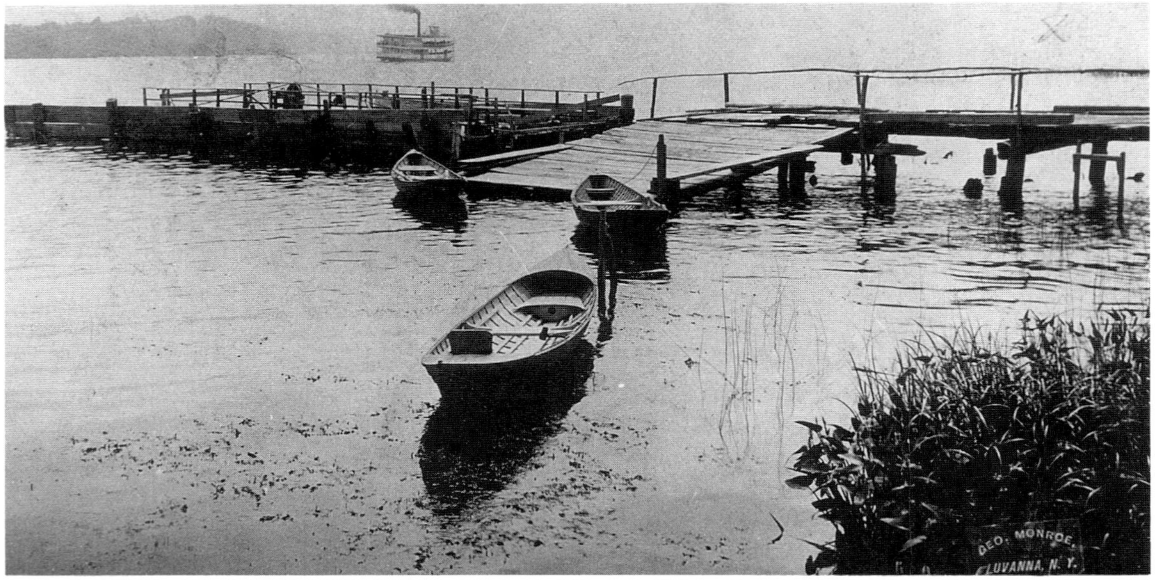

Ferry landing, Stow, ca. 1905. Stow was long known simply as "the landing." An attempt at development under the name "Lakeland" never succeeded. The *City of Cleveland* is in the distance. *FHS*

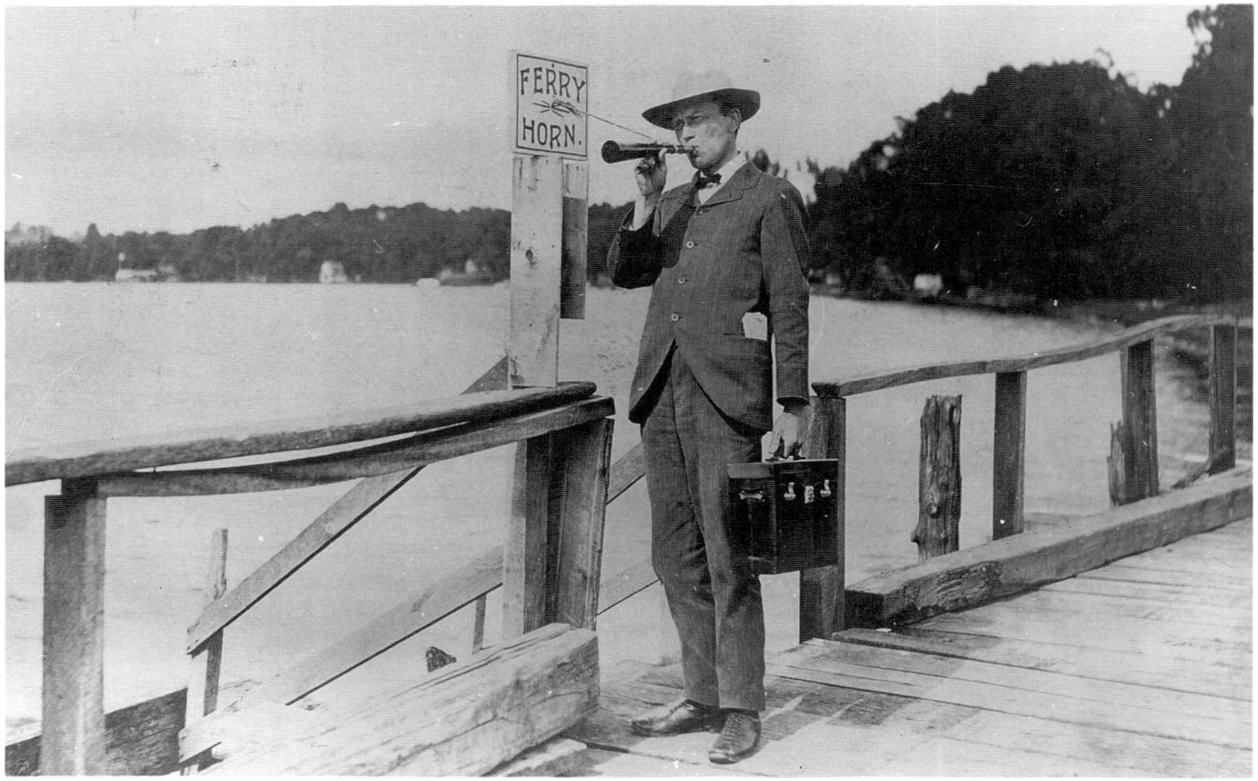

Ferry landing, Bemus, ca. 1905. Mr. Ballinger, Meadville druggist, summons the ferry from across the lake. Mr. Ballinger was a friend of Bemus Point Physician Dr. Earl Scofield. He is carrying a camera case. *RW*

Stow, ca. 1907. A view of C.W. Slayton's "Farmers Exchange" and the Chautauqua Traction Company's tracks. Mr. Slayton's store sold boots and shoes, dry goods and groceries. It also boasted a public telephone. The road adjacent to the store leads to the ferry landing. *RL*

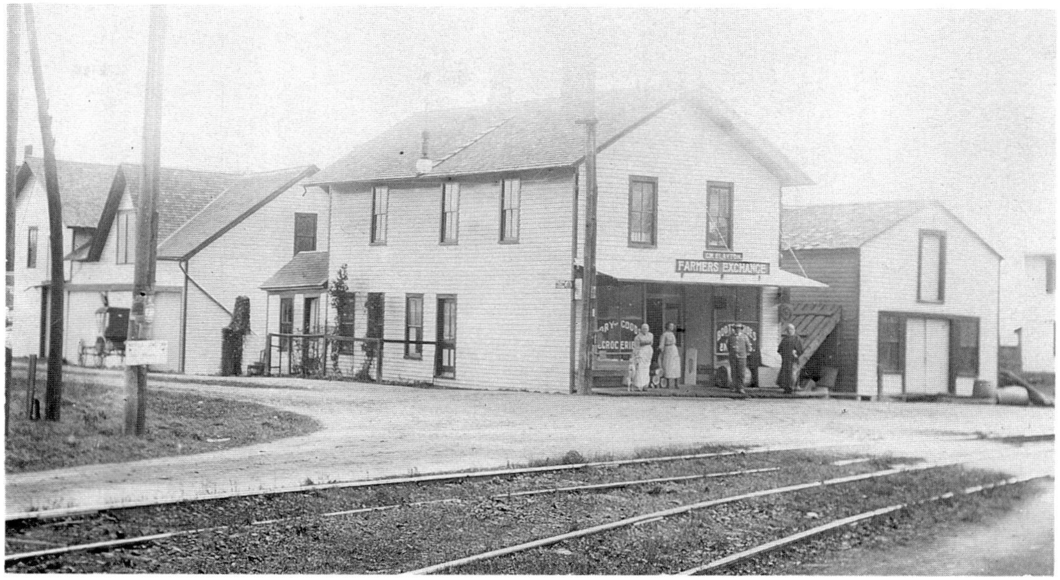

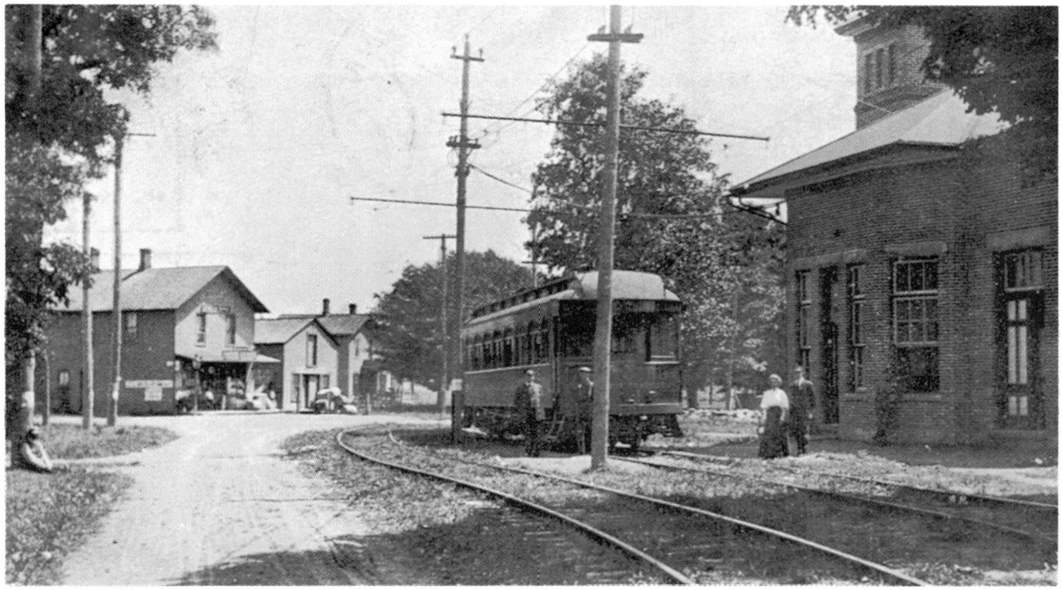

Stow, ca. 1907. What was Stow's main road lay behind Hogan's Hut and the Traction Company's station. The station contained a power house for boosting voltage output. Because of Stow's "remote" location, brick for the construction of the station had to be transported by rail to Bemus Point and carried by wagon to the ferry. The station house is still standing. *RL*

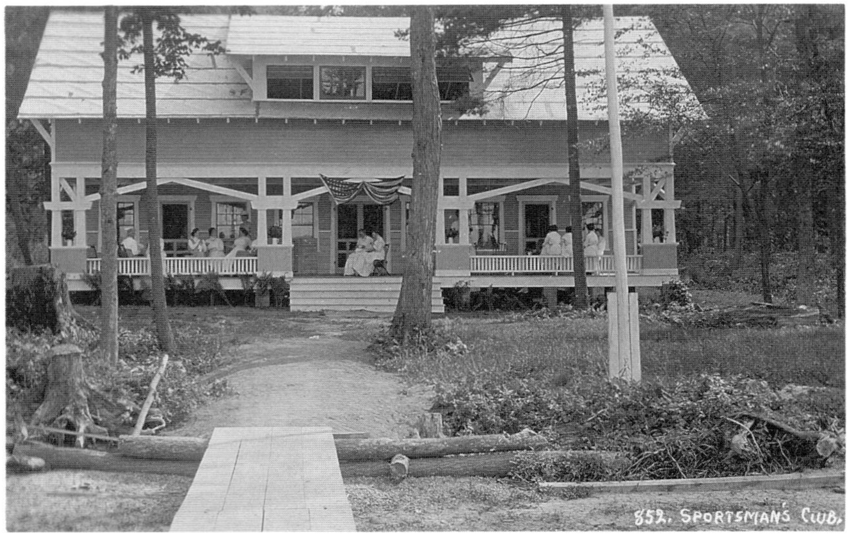

Clubhouse, Sportsman's Club, ca. 1910. The Sportsman's Club, still in existence today, is a private club whose membership includes some of Chautauqua's most prominent citizens. The clubhouse is located near Tom's Point and the Power Squadron facilities. This building burned in the 1930s and was replaced by the current clubhouse. *RL*

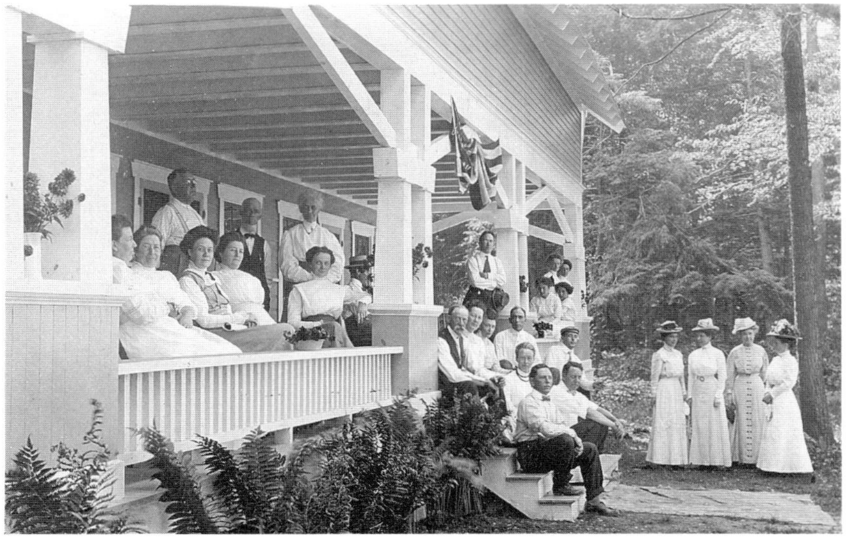

Members pose on the porch of the Sportsman's Club. The clubhouse could be reached by the Chautauqua Traction line. These folks undoubtedly dressed before arriving. Today a private road provides access to the clubhouse. *RL*

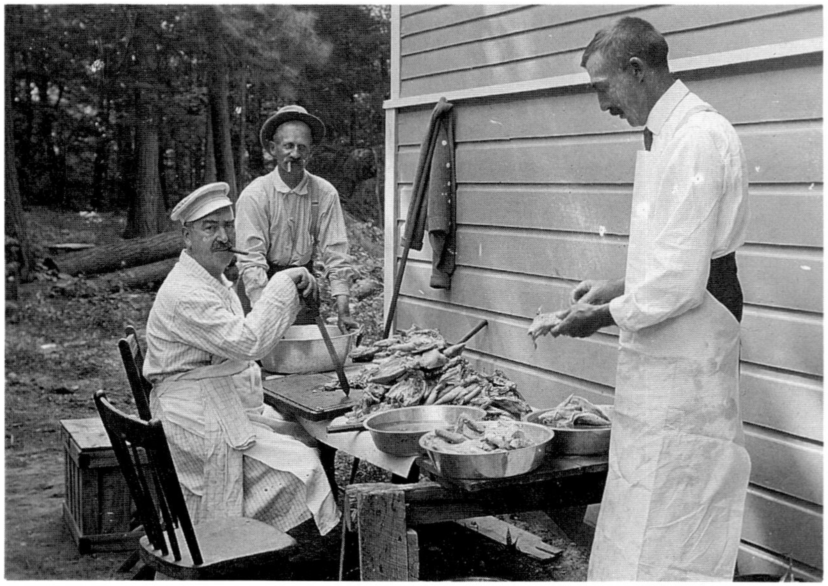

Preparation of the day's catch? A close inspection reveals it to be not fish, but chicken! *RL*

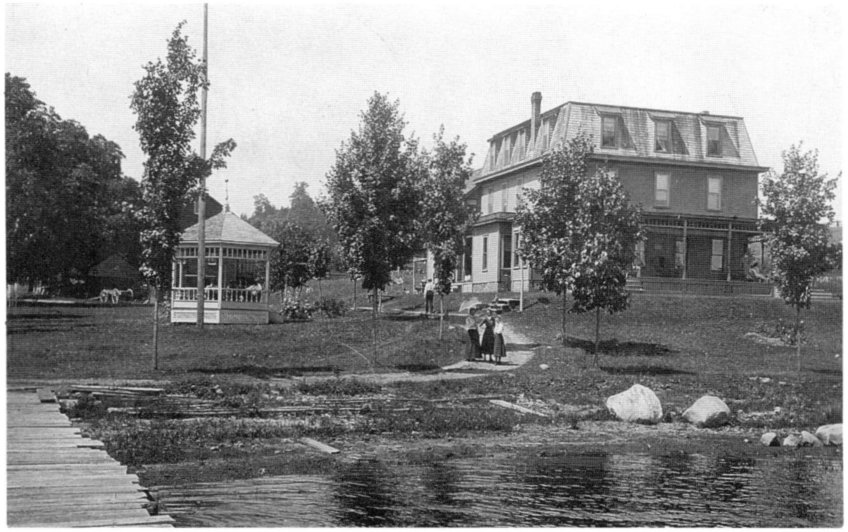

Victoria Hotel, ca. 1893. The Victoria had the reputation as a "handsome" hotel. Built in 1890, the 25-room hotel was served both by the lake steamers and the Chautauqua Traction Line. It was equipped with all the modern conveniences. Choice dishes were served and by the late 1890s, the establishment became noted for its fish dinners. Rates were $1.50 per day. The hotel enjoyed popularity for many years. It was torn down in 1931. *RL*

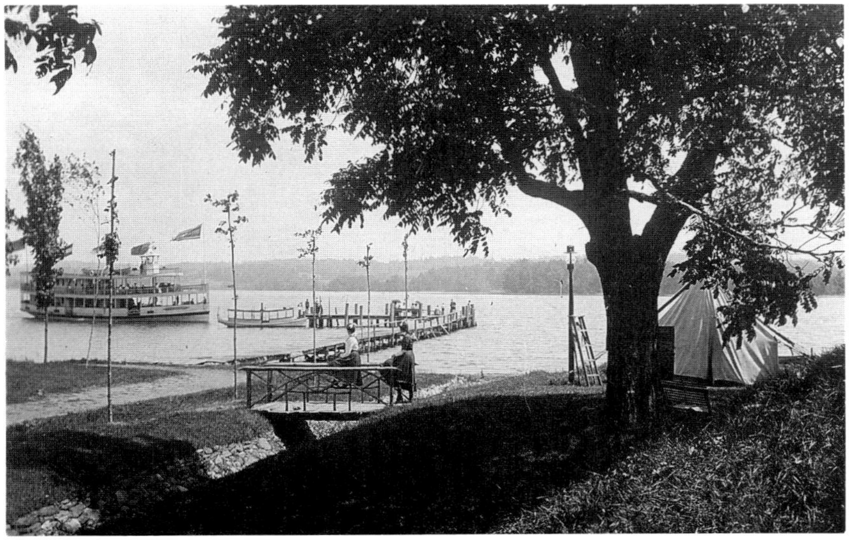

Victoria, ca. 1910. From the vantage point of Victoria's pier, visitors waiting for a steamer enjoyed a fine view of the lake including Chautauqua, Point Chautauqua and Bemus Point. *RL*

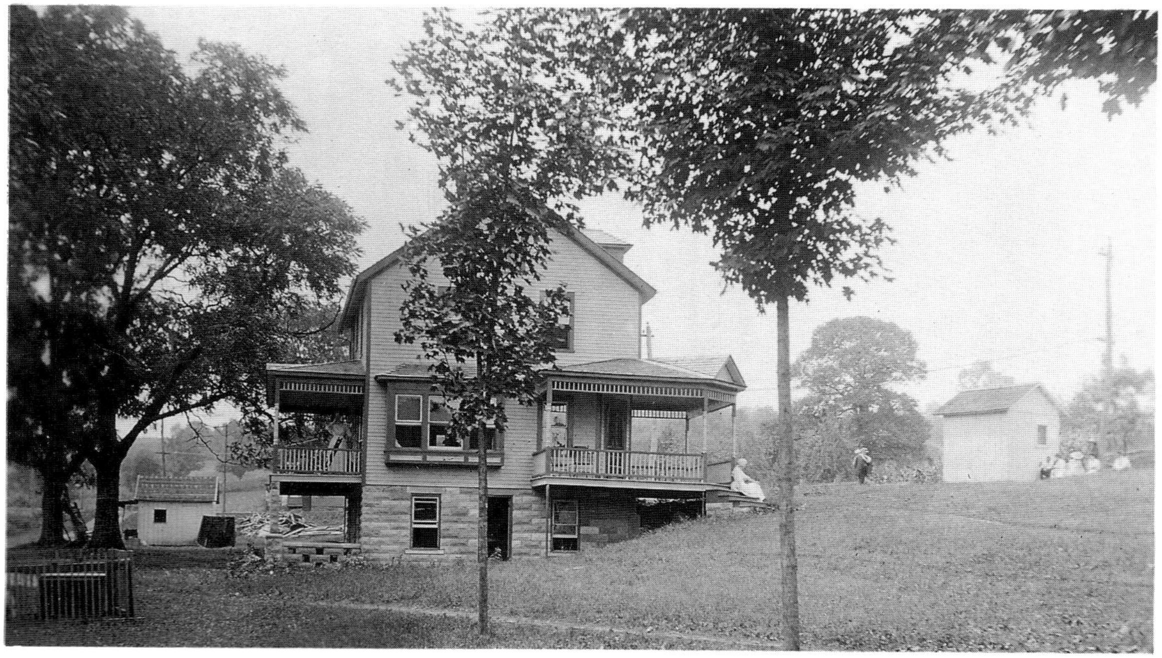

Hunt Cottage, Victoria, ca. 1896. A tranquil summer day. Hunt Cottage is more substantial than most of the seasonal cottages in the area today. *RL*

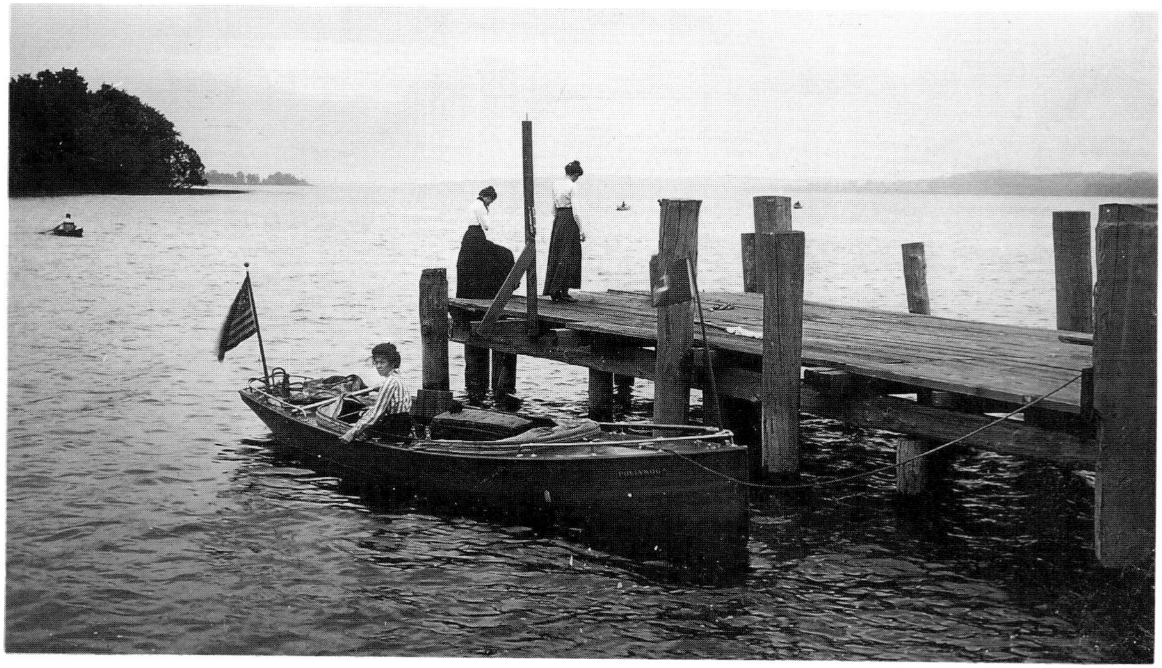

Victoria dock, ca. 1910. The romance of Chautauqua Lake at sunset looking over Victoria's dock and down the lake. These three women are emerging from the motor launch *Pollywog*. By 1910 motorboats were displacing the small steamers on the lake. Long Point is to the left. *RL*

Woodlawn Park, ca. 1910. A view of the shoreline and docks, looking down the lake from Woodlawn Park. The *City of New York* is heading for Victoria, probably having been hailed by passengers. *RL*

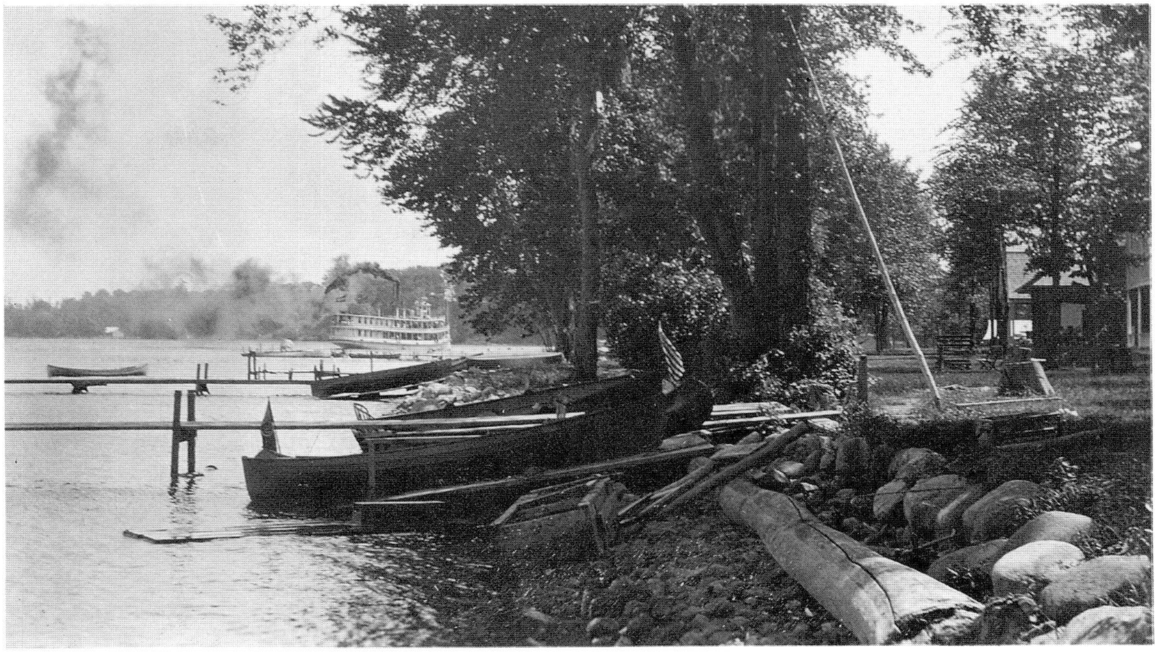

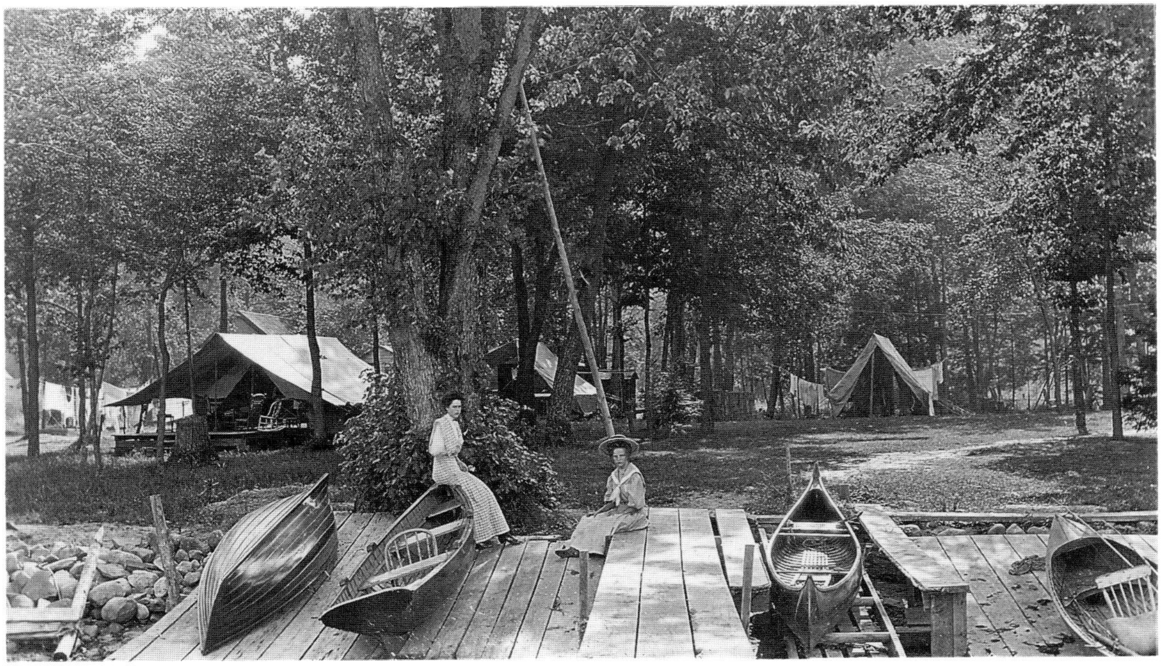

Woodlawn Park, ca. 1910. Tenting and boating at Woodlawn Park. Note that the legs have been removed from the chairs in the rowboats. The boats were rigged to troll for muskellunge. *RL*

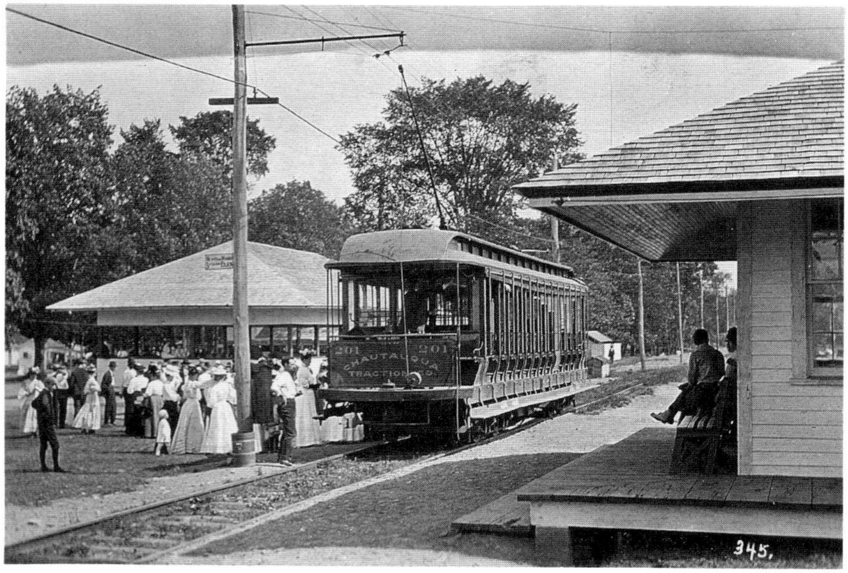

Sylvan Park, ca. 1909. Passengers await boarding at the Sylvan Park station. The Chautauqua Traction Company's tracks skirted the west side of the lake from Jamestown to Mayville and later north to Barcelona on Lake Erie. Car 201, shown in the photograph above, was an open or summer car. *RL*

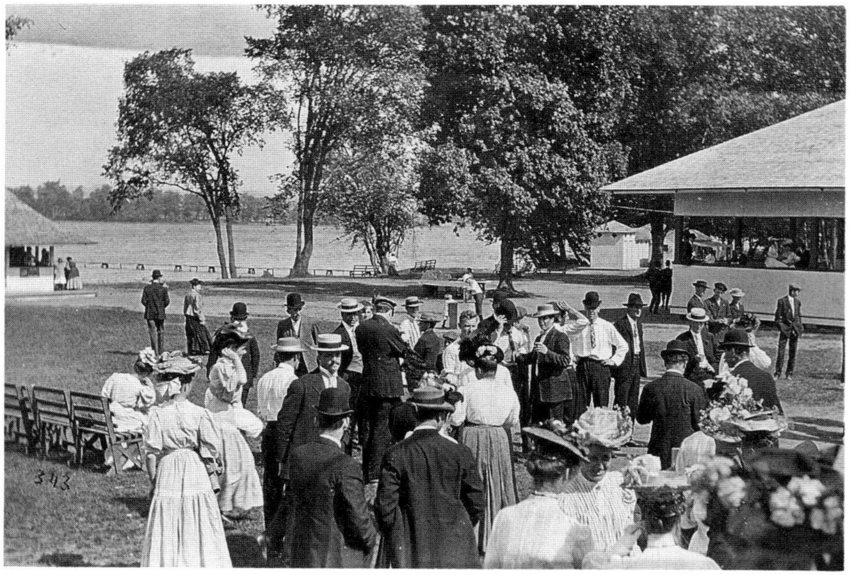

Sylvan Park, ca. 1909. Sylvan Park was a popular gathering place for church and other groups until the Traction Company suspended operations in 1926. The visitors in the photograph are dressed suitably for dancing, available on the grounds. The park was sold to private interests and became Camp Twanekotah, a high-class summer camp for girls. Camp Chautauqua occupies this site today. *RL*

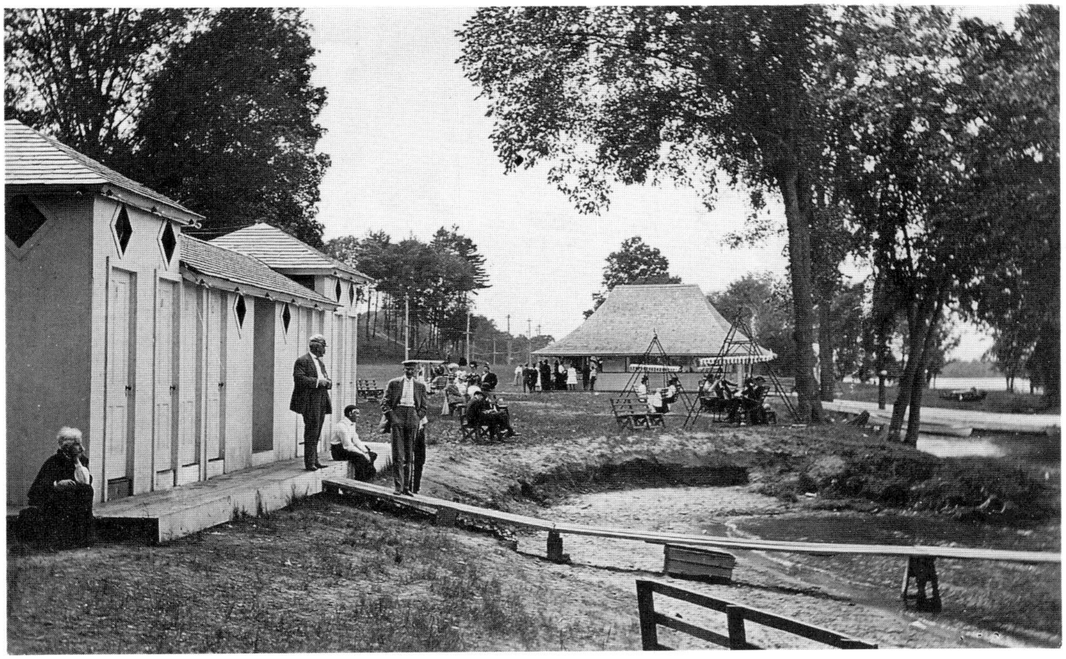

Sylvan Park, ca. 1909. One of the 16 bath houses built close to the beach. The picnic grounds also contained a baseball diamond and swings visible in the center of the photograph. Drinking water was piped into the park. The buildings and grounds were well lighted with electricity. *RL*

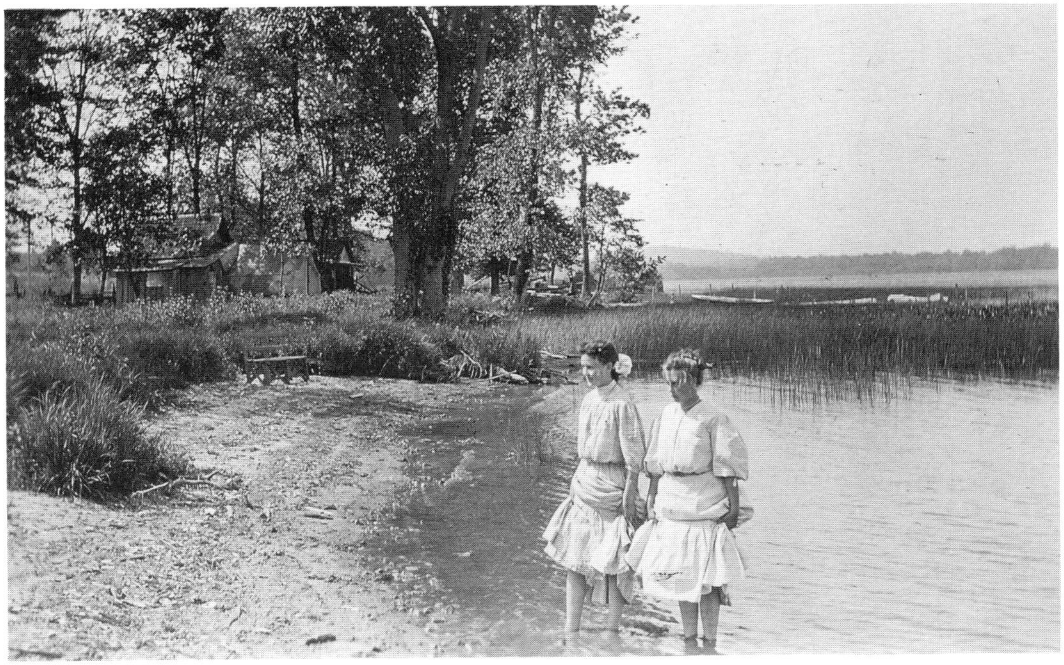

Sylvan Park, ca. 1909. Waders at the Sylvan Park beach described by the *Jamestown Journal* as "one of the finest" along the lake. *RL*

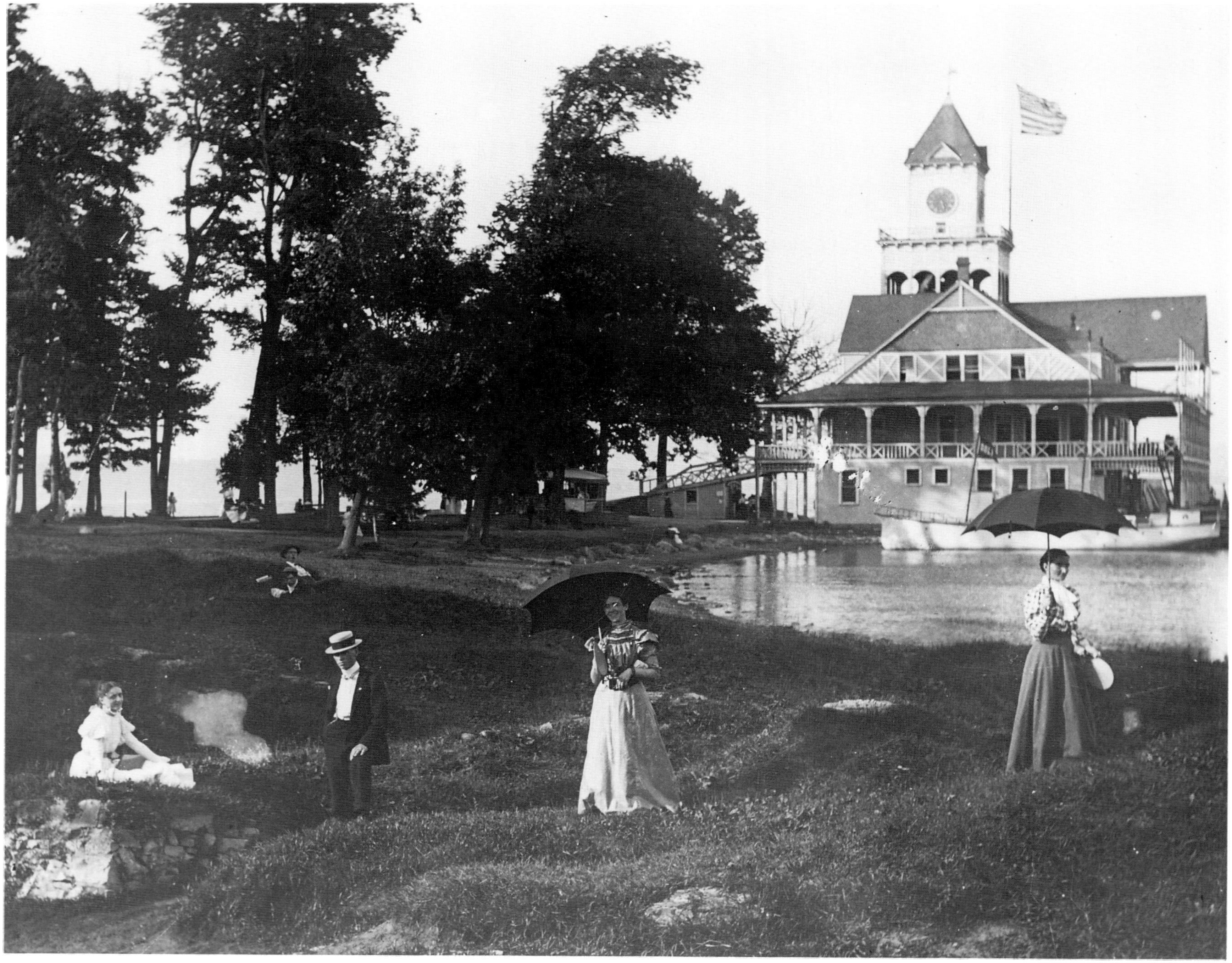

CHAUTAUQUA

Founders Lewis Miller and Bishop John H. Vincent would have been pleased with the scope and direction of Chautauqua's activities today. The modern Chautauqua Institution is an internationally recognized forum for the discussion of political and social issues as well as a regional center for the arts, entertainment, and recreation. Almost a century and a quarter has passed since the Chautauqua Lake Camp Meeting Association held its first season at the pretty piece of lake shore then called Fair Point. Mr. Miller and Dr. Vincent organized the campgrounds as a training center for Methodist Sunday School teachers. The first meeting was held August 4-18, 1874. When President Grant accepted Dr. Vincent's invitation to visit the grounds the following season, the early success of Chautauqua was assured. In 1876 the meeting was renamed the Chautauqua Lake Sunday School Assembly. The name Fair Point was formally changed to Chautauqua around 1877. The enclave became Chautauqua Assembly in 1883 and in 1902, Chautauqua Institution. Dr. Vincent's stated purpose was "to promote the intellectual, social, physical, moral and religious welfare of the people." The "Chautauqua idea" was the pursuit of knowledge in a setting unsurpassed in beauty. Its immediate success hastened development all around the lake. Preparing to enter the twenty-first century, Chautauqua Institution continues the pursuit while closely guarding its celebrated nineteenth century ambience.

Miller Park and the Steamboat Pier, ca. 1898. Late Victorian visitors stroll among the hills of Palestine Park. The small steamboat *Dolphin*, nee *Olivia*, is docked at the pier. *FHS*

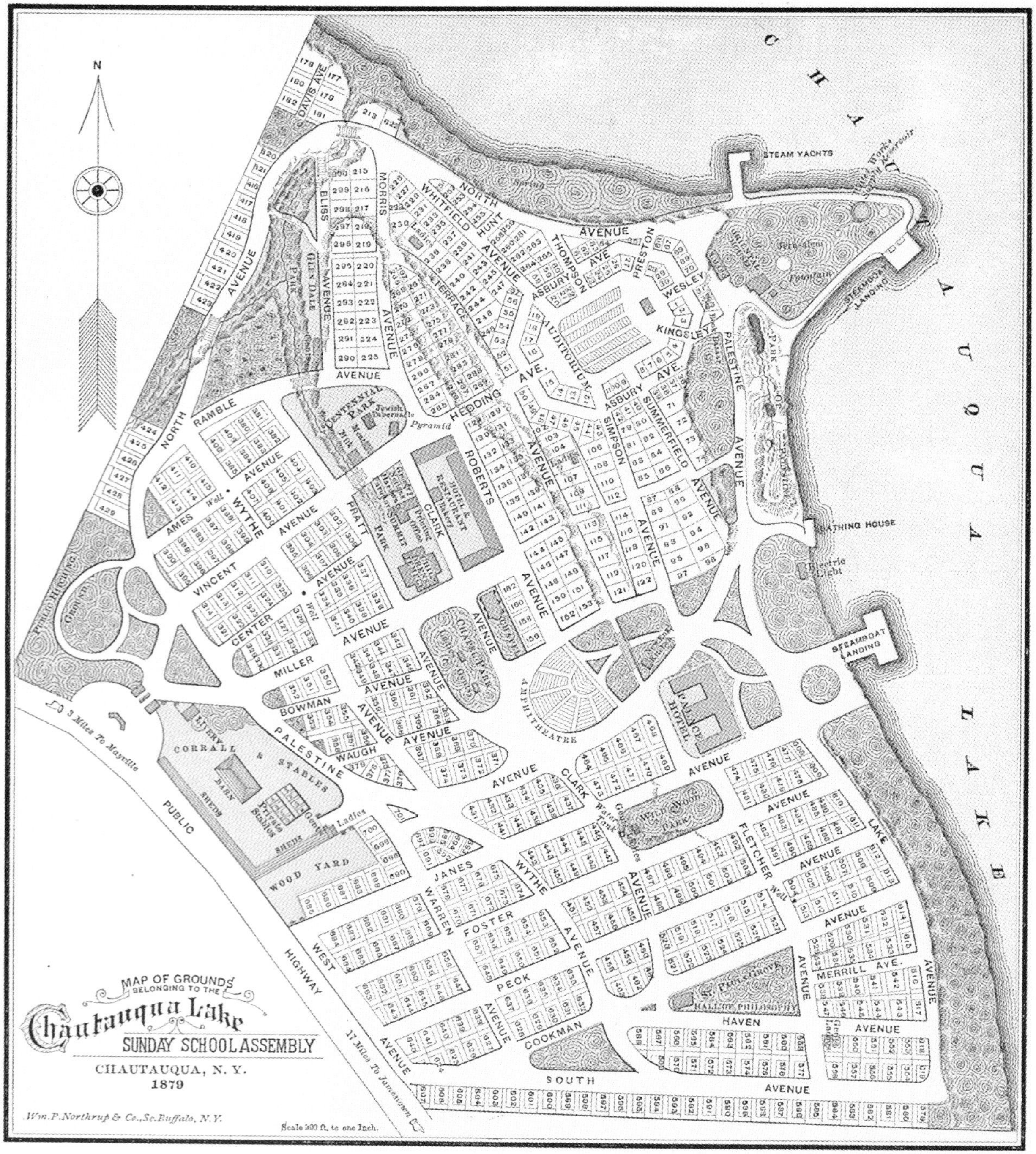

This map of the grounds of the Chautauqua Lake Sunday School Assembly shows what the community looked like in 1879. Note that little has changed in the more than 120 years of Chautauqua's existence. *PL*

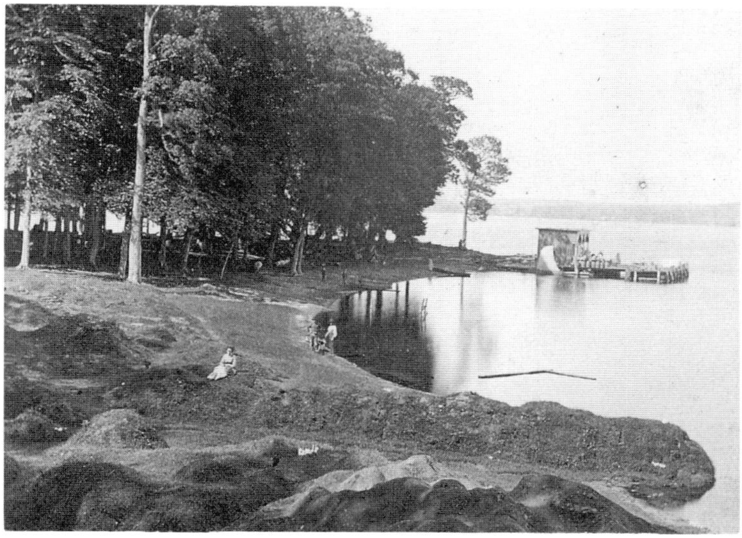

Fair Point, ca. 1874. It was the beauty of this small point extending into Chautauqua Lake that convinced John Heyl Vincent to change his original plan for a conference of Sunday School teachers from a city setting. *CCHS*

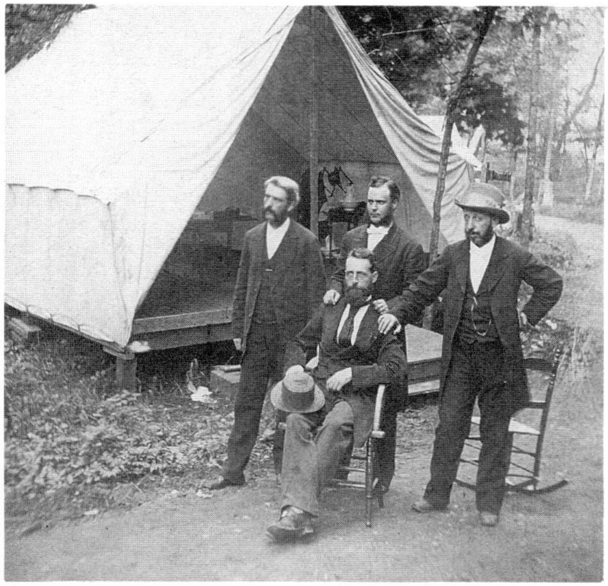

Fair Point, 1875. Before cottages, hotels and boarding establishments were built, visitors to Fair Point were housed in tents. Left to right are J.L. Hurlbut, J.A. Worden, Frank Beard, and J.L. Hughes. *CCHS*

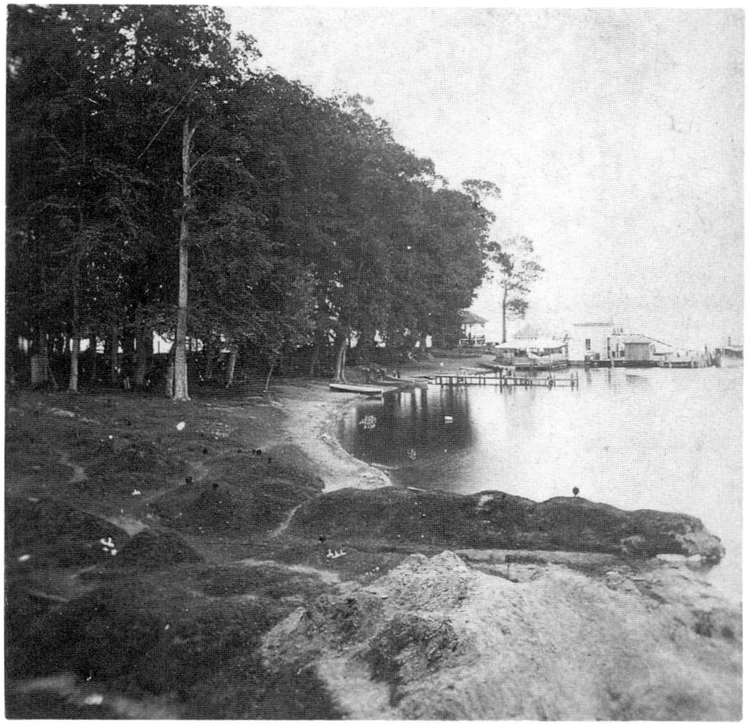

Fair Point, 1875. A view of the dock at Fair Point taken from Mt. Hermon in Palestine Park. Palestine Park was a scale replica of the Holy Land constructed near the shoreline the year the camp meeting opened. The Park was popular with visitors but was difficult to maintain, and little is left of what was then called an "artistic achievement." This is the scene that greeted President U.S. Grant when he visited Fair Point in 1875. *CCHS*

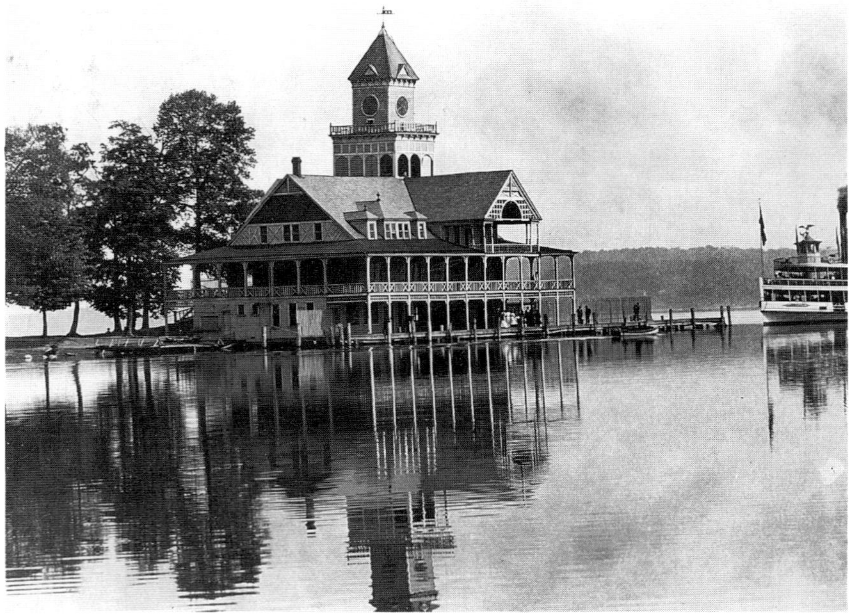

Chautauqua pier, ca. 1905. High water and the *City of Cleveland* approaching from up the lake. *RL*

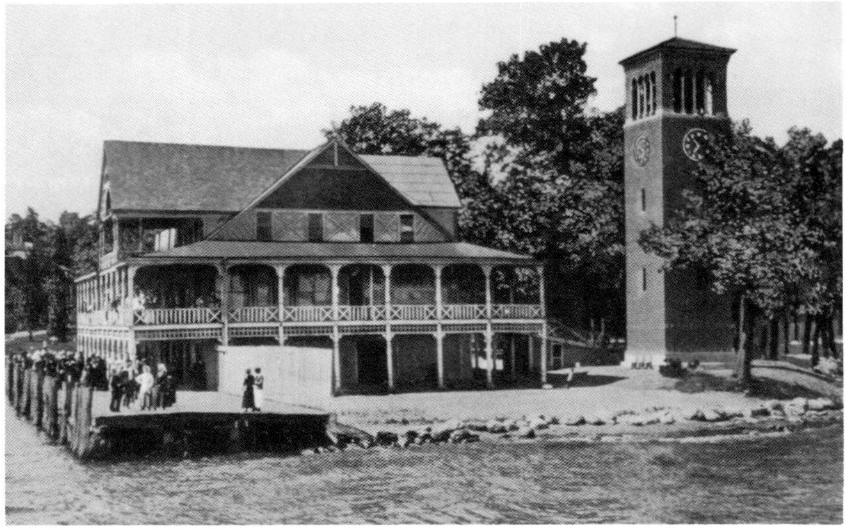

Chautauqua dock and tower, ca. 1912. The Miller Bell Tower, a memorial to Lewis Miller, has been a symbol of Chautauqua Institution since 1911. Of Italianate design, the landmark is 69 feet tall and 16 feet square. The tower is visible from both land and water, and the toll of its Westminster chimes is a familiar sound to visitors to the Institution. *RL*

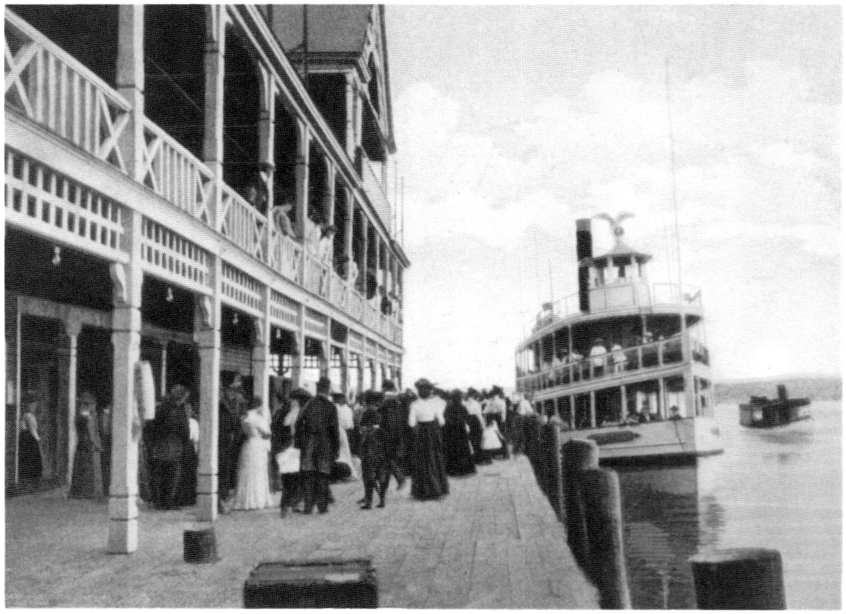

Chautauqua pier, ca. 1906-1910. Chautauqua's picturesque pier, built in 1886, welcomed visitors arriving on the lake steamers. Three stories in height, its belfry housed the Chautauqua chimes. Vacationers could shop at stores on the upper balcony. The pier building was removed in 1916. *RL*

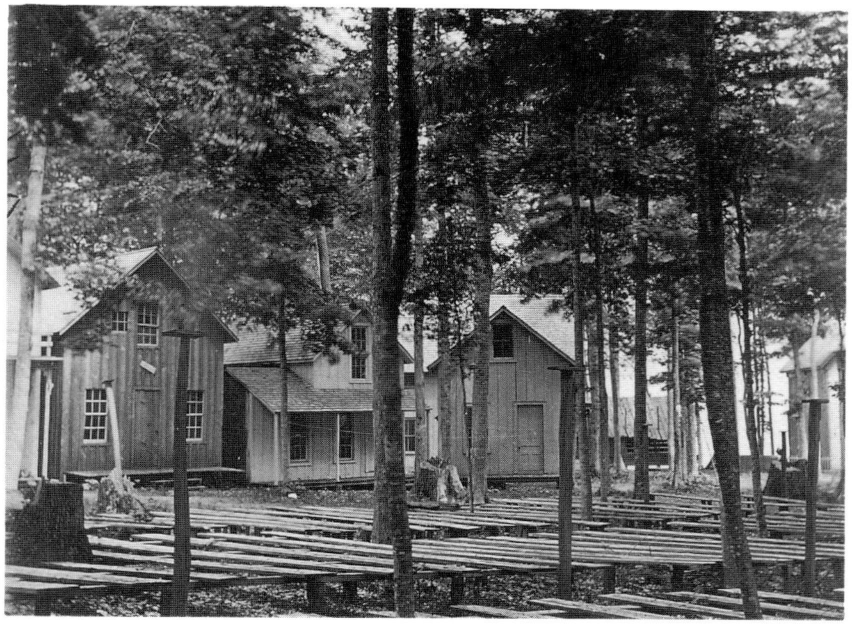

Fair Point, ca. 1876. A peaceful day at Fair Point Camp Grounds. Early cottages were built in groves of shade trees. The benches in the foreground are seats for an open air auditorium. *CCHS*

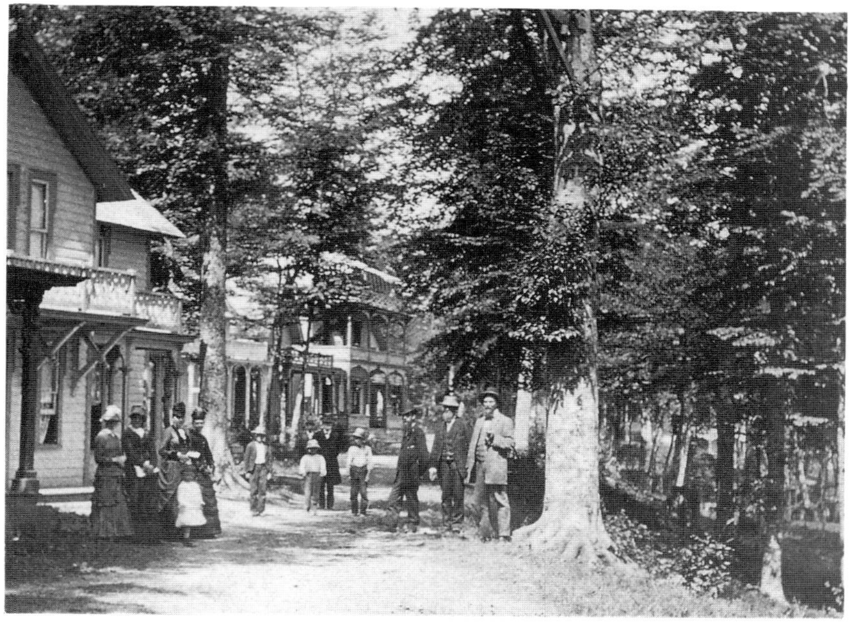

Chautauqua Assembly, ca. 1885. One of the paths traversed by early Chautauquans. After ten years, these more substantial homes reflect the success of Chautauqua. *CCHS*

St. Elmo Hotel, ca. 1910. The original St. Elmo Hotel was built in the 1890s and was a residence until 1896. Located on the corner of Pratt and Ames Avenues, its appointments were described as "elegant, with every modern appliance for comfort and convenience." Advertisements of the day praised its dining room as "one of the most pleasant on the grounds" with "cuisine above criticism." Reasonable rates coupled with an easy walk to the Amphitheater made the St. Elmo a popular spot for summer visitors. *RL*

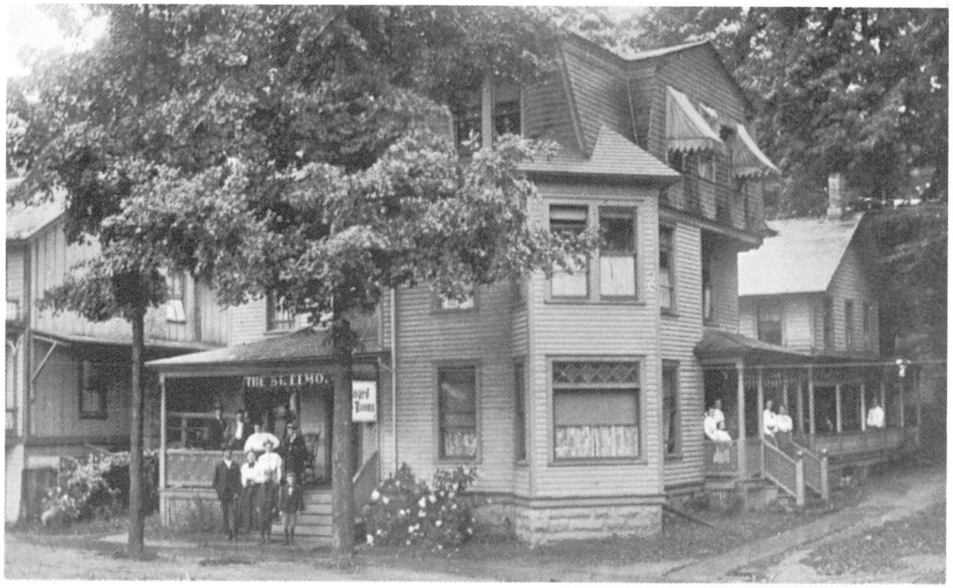

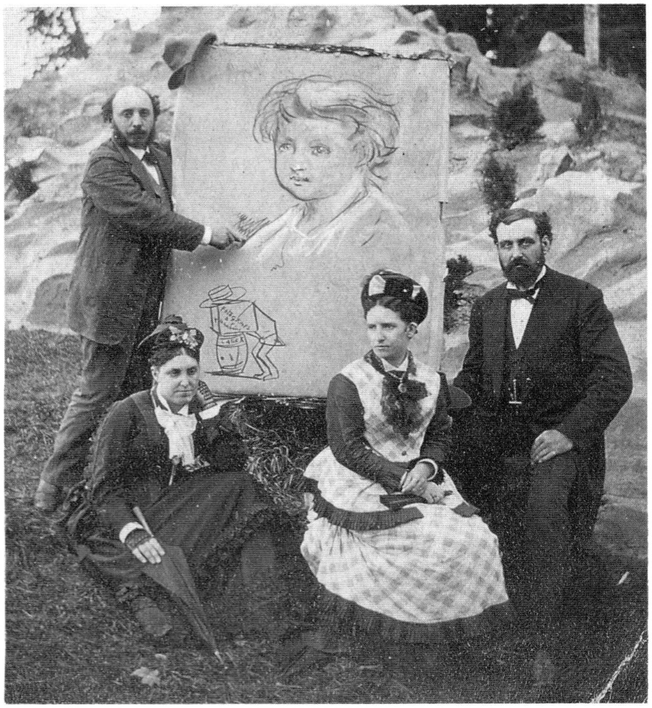

Fair Point, August, 1876. The reverse of this stereopticon view identifies Mr. and Mrs. P.P. Bliss at Fair Point during the Sunday School Assembly. The others are artist Frank Beard and his wife, Helen. Beard was a caricaturist who would often draw his portraits before an audience. Jesse Hurlbut tells how "He would draw ... a striking picture, seemingly serious and then in a few quick strokes transform it into something absurdly funny." *CCHS*

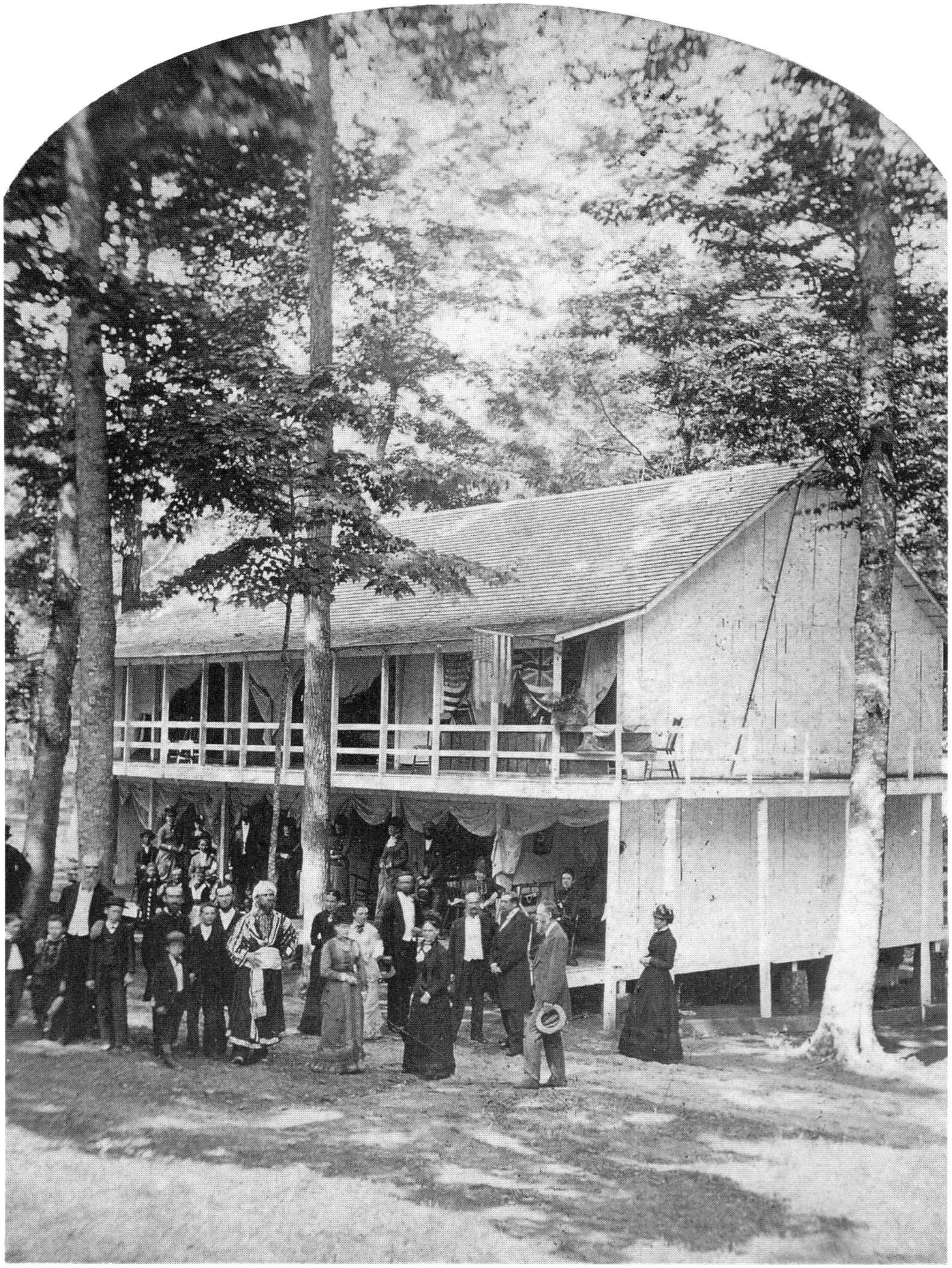

The Ark, ca. 1878. The Guest House, popularly known as "The Ark," was built around 1875. Speakers and lecturers were housed here while at Fair Point. A two-storied frame building, the living quarters were partitioned with tent cloth. Because of its many celebrated guests, the building was called "Knowers' Ark." Early guests included Edward Everett Hale and the artist Frank Beard. We can only imagine some of the stories shared by guests gathered on the porch! *CCHS*

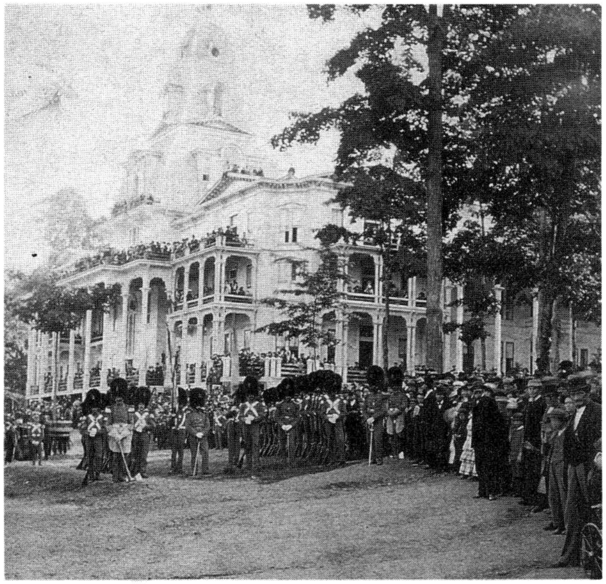

Hotel Athenaeum, ca. 1885. Guests of the lake hotels would frequently be treated to the spectacle of visiting drill teams or the summer encampments of military groups. The Seward Guard from Westfield often held drills at the Hotel Athenaeum. Organized in 1876, it was part of the 31st Brigade and 8th Division of the New York State National Guard. The unit was named for William H. Seward, President Lincoln's Secretary of State, who owned a home in Westfield. The spectators on the roof have a great view! *CCHS*

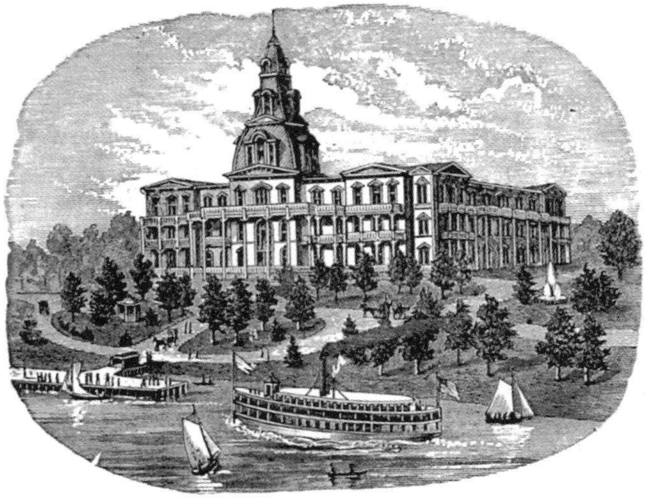

Woodcut of Athenaeum. *RL*

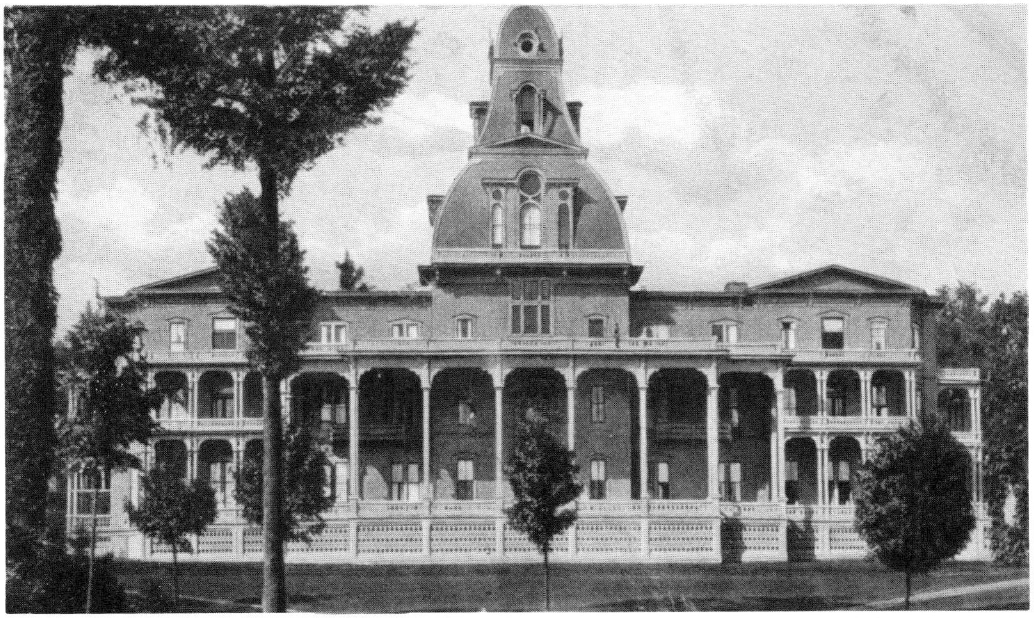

Hotel Athenaeum, ca. 1890. In all its Victorian splendor, the Hotel Athenaeum stands as a memorial to the golden days of Chautauqua Lake's great hotels. Built in 1881, it was a hotel of "the first grade." Its cuisine was excellent and visitors were pampered with all the amenities including an elevator, gas, electric bells, baths, and telegraph service. Rates for room and board were from $14.00 to $28.00 per week, depending on location. The hotel's picturesque verandah and rocking chairs are still popular with guests. Many distinguished visitors have stayed at the Athenaeum including President Bill Clinton in 1996. *RL*

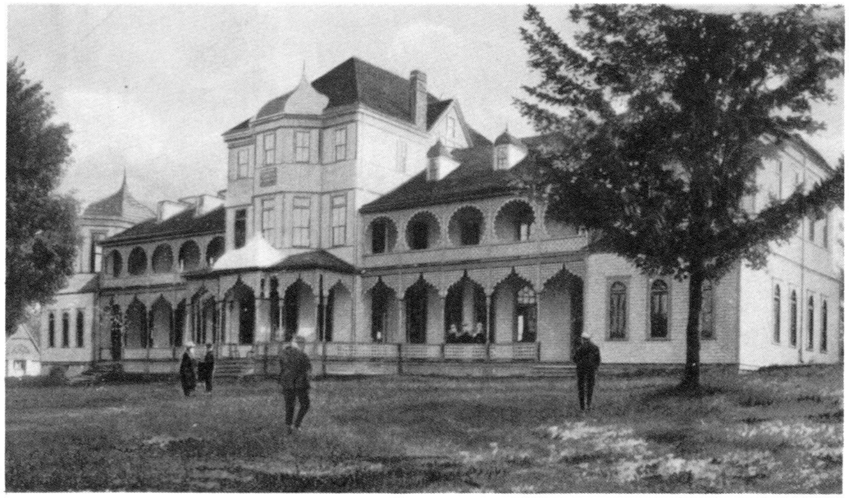

Chautauqua College of Liberal Arts, ca. 1900. Known as "The Moorish Barn," this building was built in 1887. It stood on College Hill and consolidated Chautauqua's educational programs under one roof. The building was razed in 1919 and the Arts and Crafts Building took its place. *RL*

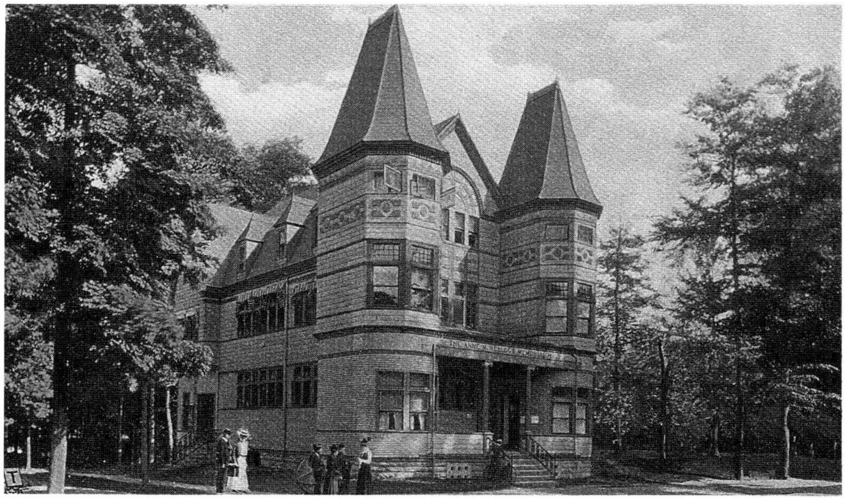

Anne Kellogg Memorial Hall, ca. 1900. Kellogg Hall originally stood on Vincent Avenue where the Colonnade Building now stands. It was built by James H. Kellogg, a wealthy merchant from Troy, New York, in memory of his mother. Dedicated to women's work, the building at one time housed the Woman's Christian Temperance Union. Kellogg Hall was moved to its present location at Ramble and Pratt Avenues in 1905. It is now headquarters for the summer school offices. *RL*

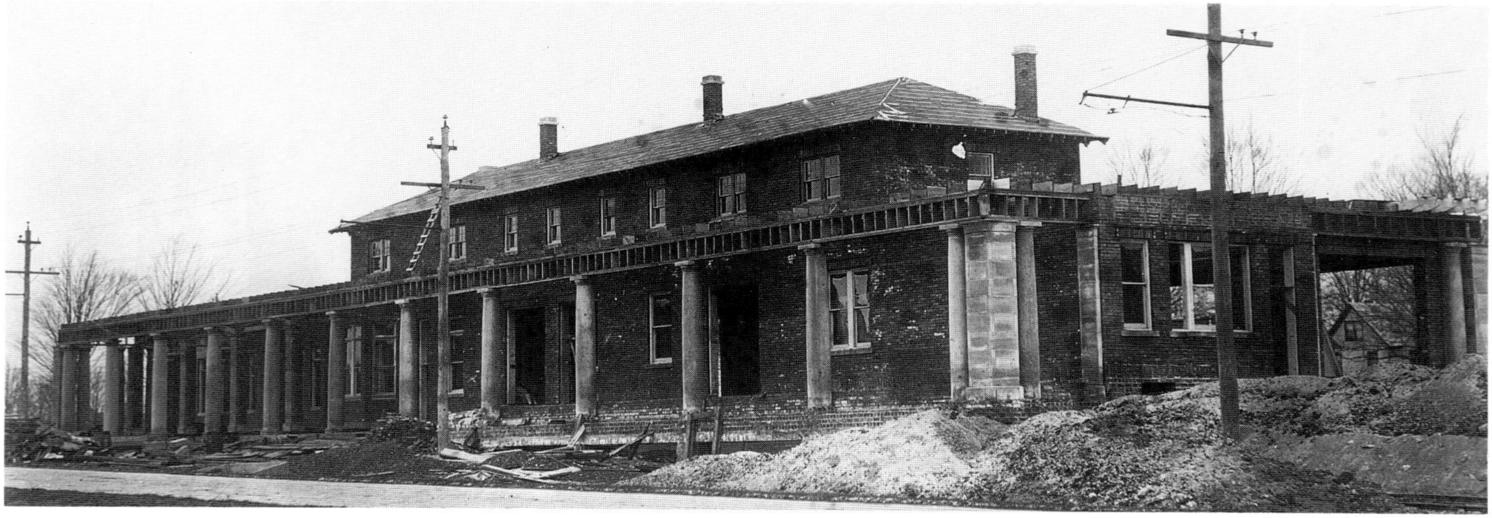

Chautauqua Traction Company stop, Chautauqua, 1917. The new station, costing $40,000.00, was under construction at this time. The station became the main gate building. The gate and entrance have been upgraded for the 1997 season. *FHS*

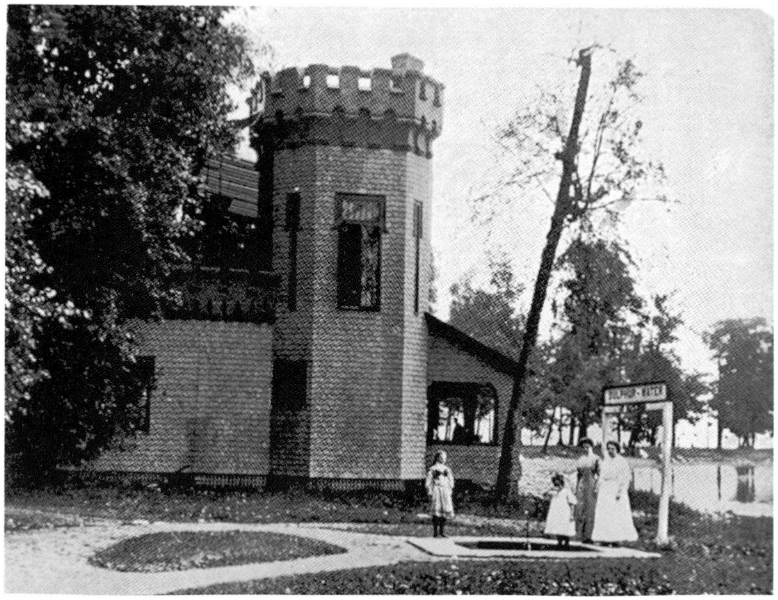

Men's Club House, ca. 1900. Built in 1893, the house, located on the lakefront near Palestine Park, was a social club offering indoor and outdoor "amusements" including chess, checkers, roque, tennis and golf. The Sports Club, open to both men and women, was its successor. *RL*

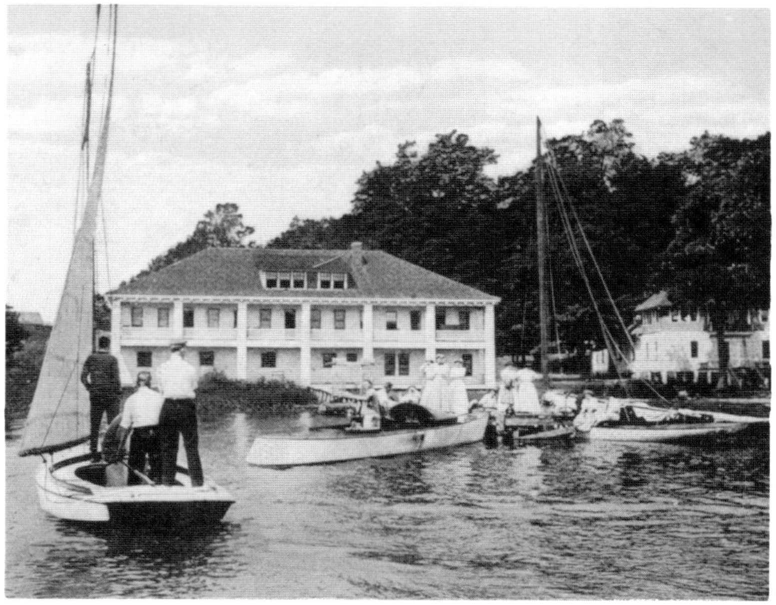

Athletic Club, ca. 1910. The Athletic Club, built in 1905, was located at the south end of the grounds just below the athletic field. The clubhouse contained bowling alleys, billiard and pool tables, lockers, a reading room, and a boat room. Today it is the headquarters for the Boys' and Girls' Clubs. Boating, especially sailing, remains a traditional summer pastime of Chautauquans. *RL*

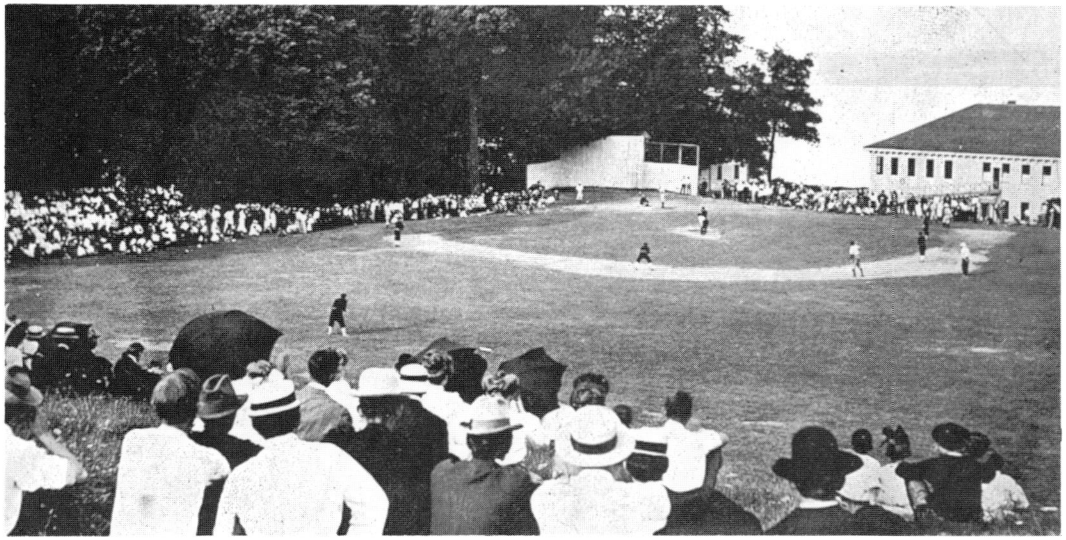

Early Chautauquans loved baseball. The baseball field was located at the south end of the grounds on the lakefront. *RL*

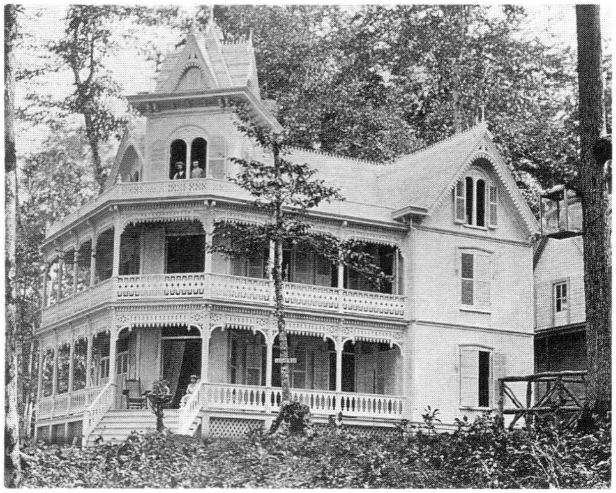

This cottage in the Queen Anne style with gingerbread embellishments is typical of the Victorian era architecture at Chautauqua Institution. *CCHS*

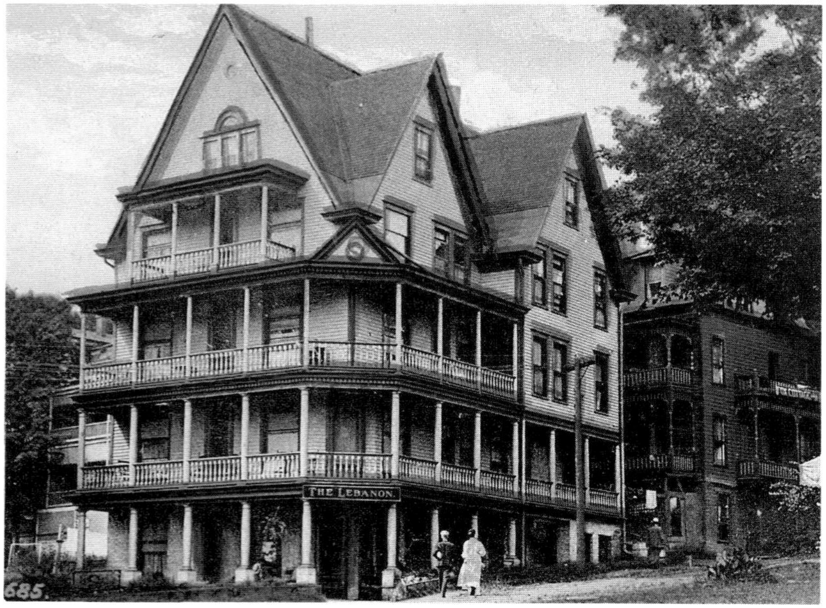

Lebanon Hotel, ca. 1900. Numerous smaller hotels continue to provide guests with comfortable lodging at Chautauqua. The Lebanon Hotel at 14 Lake Street, now 14 South Lake Drive, is today the William Baker Hotel. *RL*

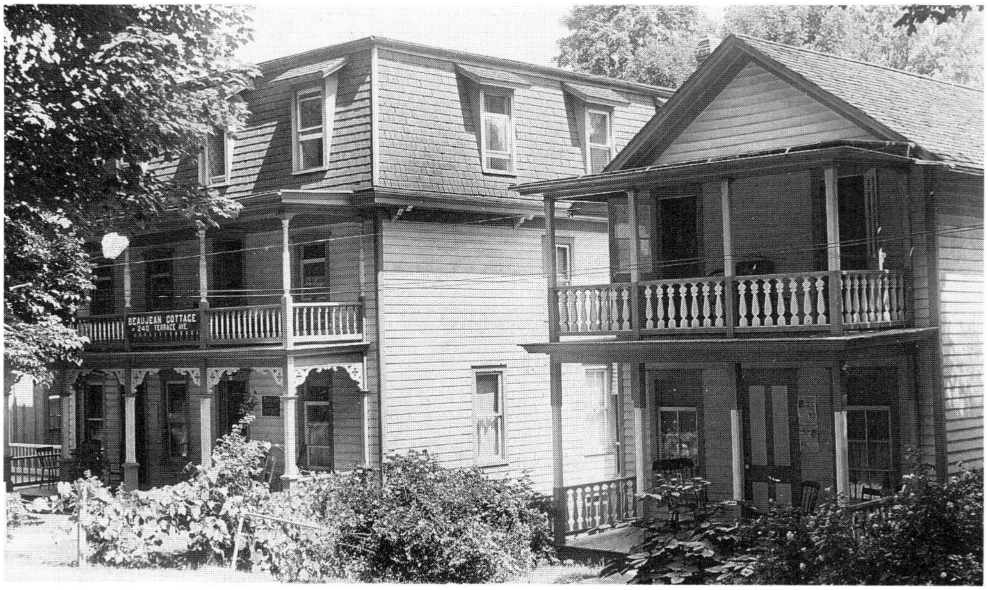

The Beaujean Boarding Cottage, ca. 1900. Located at 16 North Terrace, the cottage was built by Sanford Beaujean in 1876. It had three floors, a mansard roof and porches with the decorative gingerbread of the times. The Beaujean enjoyed a reputation as "one of the prettiest, neatest, most homelike and pleasant" of the boarding cottages at Chautauqua. Verandahs offered an excellent vista of the lake, and guests were close to the pier, Amphitheater, post office, and college. Visitors returned year after year to enjoy the large and airy rooms, excellent well water and fine cuisine. Beaujean operated a shoe repair business in the cottage adjacent to the boarding house. *RL*

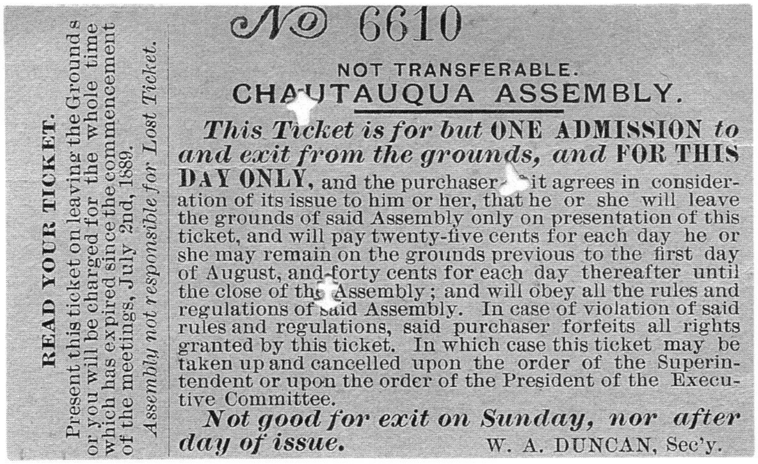

READ YOUR TICKET.

Present this ticket on leaving the Grounds or you will be charged for the whole time which has expired since the commencement of the meetings, July 2nd, 1889.

Assembly not responsible for Lost Ticket.

№ 6610

NOT TRANSFERABLE.

CHAUTAUQUA ASSEMBLY.

***This Ticket is for but* ONE ADMISSION *to and exit from the grounds, and* FOR THIS DAY ONLY**, and the purchaser of it agrees in consideration of its issue to him or her, that he or she will leave the grounds of said Assembly only on presentation of this ticket, and will pay twenty-five cents for each day he or she may remain on the grounds previous to the first day of August, and forty cents for each day thereafter until the close of the Assembly; and will obey all the rules and regulations of said Assembly. In case of violation of said rules and regulations, said purchaser forfeits all rights granted by this ticket. In which case this ticket may be taken up and cancelled upon the order of the Superintendent or upon the order of the President of the Executive Committee.

Not good for exit on Sunday, nor after day of issue. W. A. DUNCAN, Sec'y.

This is not a Twenty-four Hour Ticket but is good for One Admission and Exit on the day of issue only.

☞ The Assembly not responsible for lost tickets.

Take care of this ticket. The loss of it may cost you $5.00, or the price of a season ticket.

PATTERSON LIBRARY

TUESDAY JUL 1889

25

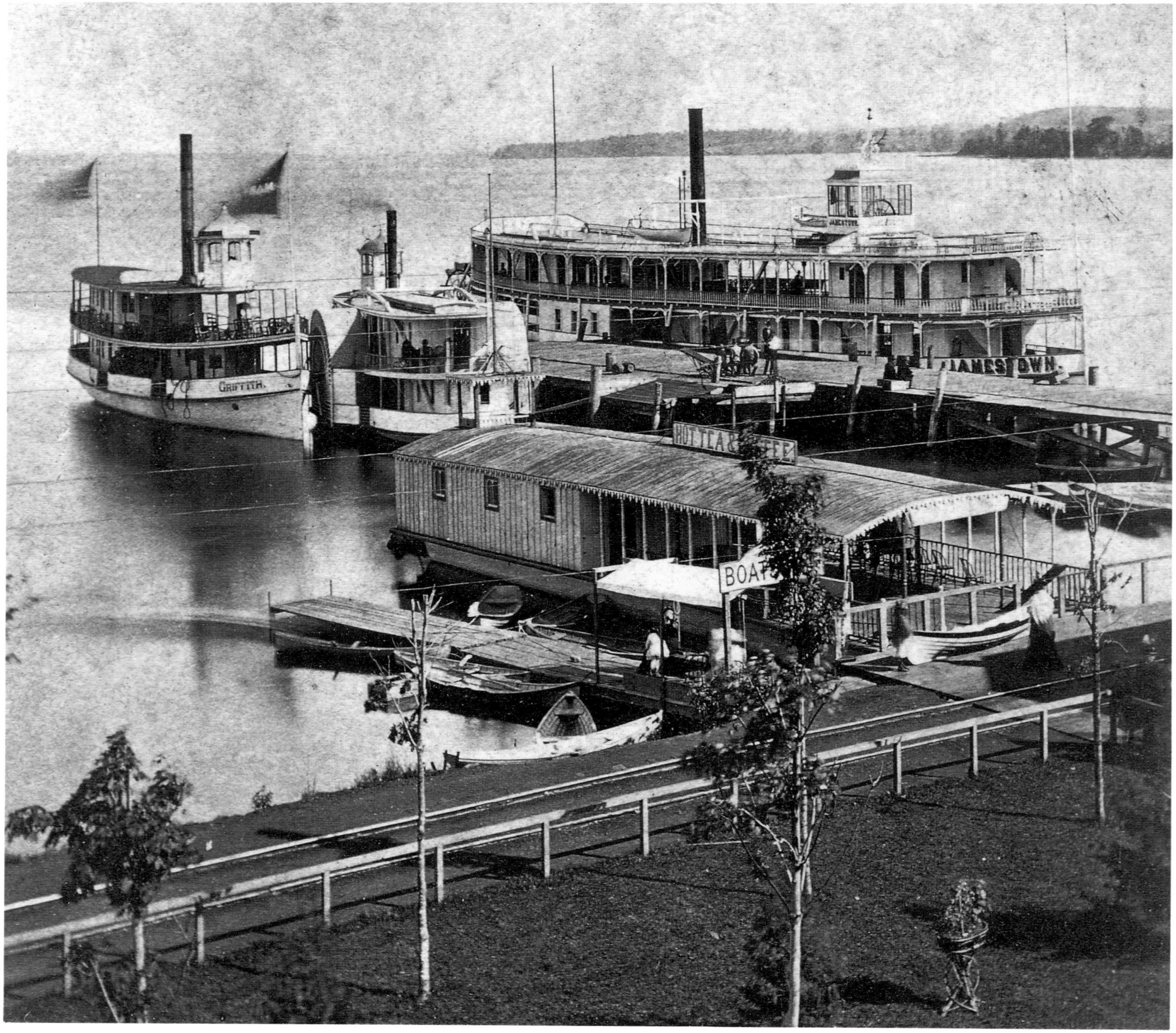
GRIFFITH.
JAMESTOWN

MAYVILLE

LIGHTHOUSE POINT HARTFIELD

The pretty village of Mayville, situated on a hill at the head of the lake, was first settled in 1804. It was designated the county seat in 1811, and the county courthouse and jail are still located here. The village was incorporated in 1830. Mayville was hailed as both "beautiful and delightful." It had one of the finest vistas of Chautauqua Lake, its lands sloping gently to its shores. It was to become the largest town located on the lake. In 1868 the Buffalo, Corry, and Pittsburgh (Crosscut) Railroad established a station stop along the waterfront. That same year, the Chautauqua House, the lake's first resort hotel, was completed at the foot of Erie Street. The Chautauqua House had a prime location just above the depot. Steamboats had been running the lake between Jamestown and Mayville for forty years before the railroad arrived. Easy connections between train and steamer made Mayville the lake's busiest port. Both the railroad and the Chautauqua House had a dock, and a third dock below the depot was available for the steamboats to coal up. The railroad also serviced the ice trade that flourished along the lake shore until well into the twentieth century.

By 1887 Jamestown and Mayville were connected by rail through the Chautauqua Lake Railway, providing further access to the resorts springing up on the lake's east shore. The Chautauqua Traction Company's electric line on the west shore completed a transportation system that encircled the lake. Mayville, with its steamboats, docks, and depot was a colorful place. Though quieter today, the little village remains every bit as lovely.

Lighthouse Point, part of a development by a group of summer residents from Pittsburgh, is located between Chautauqua Institution and Mayville. The developers called the area Duquesne Heights. The Lighthouse Point Hotel was part of the development. The gas lighthouse at the end of the dock was visible to Mayville. Just east of Mayville lies the village of Hartfield, distinguished in the late nineteenth century for the "Big Inlet" and its famous hermit.

Mayville dock, 1876. A stereopticon view of the Mayville dock taken from the Chautauqua House. Visible are the boat livery, the *Floating Bird, M.A. Griffith, May Martin* (stern), and *Jamestown.* The *Nettie Fox* became the *Jamestown* in 1876. Fair Point (Chautauqua) is in the distance. *CCHS*

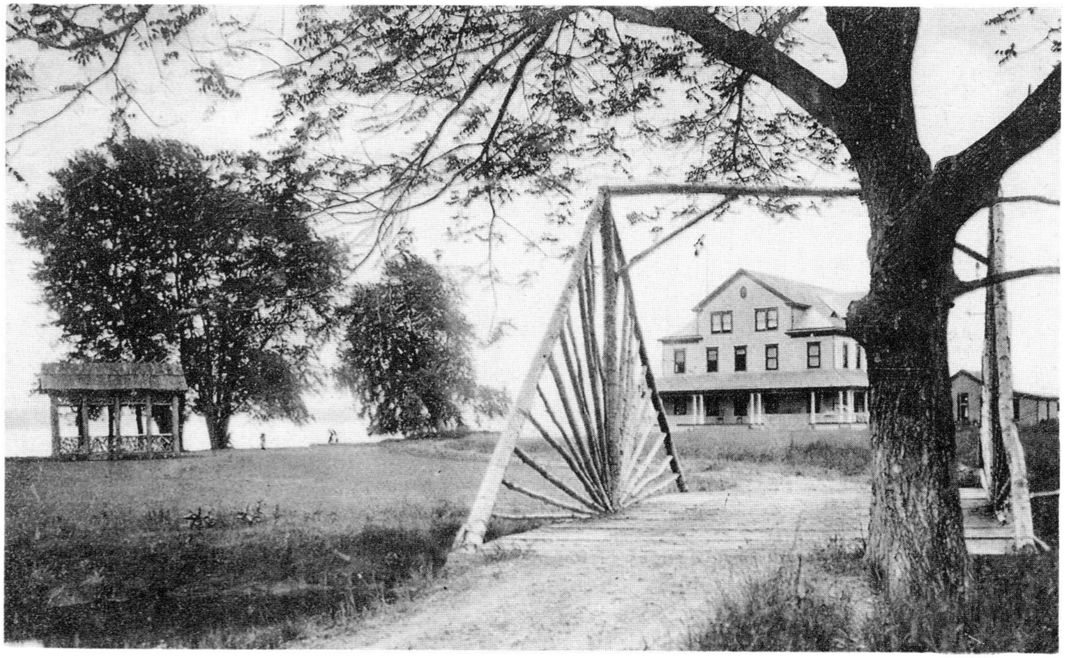

Lighthouse Point Hotel, ca. 1909. This hotel was especially attractive to certain Chautauqua Institution guests, for it offered both alcohol and dancing, both of which were forbidden on the Institution grounds. The twig style of the bridge and pavilion were common in the nineteenth century. The hotel burned in 1919. *RL*

Lighthouse Point, ca. 1906. Looking across the lake toward Point Chautauqua. The location derived its name from the acetylene gas lighthouse located at the end of the dock. In 1904 Lighthouse Point became one of the station stops on the Chautauqua Traction Line. Today the popular Lighthouse Point Grocery occupies the former station. *RL*

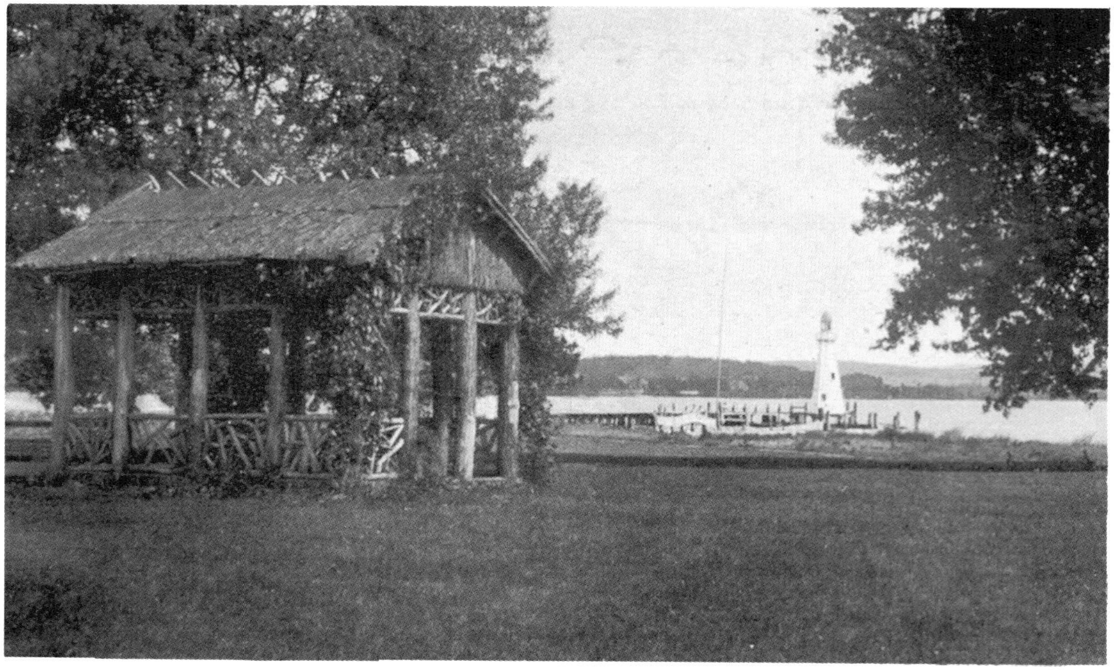

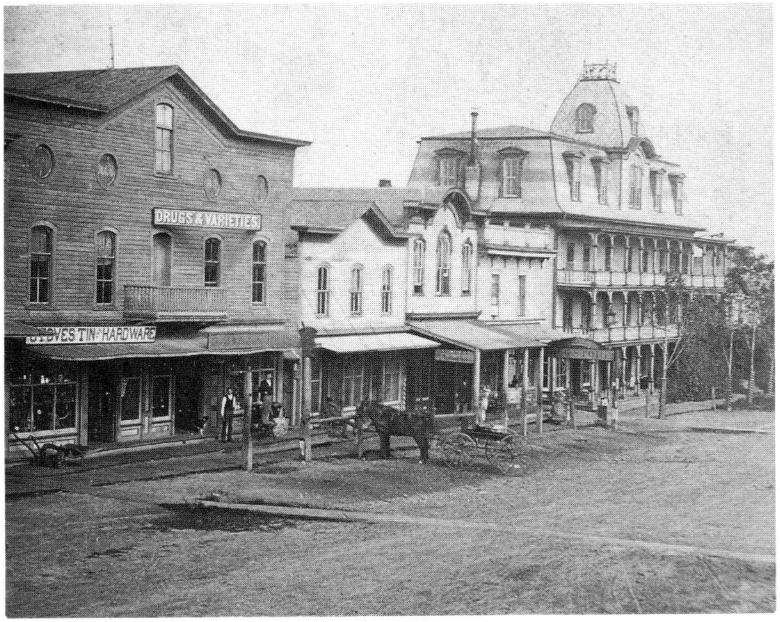

Mayville House, ca. 1879. This first-class establishment began its history in 1850 as the Hammond House, erected by Mr. E. Hammond on the site of the old Temperance House. Later the Fox Hotel, it was situated in Mayville's business district near the County Courthouse and offices on the east side of Main Street. "Large and commodious," the Mayville House contained four stories, sixty-six sleeping rooms and could accommodate 100 - 125 guests. A mansard roof and tower observatory provided one of the finest views of the lake anywhere. The hotel was noted for excellent cuisine and modern amenities at popular prices. When this stereopticon view was taken, the hotel was called the Robertson House after its proprietor John R. Robertson, a former County Clerk. It burned in 1914. Mayville's Quality Market occupies the site today. *CCHS*

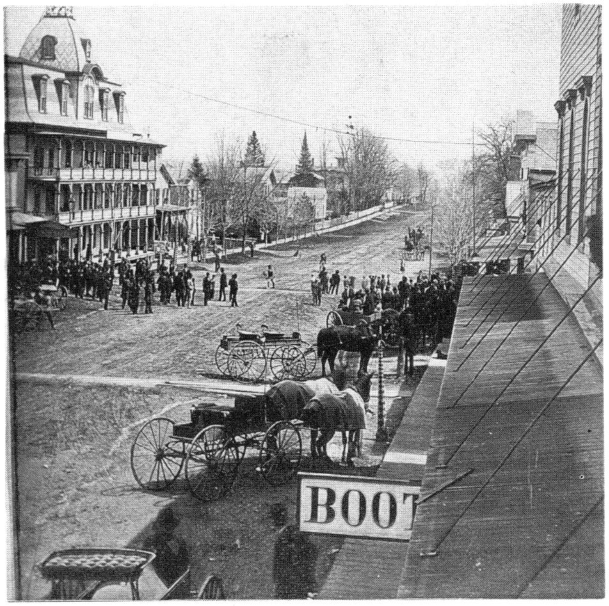

Mayville, ca. 1875. Professor Leon is barely visible on a tightrope above Main Street. The Mayville (Robertson) House is to the left, the lake to the rear. *CCHS*

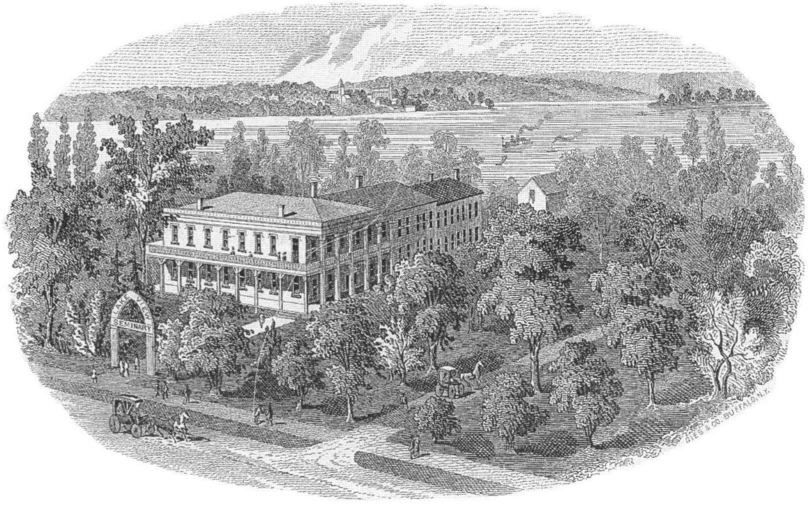

Lake View Seminary, ca. 1883. This building, constructed by William Whiteside, was purchased by R.W. Bemus for a boarding house/hotel. On September 15, 1881 it opened as the Mary Washington School, a Christian school for women operated by the Episcopal Diocese of Western New York. The school was located close to the Mayville docks near the corner of South Erie Street and Washington. It was succeeded by Lake View Seminary, a boarding and day school for "young ladies" operated by Rev. H.A. Duboc. The seminary was destroyed by fire on September 14, 1886. *CCHS*

Chautauqua House from the *Nettie Fox*, 1875. South Erie Street (Main Street) is to the right. The Crosscut Railroad depot (not visible in the photo) is to the left. The barge in front of the hotel was for a time a pleasure craft towed around the lake by a steamer. Anchored here, it was a snack shop. The barge was called the *Floating Bird*. *CCHS*

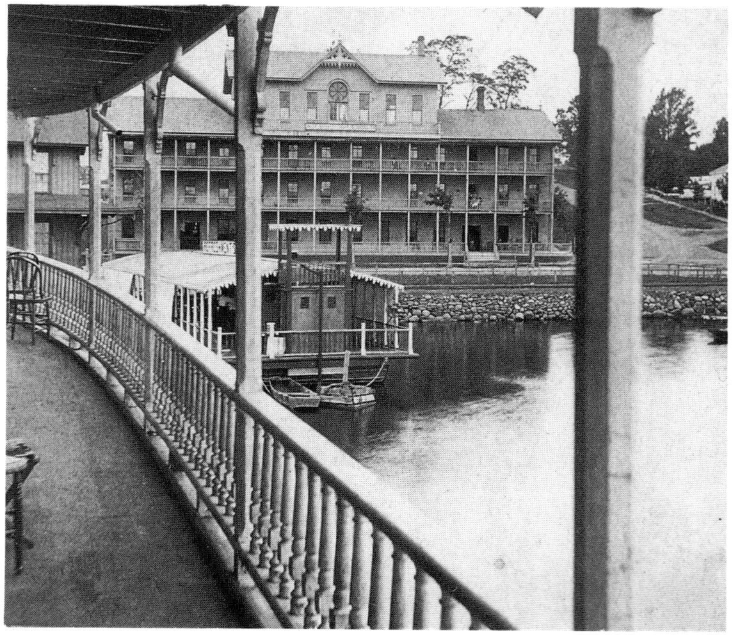

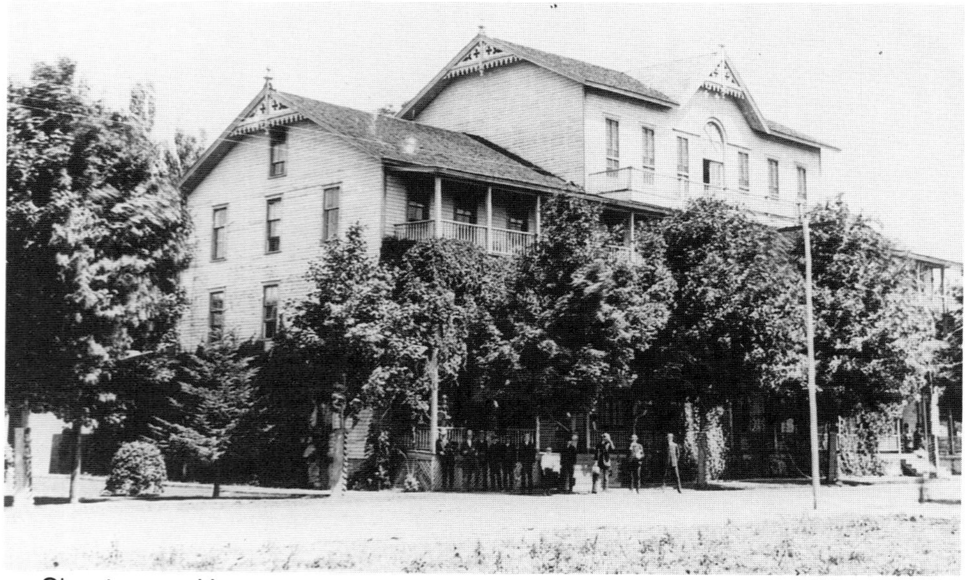

Chautauqua House, ca. 1879. The Chautauqua House opened for business in 1868, the same year a station stop for the Crosscut Railroad opened. The hotel was conveniently located near both the dock and railroad station. Horace Fox managed the house which became so popular that by 1870 the first-class establishment was enlarged, doubling its capacity. Fox's motto was "Let the house advertise itself." By 1887, hotels on the east side of the lake were beginning to flourish and, following the 1892 summer season, the Chautauqua House went out of business. It burned on April 27, 1894. *CCHS*

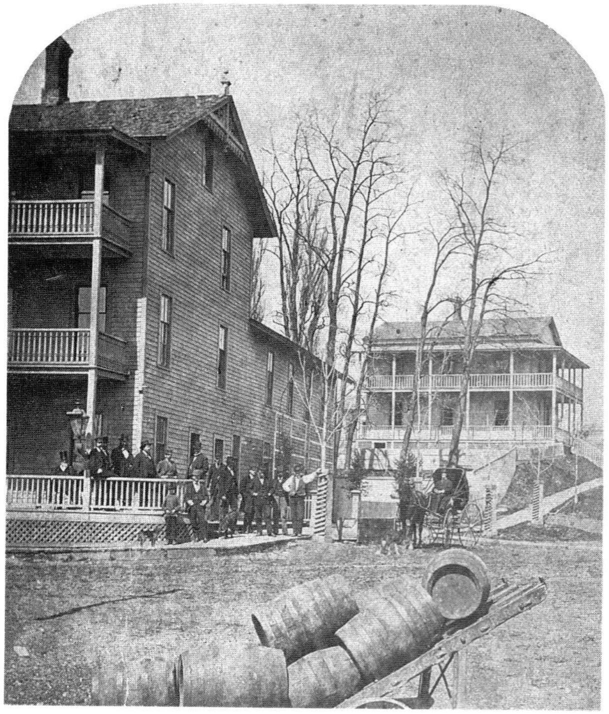

Chautauqua House, ca. 1879. The Chautauqua House cottage located just above the main building on South Erie Street. The gentlemen pictured, including Hod Fox, were Victorian Mayville's men about town. *CCHS*

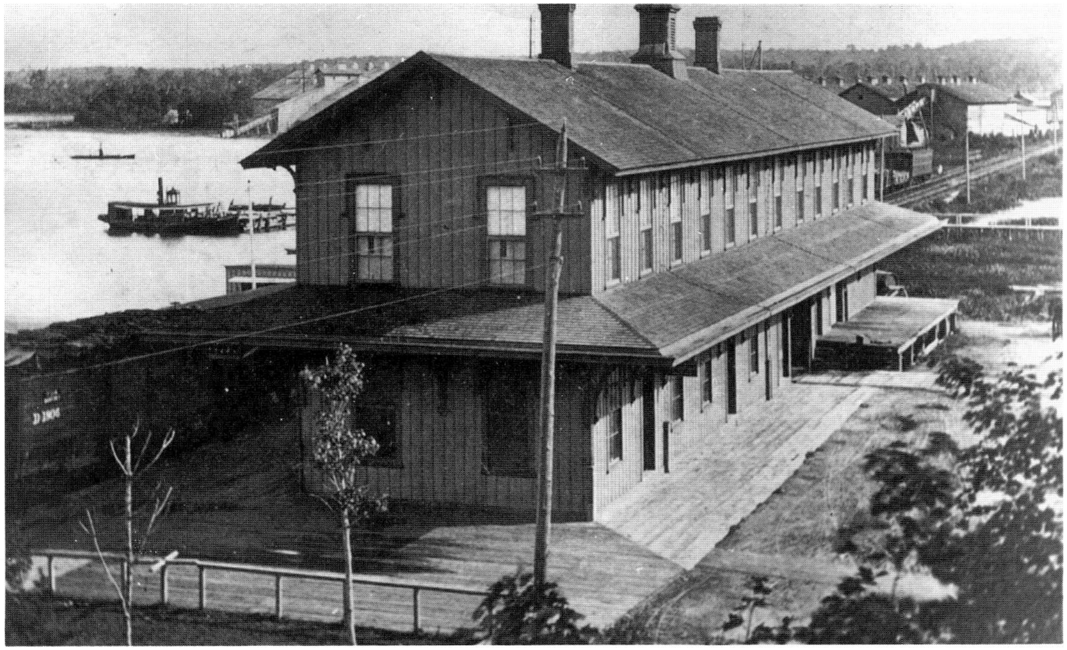

Western New York and Pennsylvania Railroad depot, ca. 1890. The Cornell and Hewes ice house is to the left and the Pittsburgh Ice Company to the right. The track bed was built on fill directly over the lake. *FHS*

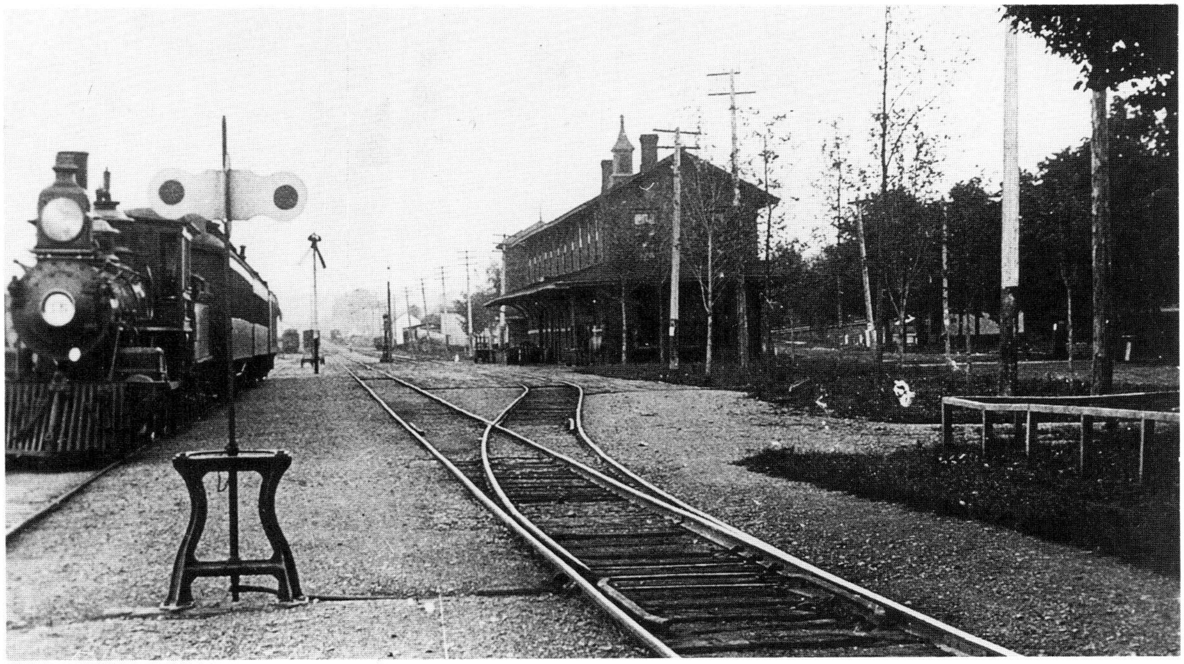

Western New York and Pennsylvania Railroad depot, ca. 1890. A train is stopped on the dock side probably waiting for a steamer to dock and discharge its passengers. *VN*

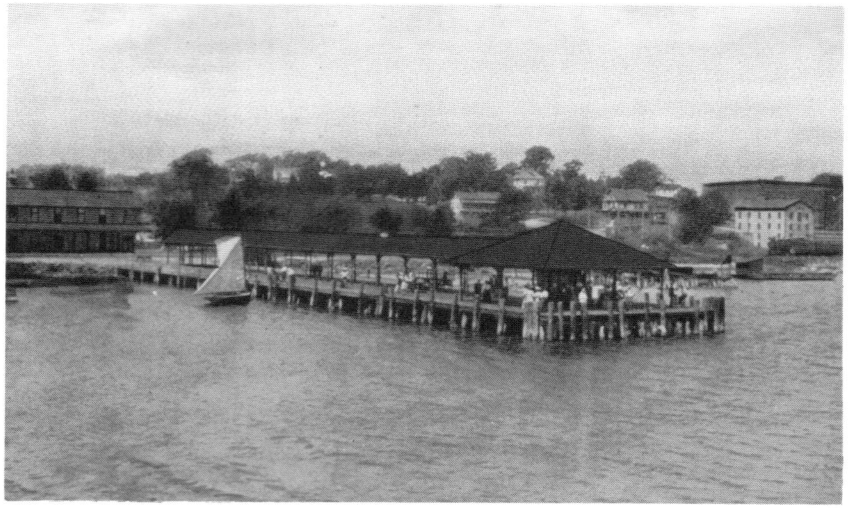

Lakefront, ca. 1913. A view of the Mayville dock and lakefront taken from a steamer. The Hopson Ice House is on the right and the railroad depot on the left. Chautauqua Lake Mills, a feed mill, is in front of Hopson's. *RL*

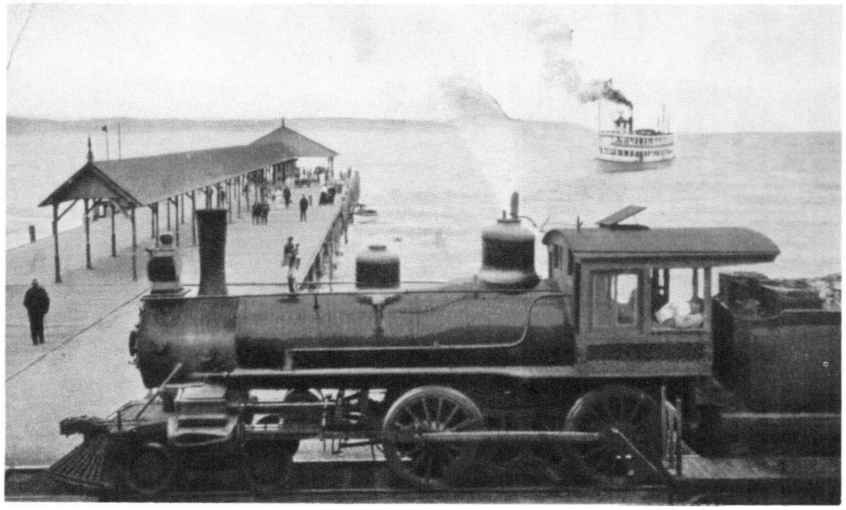

Mayville dock, ca. 1900. The Jamestown and Chautauqua Railroad engine number 4 probably awaiting arrival of the Western New York and Pennsylvania Railroad train. The J & C Railroad was one of four reorganizations of the original Chautauqua Lake Railway. Engine number four has just returned from Chautauqua Institution. The *City of Buffalo* is approaching. *RL*

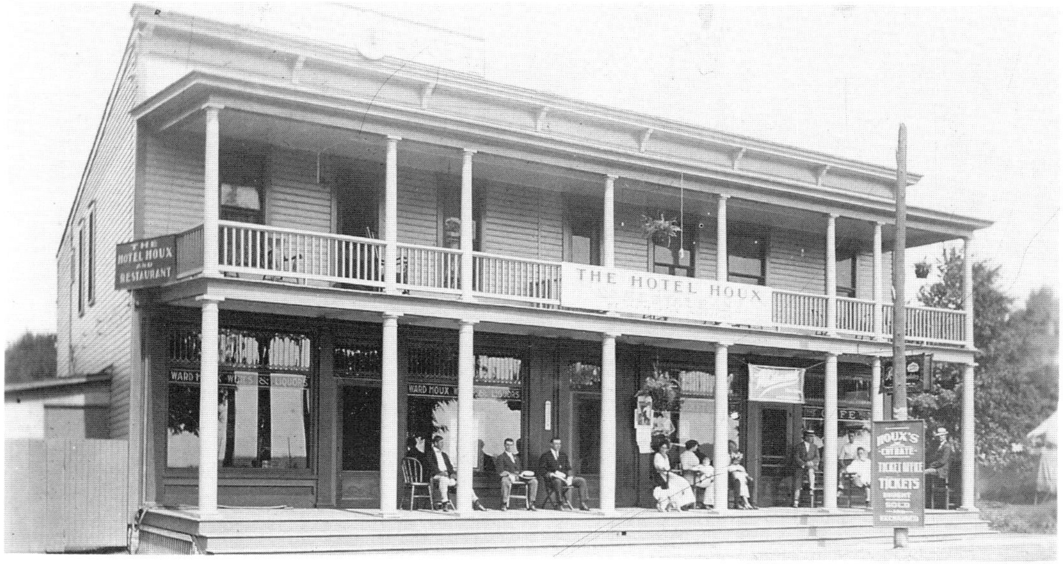

Hotel Houx, ca. 1913. Conveniently located opposite the dock and depot, the hotel offered "the proper cafe and lunch room at the head of the lake." Giambrone's Restaurant occupies the building today. *CCHS*

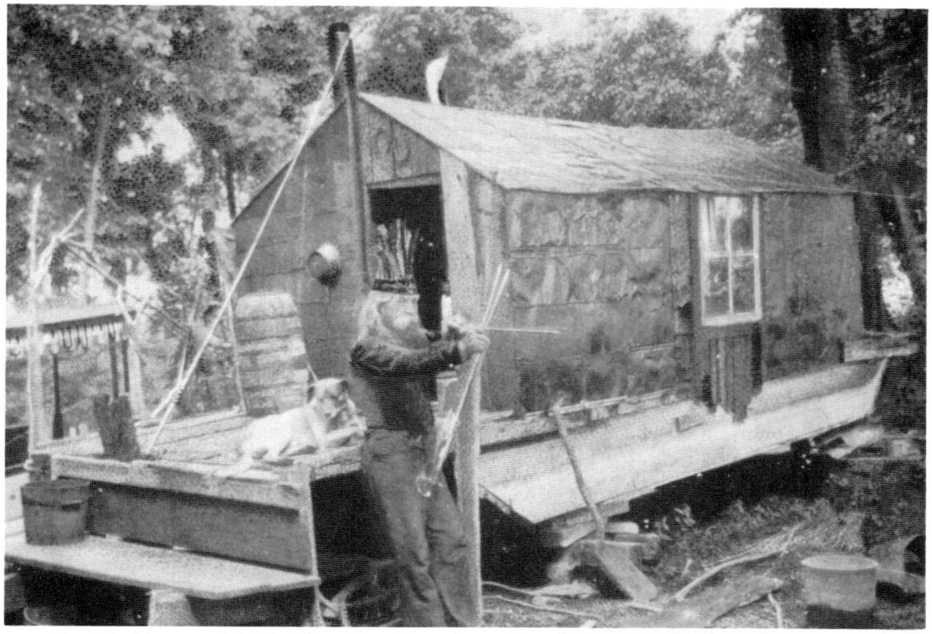

Hartfield, ca. 1904. Charlie Cowden, the "Hermit of Chautauqua Lake", at his cabin on the Big Inlet. Charlie's cabin was a barge pulled up on the shore. Like his predecessor, "Commodore" Truman Downs, who occupied the same site, he achieved some notoriety during his years as a recluse on the lake. *RL*

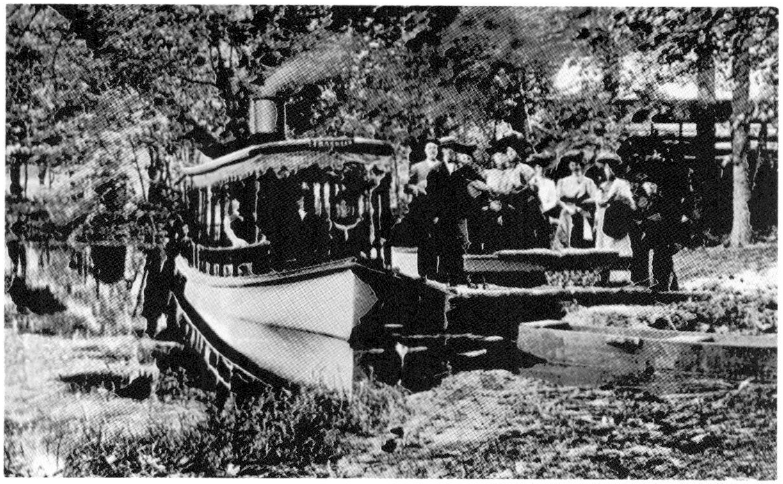

Hartfield, ca. 1905. The steamboat *Franklin* docked at the "Big Inlet." Since the inlet was wide enough to accommodate a small steamboat, vacationers sometimes travelled upstream looking for the Hermit. The Big Inlet, channeled today, is a private lakeside community. *RL*

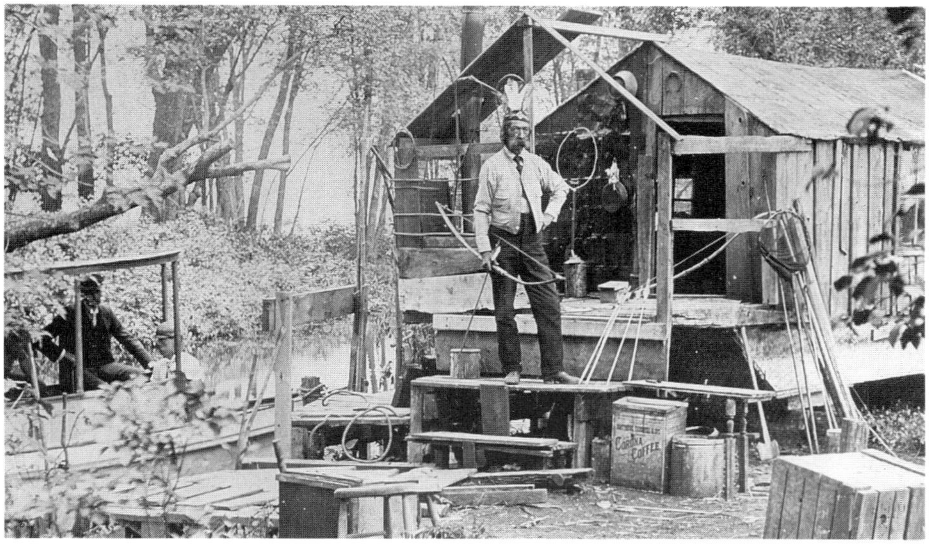

Hartfield, ca. 1905. Charlie has made some minor improvements to his cabin. Besides the cabin, he had a houseboat. He was skilled at storytelling, left handed fiddling, and wood carving. In the summer he subsisted by fishing, and in the winter he stayed with various local people. Charlie is buried in the cemetery at North East, Pennsylvania. *CMN*

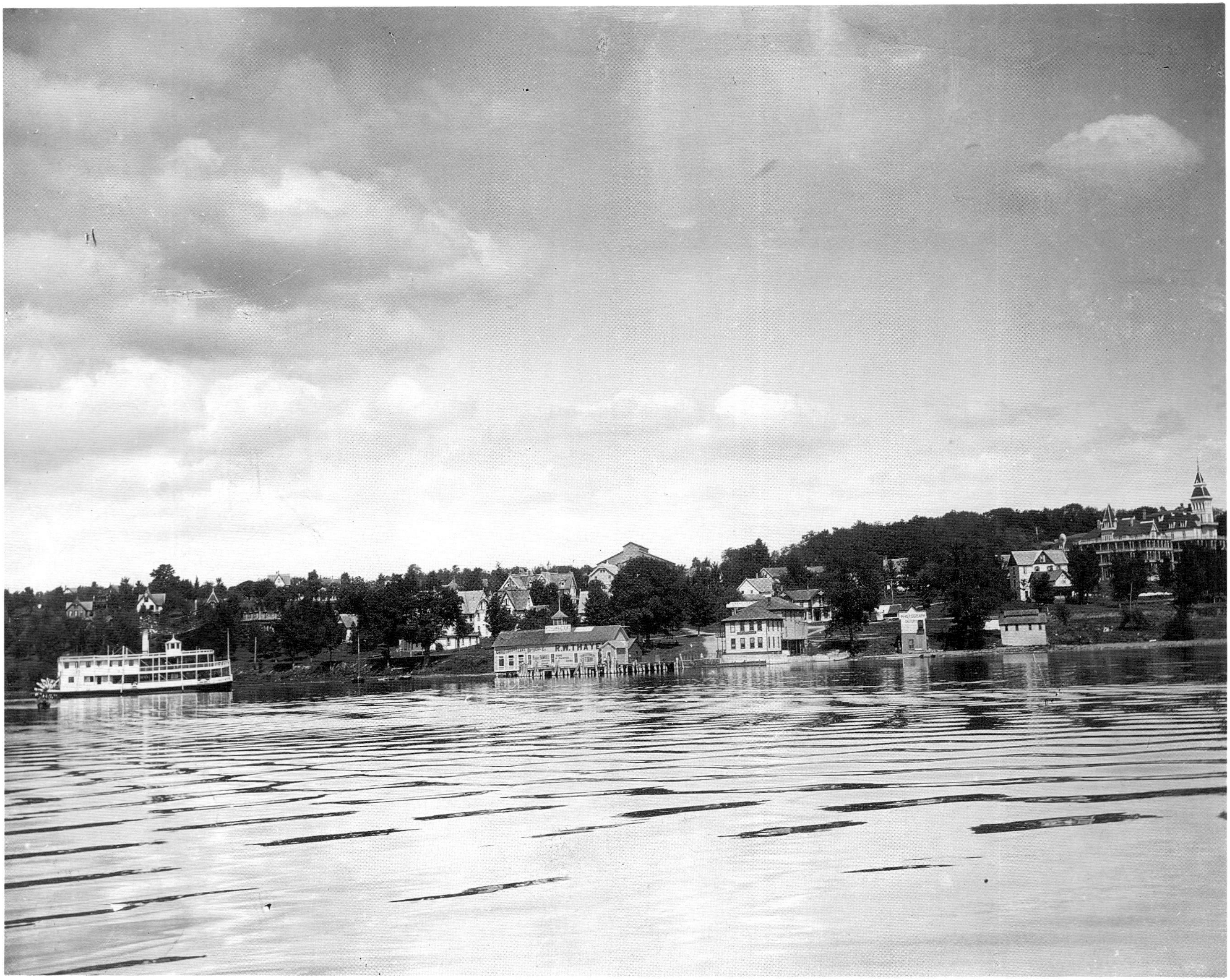

POINT CHAUTAUQUA
WOOGLIN

Point Chautauqua was designed in 1875 by landscape architect Frederick Law Olmsted, best remembered for his plan of New York's Central Park. It began as a Baptist camp and was the only religious community ever designed by Olmsted. His curving roadways and building lots conformed to the lay of the land and its relationship to Chautauqua Lake. Revival meetings were held on the grounds in a tabernacle, and groves provided shady areas for religious retreats. As at its Methodist counterpart across the lake, visitors were first housed in tents until homes and cottages were built. The religious aspect of the community faded after 1885, but Point Chautauqua prospered as a summer resort and recreation area into the early days of the twentieth century. Following the Great Depression and the Second World War, the number of vacationers declined. In the mid 1960s, Point Chautauqua saw a revival. A beautification program was begun by long time residents. Many of the Victorian era homes were restored to their original beauty and charm. New homes have been built and many of the old rooming houses have been converted to private dwellings. Ninety well kept homes, many of which are year round residences, make up the community today. As a residential community, Point Chautauqua sustains the character of Olmsted's original design. An abundance of trees, plants, wooded areas, parks, and winding streets reflects a peace and tranquillity treasured by its residents.

Point Chautauqua, ca. 1896. Point Chautauqua during its years as a pleasure resort. The steamer *Buckeye*, built in 1888 as the *Alaquippa*, approaches the dock. Note the towers of the Grand Hotel on the right and the old dock building in the center. The Breeze Hotel is to the right of the dock. *CMN*

Point Chautauqua, 1880. This map shows the layout of the grounds of Point Chautauqua when it was still a religious community. Note the curving roadways, woodland groves and parks, all part of Frederick Law Olmsted's characteristic design. The avenues were twenty-six feet wide and the plans called for 465 building lots, each 1/8 of an acre in size. Olmsted presented no specifications, however, as to the design of homes and structures. *JE*

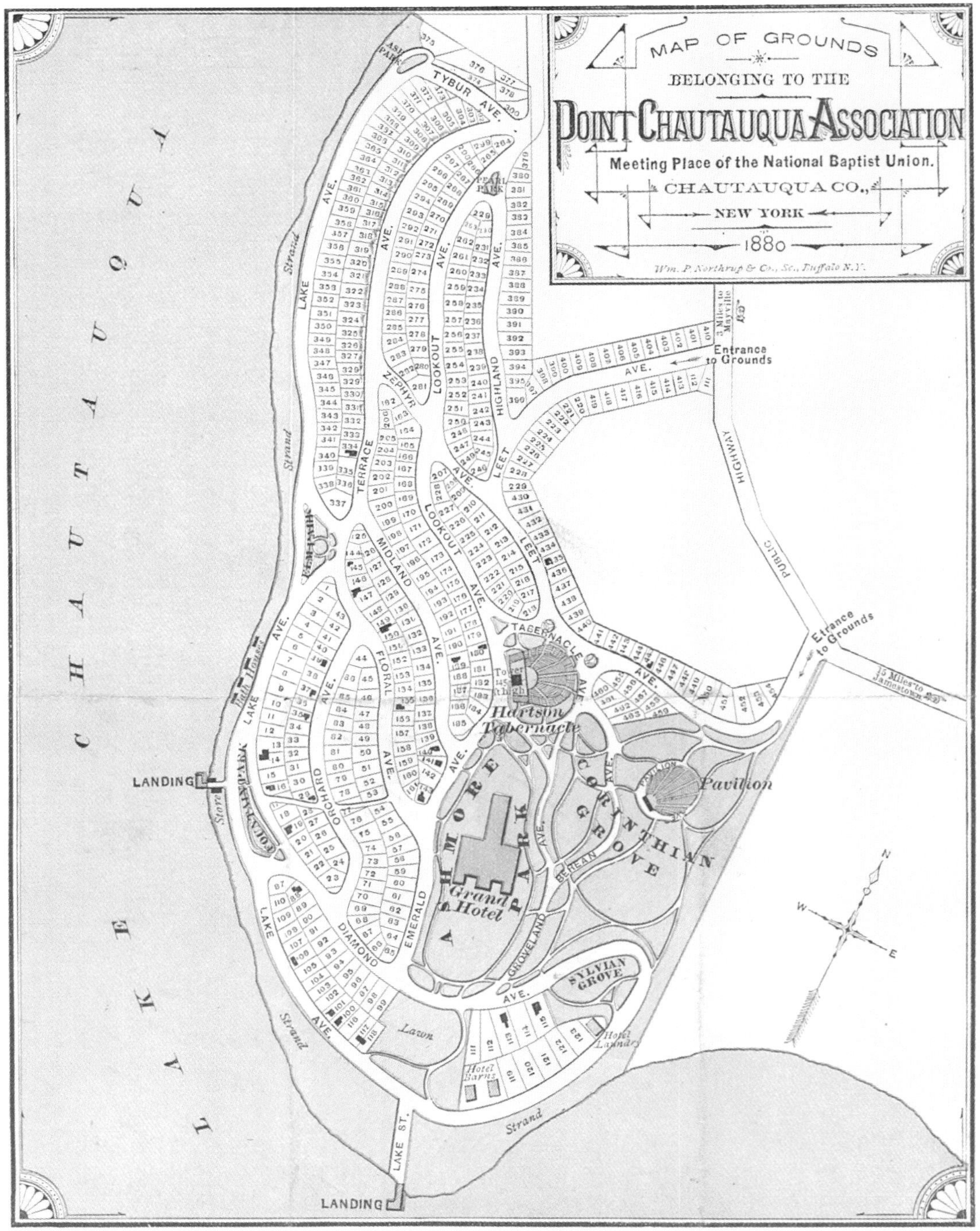

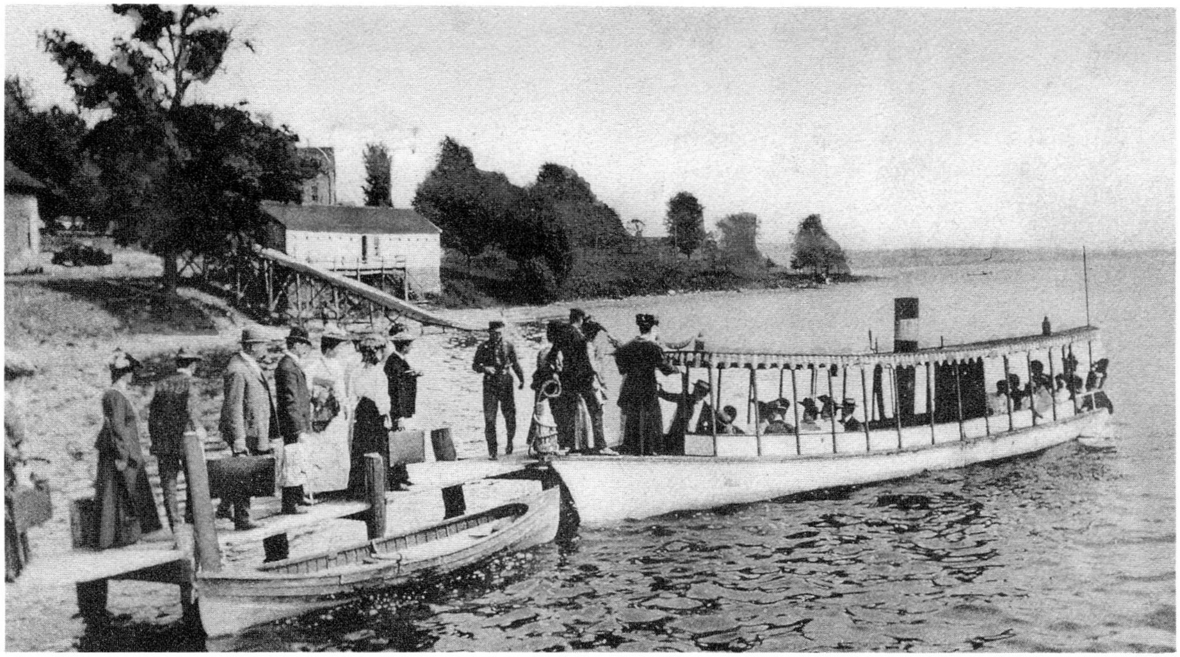

Point Chautauqua, ca. 1900. A group of well-dressed passengers with luggage board a small steamer for the first leg of their journey home. Most of Point Chautauqua's summer residents during the resort years were wealthy families from Pittsburgh. Point Chautauqua was considered a "prestigious" summer resort. Vacationers could enjoy a brief sojourn at the Point or a whole season. Families and servants would often spend the summer in their own or rented homes. Husbands would come for weekends and spend weekdays in the city tending to business. The water slide in the background is a reminder of Point Chautauqua's days as a pleasure resort. *RL*

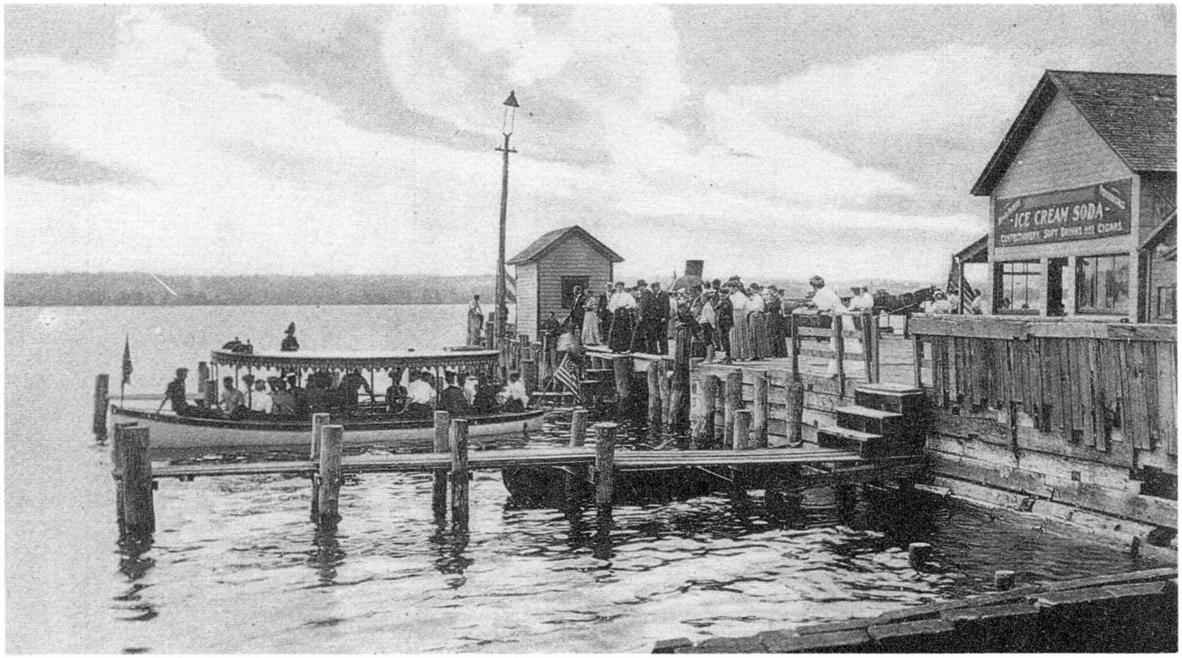

Point Chautauqua dock, ca. 1906. The ice cream parlor must have been popular on warm days. Passengers are boarding a motor launch. Most of these smaller craft ferried passengers to Chautauqua Institution. *RL*

Breeze Hotel, ca. 1900. The Breeze Hotel went through several renovations over the years. It became Point Chautauqua's post office in the early 1900s and was used for summer theater in the 1930s. The building is no longer standing. Note "Sherman's Photograph Gallery" next to the hotel. William Sherman was a Westfield photographer. *CMN*

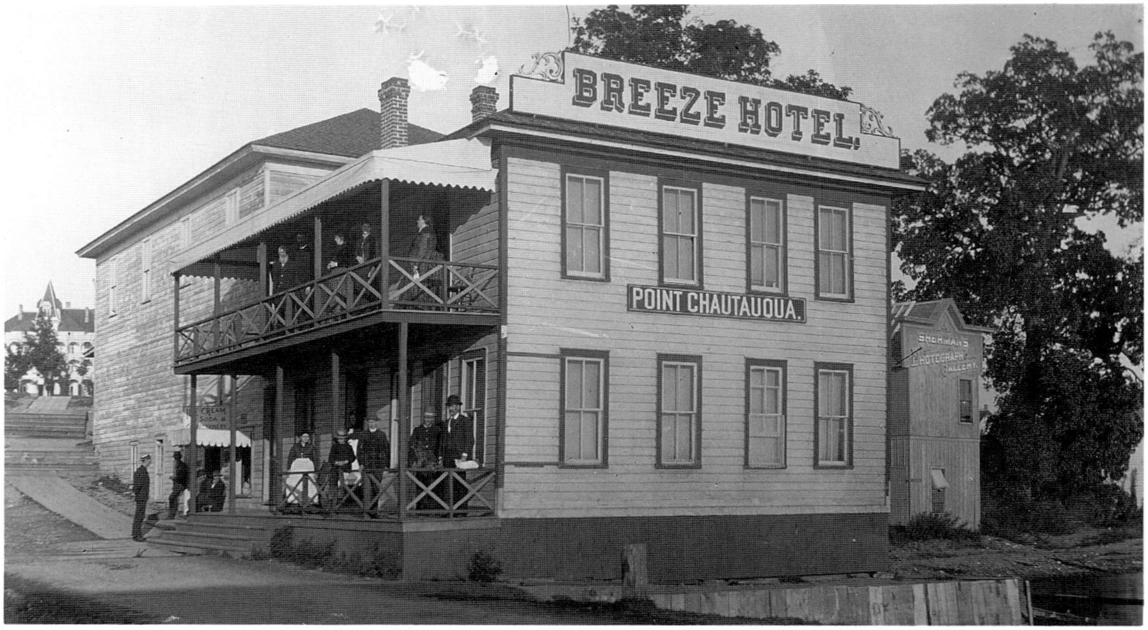

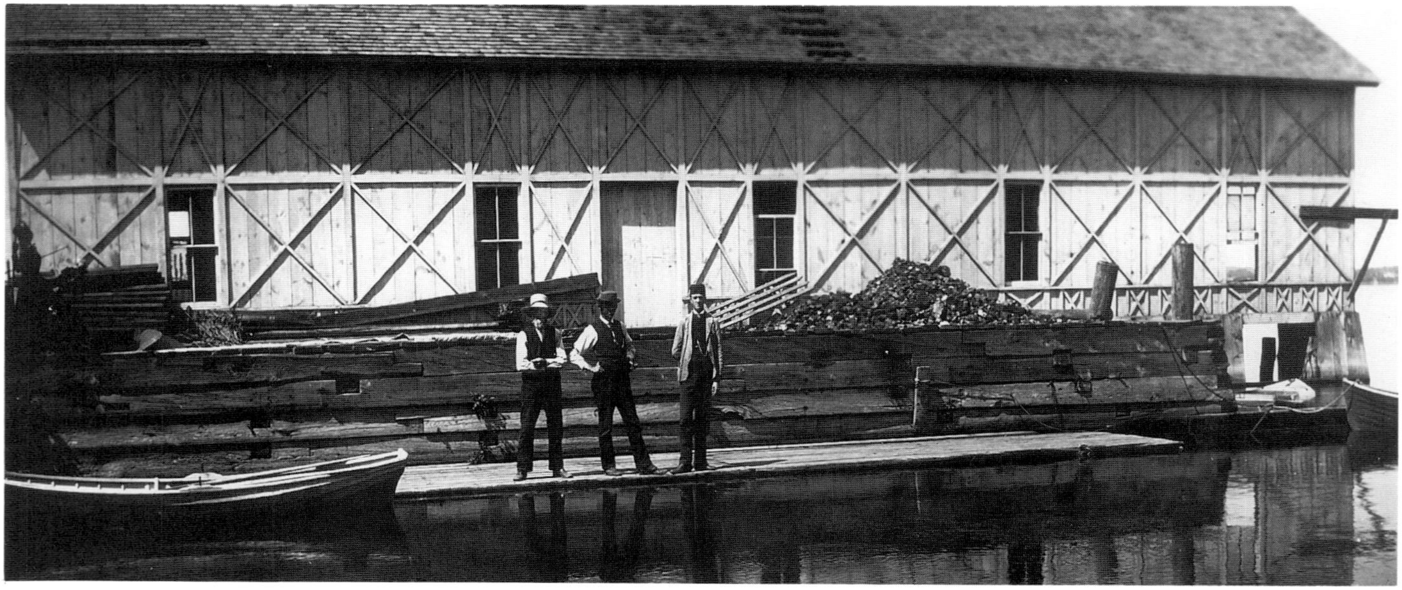

Point Chautauqua dock, ca. 1890. The structure on the dock was built around 1880 by Henry Cooper. It was used for boat rentals and storage. There were shops in the front of the building and a boat livery in the rear. Winter ice ruined the building by around 1900. The beach is located on the site today. *JE*

The Grand Hotel, ca. 1891. Construction of the Point Chautauqua Hotel began in 1878 and was completed in 1880. It originally served guests coming to Point Chautauqua for the religious program. The hotel was truly imposing and its name was later changed to the "Grand Hotel". More spacious than the Athenaeum at Chautauqua, this well-appointed establishment earned a reputation as the "largest and finest hotel in the region" and "the crowning glory of the Point." Four hundred guests could be accommodated. The Grand Hotel was equipped with all of the conveniences, including electric lighting, call bells in each room, telephone and telegraphic communications, elegant furnishings, large rooms, and a vista from its verandahs unsurpassed on Chautauqua Lake.

Unfortunately, the hotel suffered financial setbacks and fell into decline with the waning of the religious community. It was sold at auction in 1889 to a group of private investors. Completely renovated in 1891, it became a vacationer's paradise. A bus operated by the hotel would pick up passengers arriving by steamboat. However, due to heavy maintenance expenses and declining business, it entered a second phase of deterioration. On October 17, 1902, the Grand was completely consumed by flames. The blaze was determined to be arson orchestrated by one of the owners of the hotel. *CCHS, CMN*

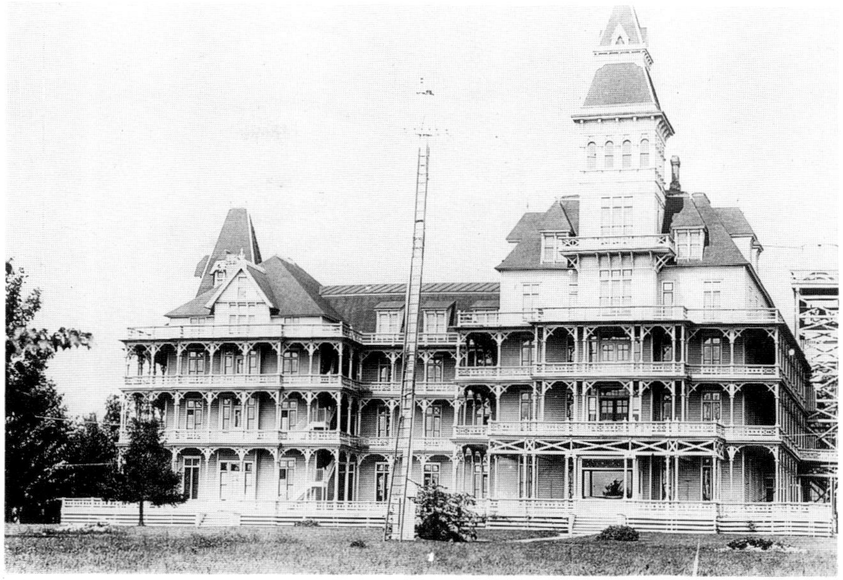

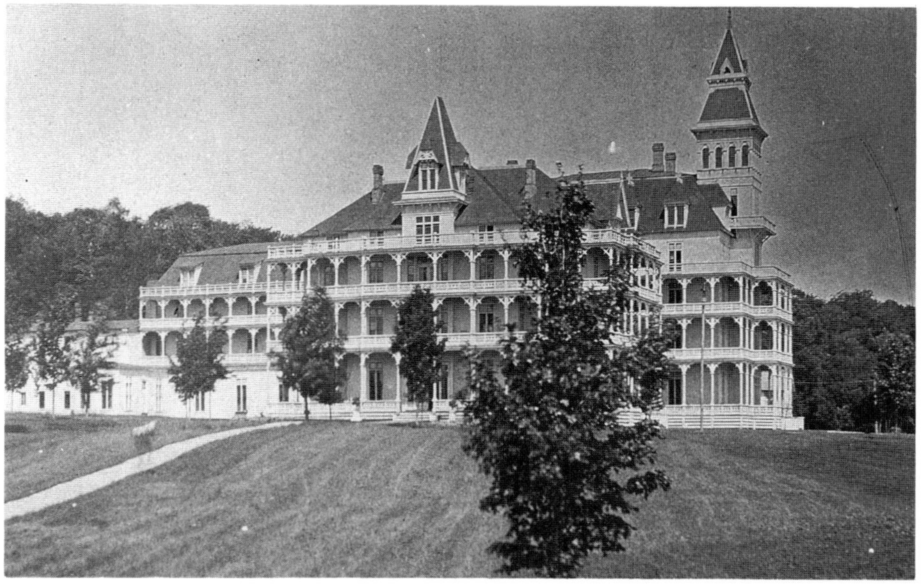

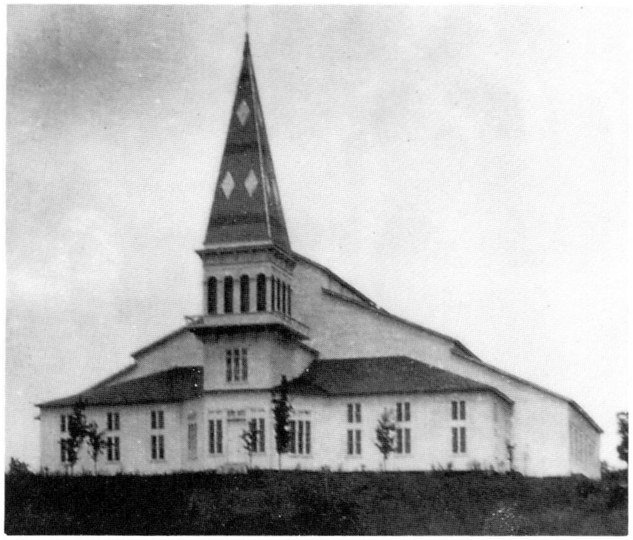

Hartson Tabernacle, ca. 1880. Built in 1878-79 and used for revival meetings. The structure could accommodate 5,000 people. It was named in memory of Horace Hartson, pastor of the Baptist Church in Jamestown. The tabernacle became the "Temple of Music" in 1886, the Maltby Cycling Academy in 1897 and finally a roller rink and summer theater during the Point's era as a pleasure resort. Its decline and deterioration paralleled that of the Grand Hotel. It was abandoned in 1900 and finally razed in 1904. *FHS*

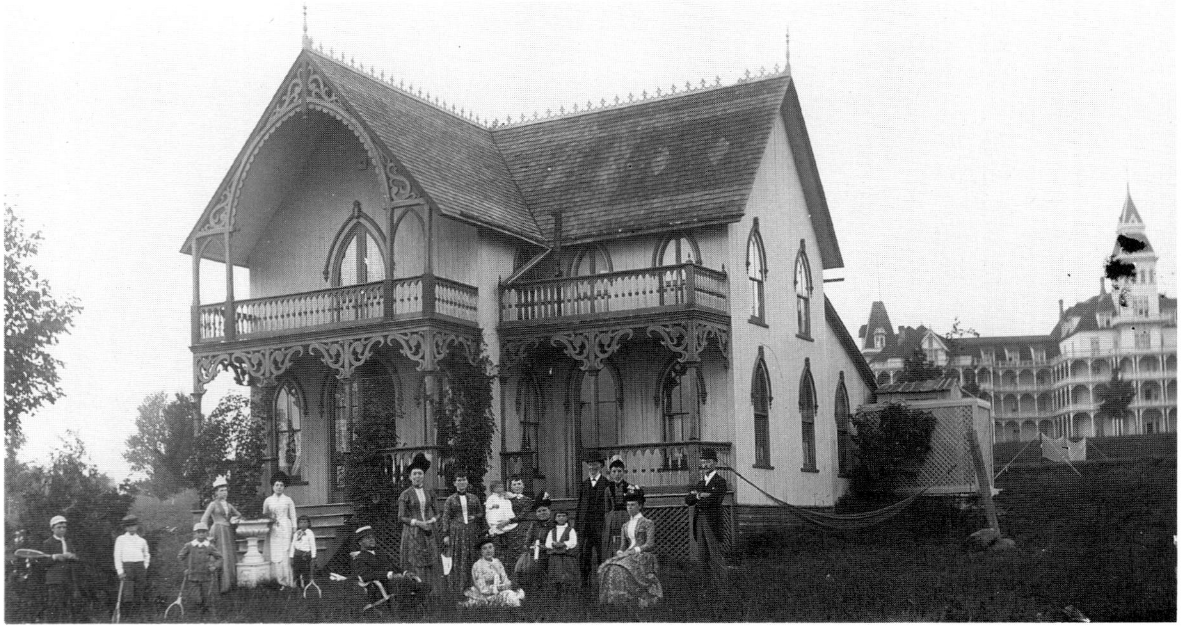

Point Chautauqua, ca. 1890. The architectural designs of the homes and cottages at Point Chautauqua reflect the periods of the community's development as well as the tastes of their owners. The Point Chautauqua Association exercised control over the character and style of structures built within the community. During the Baptist era of the 1870s and 1880s, homes were built in the Gothic Revival or Stick styles. The Grand Hotel is imposing in the background. *CMN*

Avon Cottage, ca. 1903. The loss of the Grand Hotel did little to discourage visitors from spending the summer at Point Chautauqua. Smaller inns, hotels, and boarding houses continued to provide comfortable accommodations for guests. The Avon was known for its graceful terraces and trees and gently sloping lawn. It had 35 rooms, richly furnished with handsome carpeting, fine art, and elegant accoutrements. Running water and gas, among other amenities, made it a delightful stopping place for the summer guest. By 1912 this establishment was known as The Inn. It operated under that name until the 1950s. It was demolished in 1965. *RL*

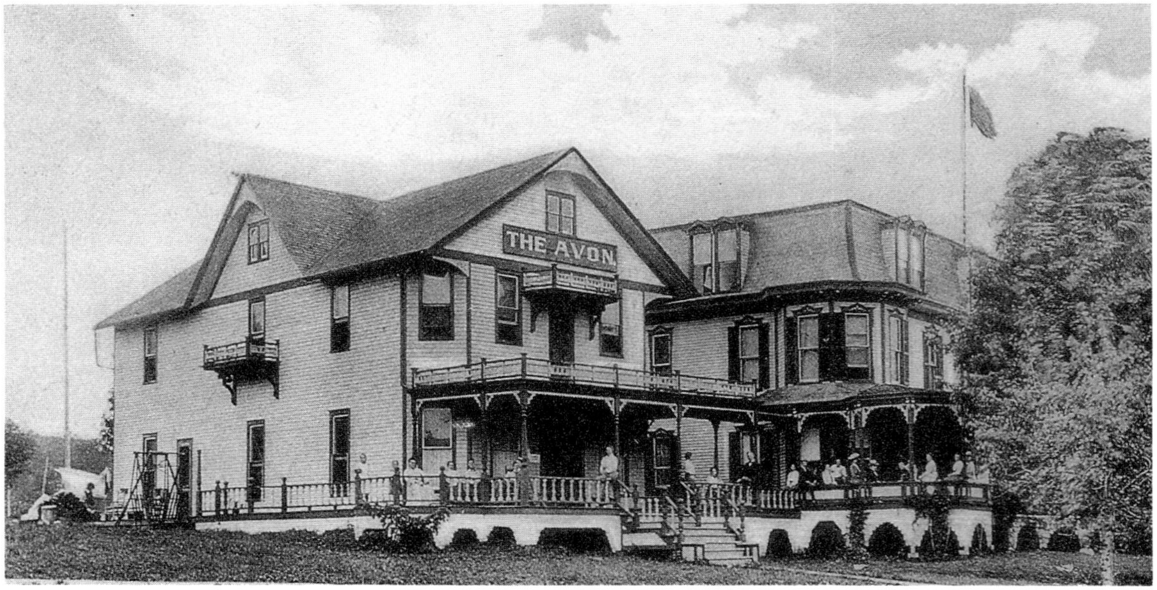

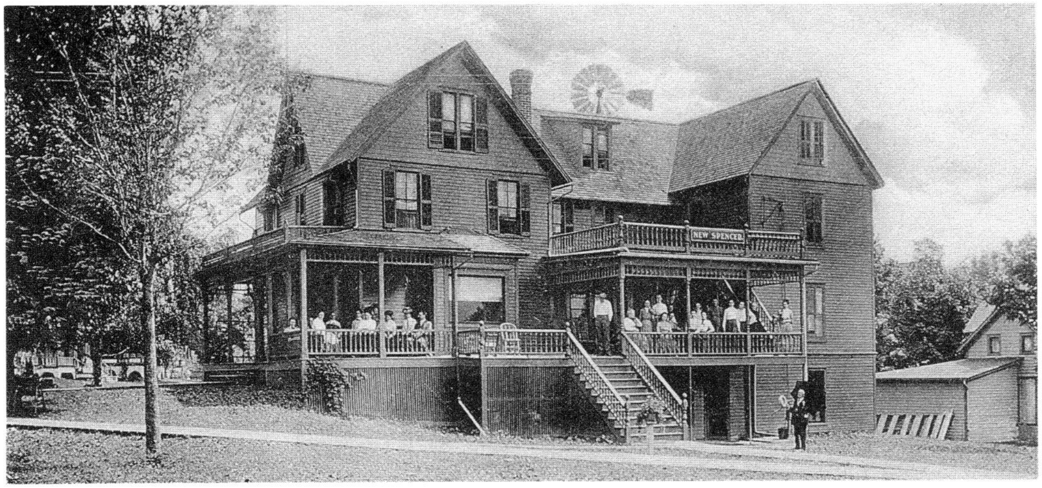

New Spencer Hotel, ca. 1905. This hotel was destroyed by fire in 1909. *RL*

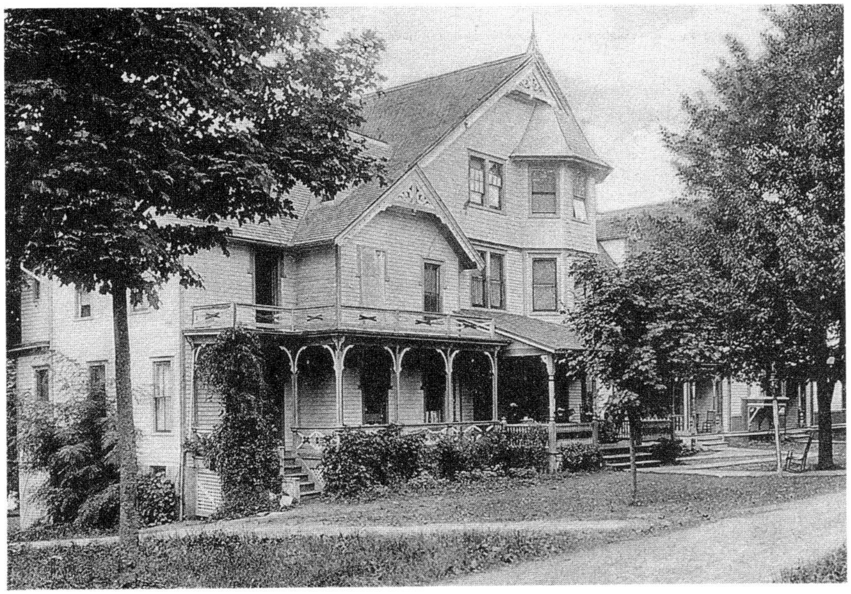

Barnes Inn, ca. 1910. Located on Floral Avenue, this small hotel burned to the ground in 1930. Buildings at Point Chautauqua were particularly vulnerable to fire since the closest fire departments were at Hartfield and Dewittville. The Mayville and Bemus Point departments were called but arrived too late. *RL*

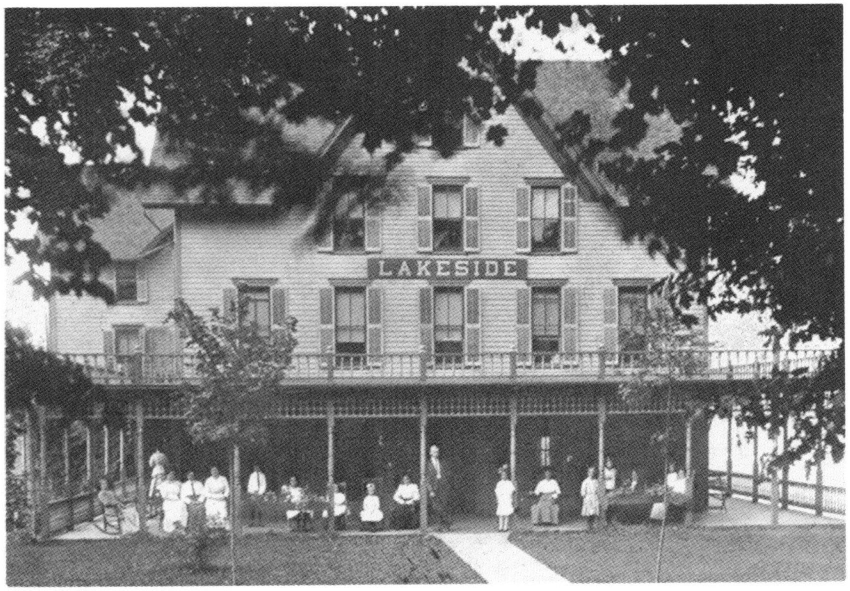

Lakeside Cottage, ca. 1913. The Lakeside was a smaller hotel conveniently located near the shore. It afforded a bird's eye view of Lake Chautauqua and environs. Imagine a relaxing summer evening basking in a cool lake breeze on one of the hotel's verandahs. The building was torn down around 1940. *RL*

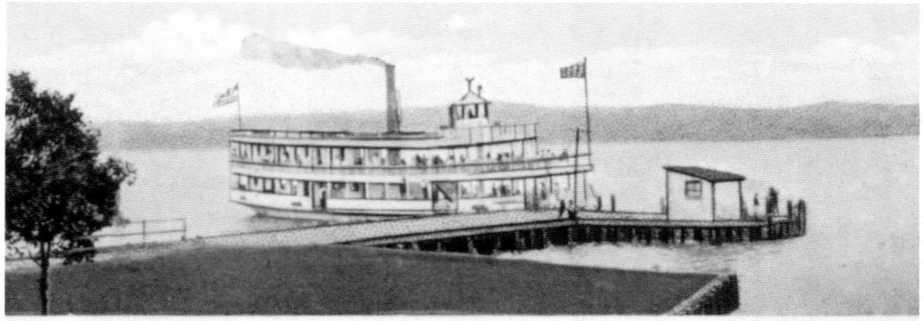

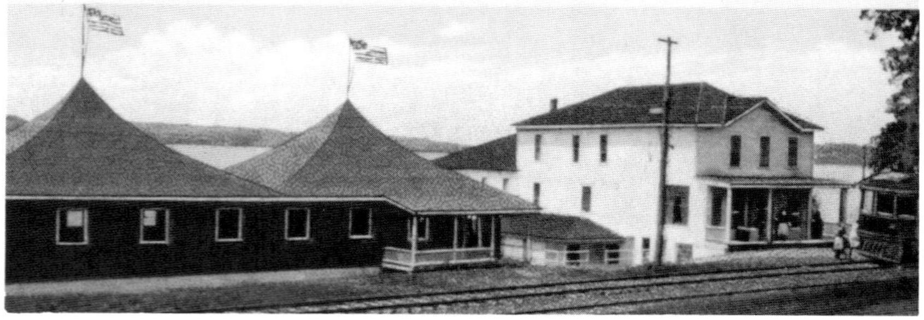

Point Chautauqua. Methods of transportation to points around the lake changed over time. Steamboats served as the primary means of travel until competition from railroads caused their decline. Trolley service from Jamestown arrived at Point Chautauqua in 1914 when the Jamestown, Westfield and Northwestern Railroad pushed north from Bemus Point. The tracks ran along the lake side of Lake Avenue. Cars stopped at the dock allowing passengers to alight or board. The J.W. & N.W. ceased passenger operation on November 30, 1947. *RL*

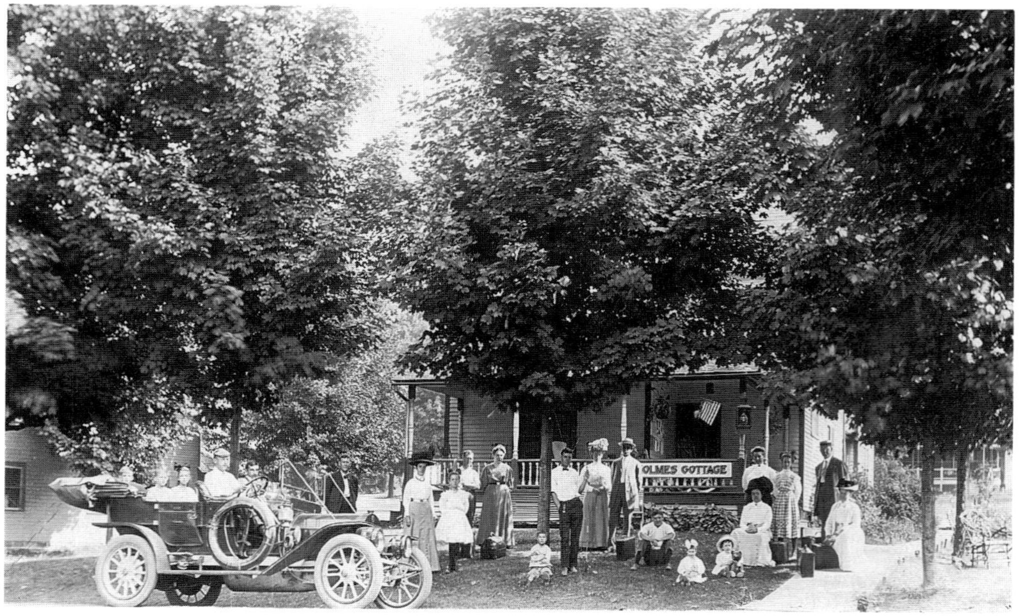

Holmes Cottage, ca. 1913. Guests, including children, in fine dress and with satchels about to enjoy an outing. The flag flying on the porch perhaps signifies the Fourth of July. Trees in full leaf denote high summertime. The touring car lends a certain jauntiness to the occasion. *RL*

Wooglin Inn, ca. 1890. Beta Theta Pi, a national fraternity, built the Wooglin Inn as a summer clubhouse in 1884. Located between Point Chautauqua and Hartfield, the Wooglin offered public rooms for meals, reading, socializing and dancing on the first floor. On the second floor were single rooms and small apartments for families. The fraternity continued the operation through the 1894 season, then, because of financial problems, sold the establishment. After a brief and unsuccessful attempt as a public hotel, the building was abandoned in 1899. It was struck by lightning and burned in 1901. *JE*

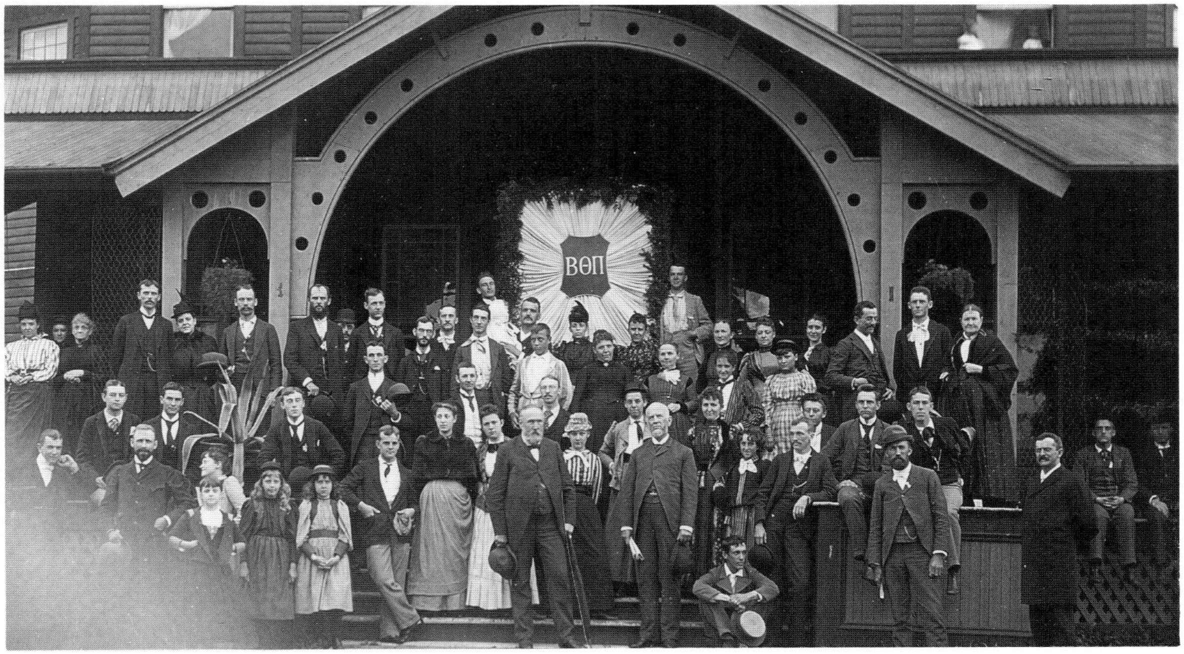

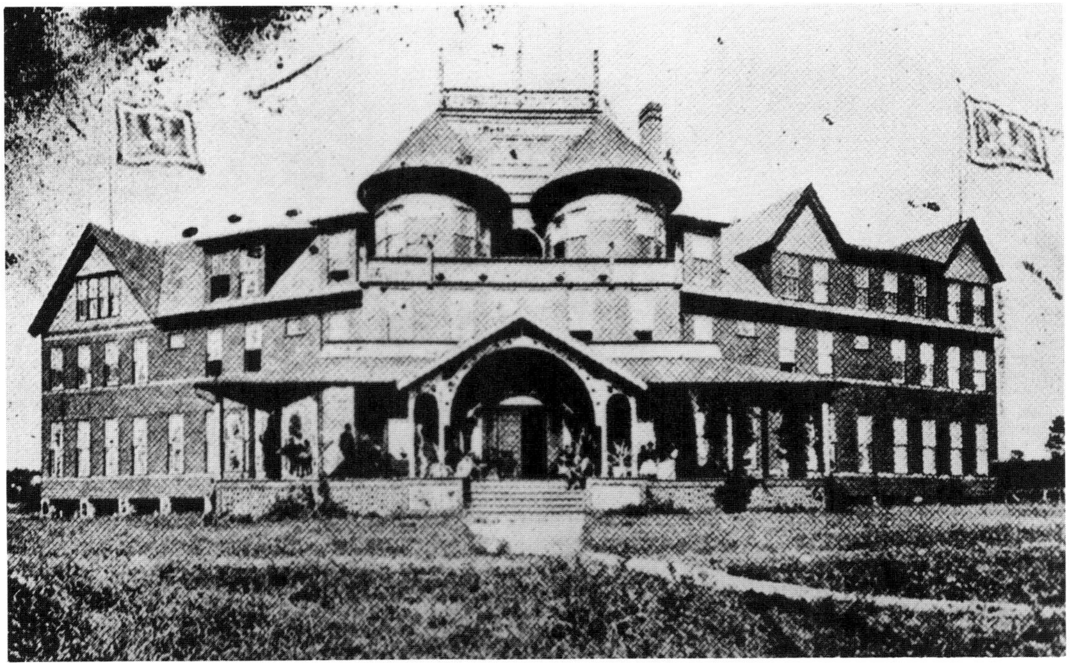

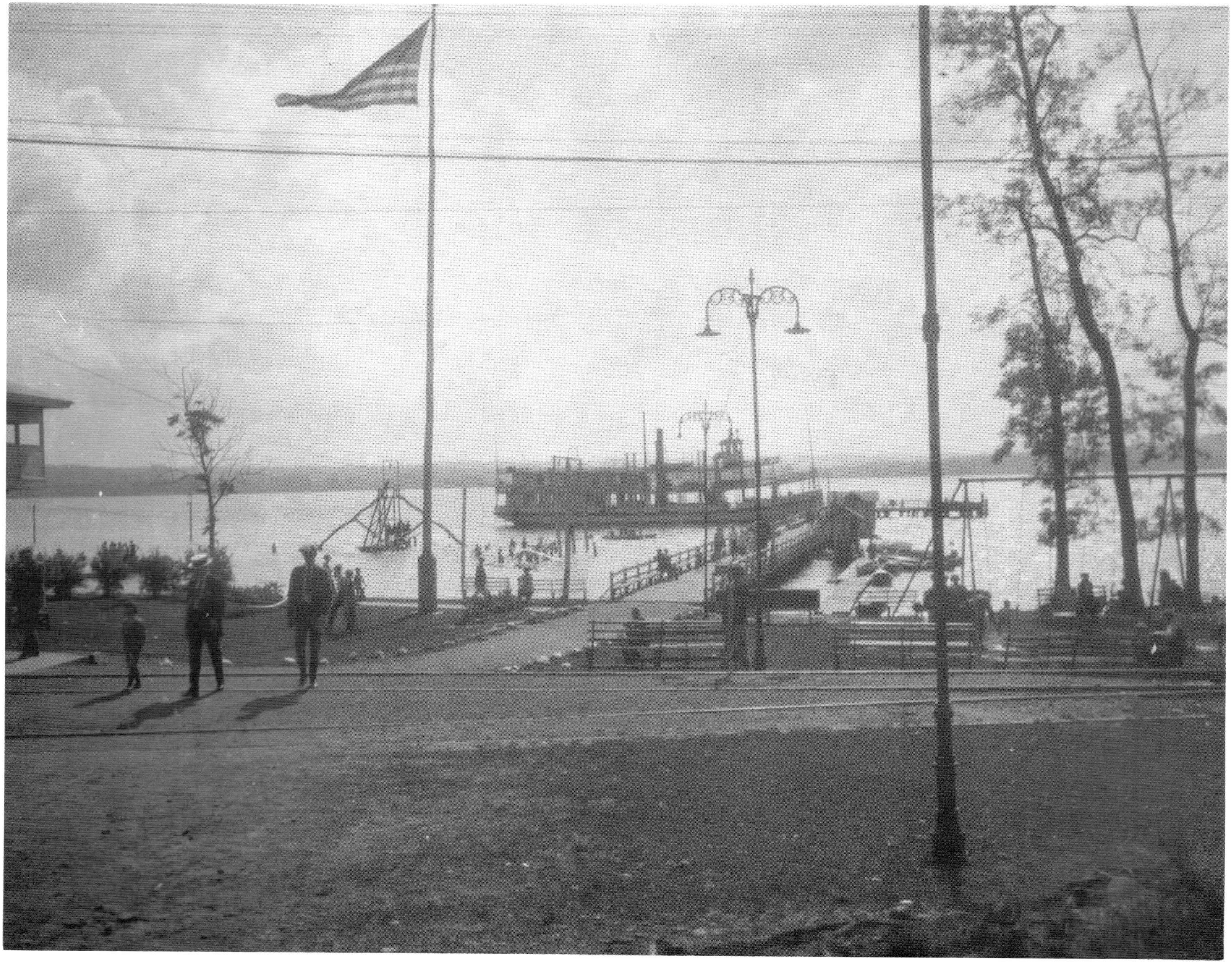

MIDWAY PARK   MAPLE SPRINGS
POINT WHITESIDE

Chautauqua Lake's popular amusement center will celebrate its centennial in 1998. Undoubtedly influenced by the success of Celoron, the Jamestown and Lake Erie Railroad, formerly the Chautauqua Lake Railway, leased seventeen acres of prime lakefront between Dewittville and Long Point for its own picnic grounds and amusement center. Midway, which opened formally on July 12, 1898, boasted a "sandy" beach for bathing, a dance pavilion, and a dining room. Tennis courts, bath houses, and a ballpark were also planned.

The name "Midway" derives from the long dock built in 1894 that serviced the Hotel Whiteside and the Maple Springs Inn, small resort hotels located just below the park. Each hotel maintained its own dock until 1894 when a new and longer dock called "Midway" was constructed between the two. The dock became a regular steamboat and railroad stop. When the two hotels failed to open during the first few years of the twentieth century, the name was changed to "Maple Springs" for its large number of stately maple trees and water springs. The area was considered one of the most naturally beautiful on the lake.

In 1905 a Jamestown real estate firm developed Maple Springs into a residential community. A separate pier was built at the Midway picnic grounds. In 1913 the Broadhead brothers purchased the railroad, and the following year converted the steam into an electric railway called the Jamestown, Westfield and Northwestern Railroad. The Chautauqua Lake Navigation Company, a railroad subsidiary, purchased the park in 1915. Running time to Midway from Jamestown on the J.W. & N.W. was about twenty-eight minutes, compared to two hours by steamer. The cars stopped just outside the fancy new pavilion built in 1915. Today Midway Park is owned and operated by Michael and Janis Walsh, the second generation of the Walsh family to carry on the business. Maple Springs is today a quiet enclave of homes and cottages.

Lakefront, Midway Park, ca. 1922. The *City of New York* laying off at the end of the dock after depositing its passengers. The bath house is to the left behind the J.W. & N.W. tracks. *FHS*

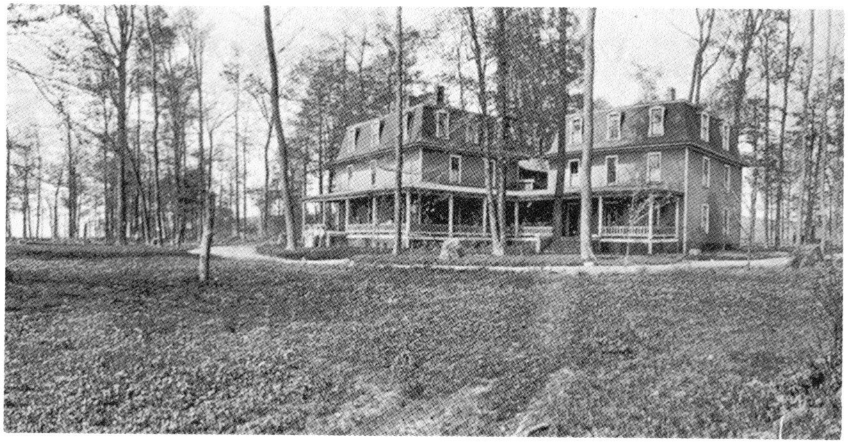

Hotel Whiteside, ca. 1905. Built by William Whiteside, this small hotel began operations in 1879. Its cool, shady verandahs afforded a picturesque view of the lake. With both a steel pier and a station for the Chautauqua Lake Railway, later the J.W. & N.W., the inn flourished. Hotel guests enjoyed its tennis court and croquet grounds along with its excellent cuisine. During the 1920s, the hotel was enlarged and modernized. The once popular resort hotel was demolished in 1984. *RL*

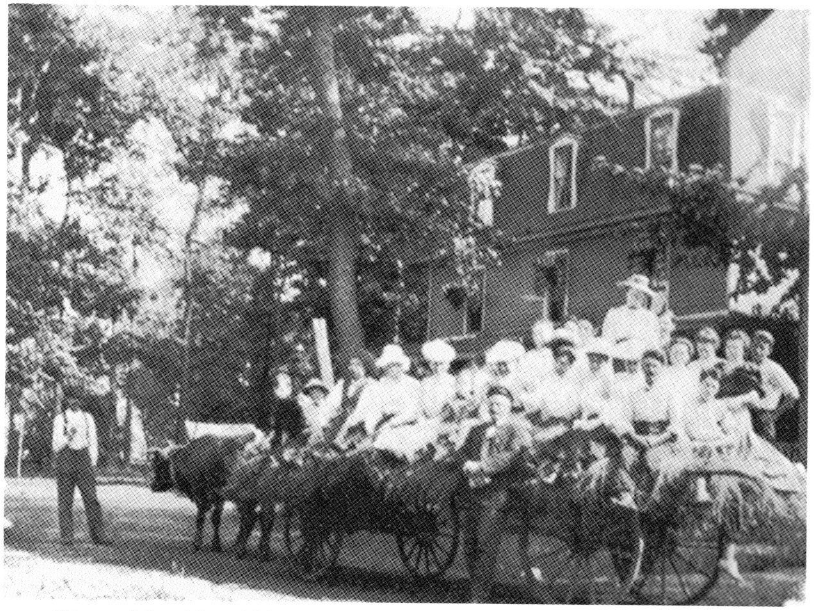

Strawride, Hotel Whiteside, ca. 1900. Diversions at the turn of the century were more subdued than they are today. Without the motor car, radio, and television - to say nothing of air travel - people enjoyed simpler pleasures. Boat rides, walks along the shore, theatricals, parades, dances and "strawrides" were popular pastimes. *CCHS*

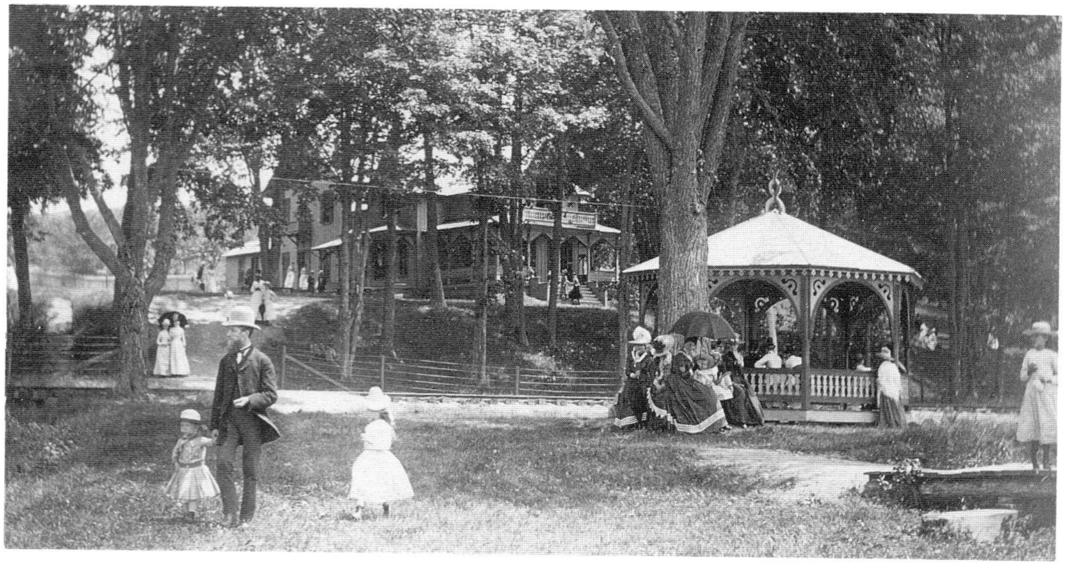

Maple Springs Inn, ca. 1890. The "Gay Nineties" at Chautauqua Lake. The Maple Springs Inn declined after the development of Maple Springs around its competitor, the Hotel Whiteside. *FHS*

Midway Park, ca. 1913. The picnic grove at Midway Park seen from the dock, and coaches of the Jamestown, Chautauqua and Lake Erie Railroad formerly the Jamestown and Lake Erie Railroad. The J.C. & L.E. was a reorganization of the original Chautauqua Lake Railway. It became the J.W. & N.W. in 1914. The Midway bath house was built just below the tracks and to the right of the dock a few years after this photo was taken. *RL*

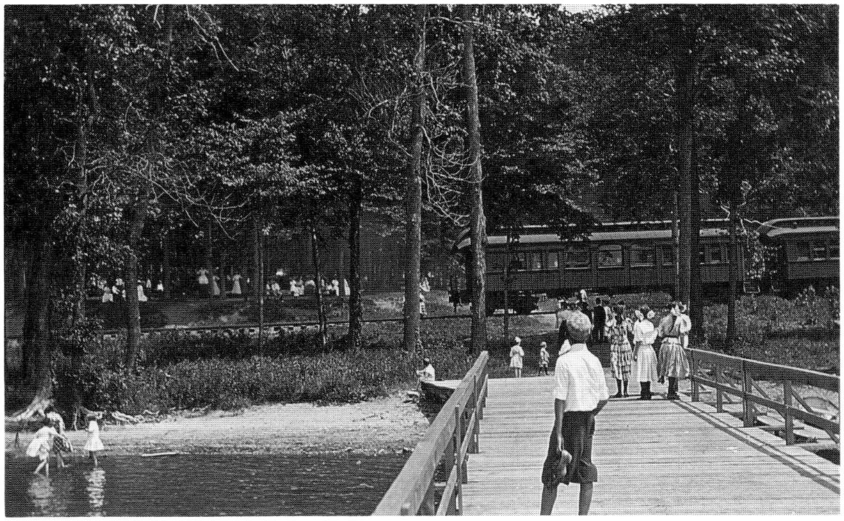

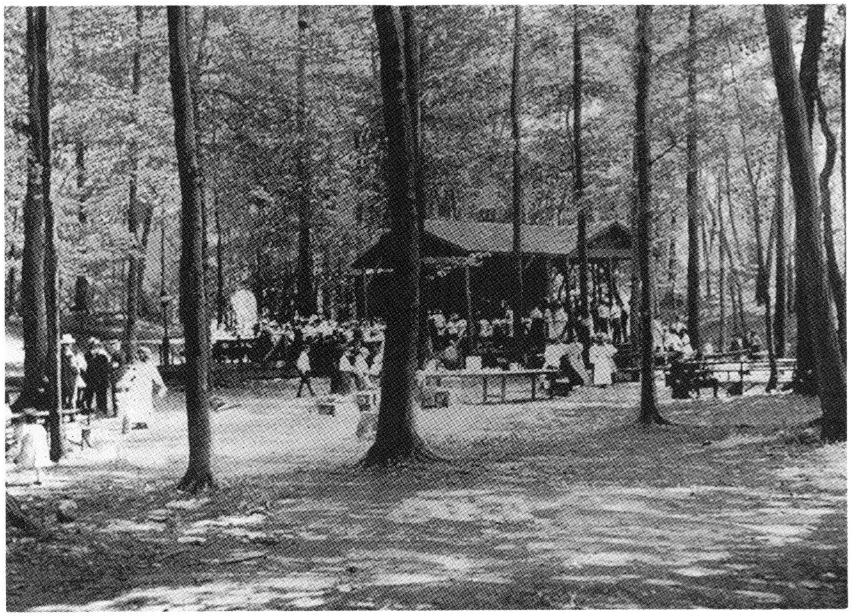

Pavilion, Midway Park, ca. 1900. Ladies in fine dress enjoy the picnic grove which looks today much as it did when this photograph was taken. *FHS*

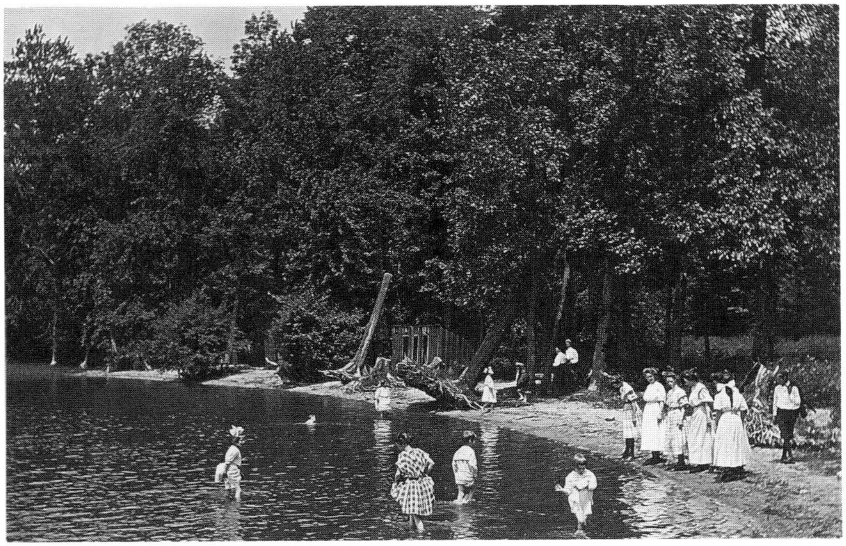

Midway Park, ca. 1908. The park's "sandy" bathing beach looking up the lake from the steamboat dock. *RL*

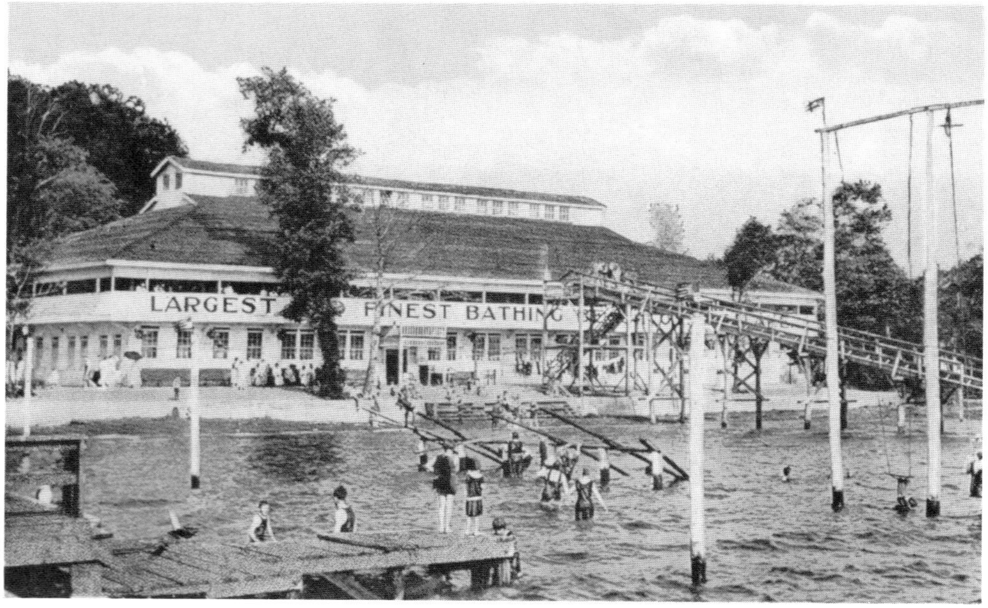

Bath house, Midway Park, ca. 1925. The Midway Park bath house, built in 1915, featured a toboggan slide which was removed each year before the winter season. The first floor of the bath house contained two dressing rooms for bathers, a large dining room and kitchen, and various concessions. The upper story was a marvelous skating rink and dance floor. The windowed superstructure, a ventilation system, was blown off by a tornado in the 1940s. The building today houses the arcade, Midway's own museum and the ever-popular roller skating rink. *CCHS*

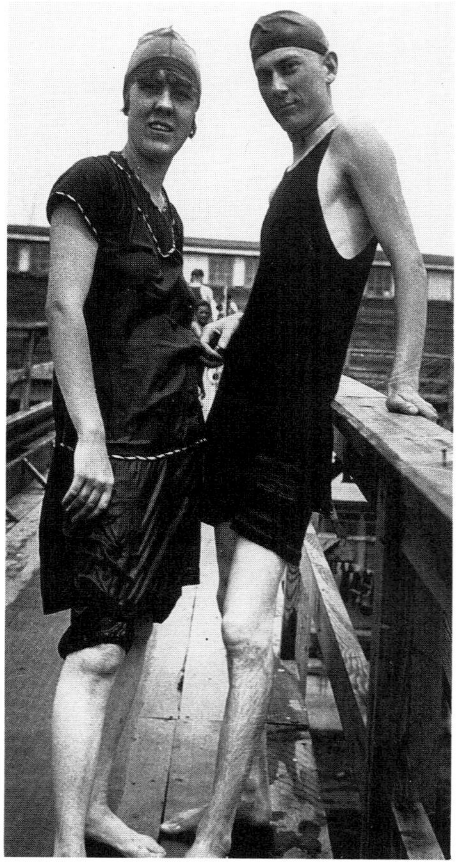

Midway Park, 1917. Marie Johnson Norton and Merton Johnson, Vic Norton's mother and uncle, on the toboggan slide. *VN*

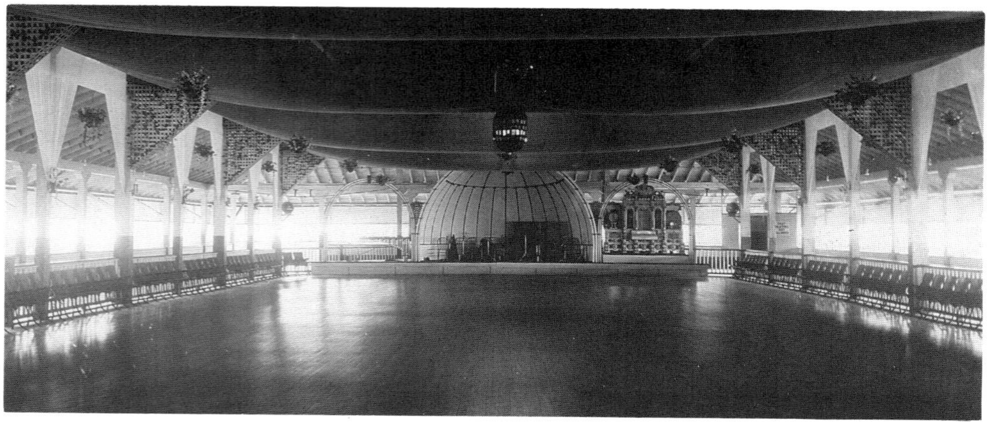

Skating rink interior. Lanes behind the rails on either side were reserved for experienced skaters. Many a young man met his future bride at the Midway skating rink. *FHS*

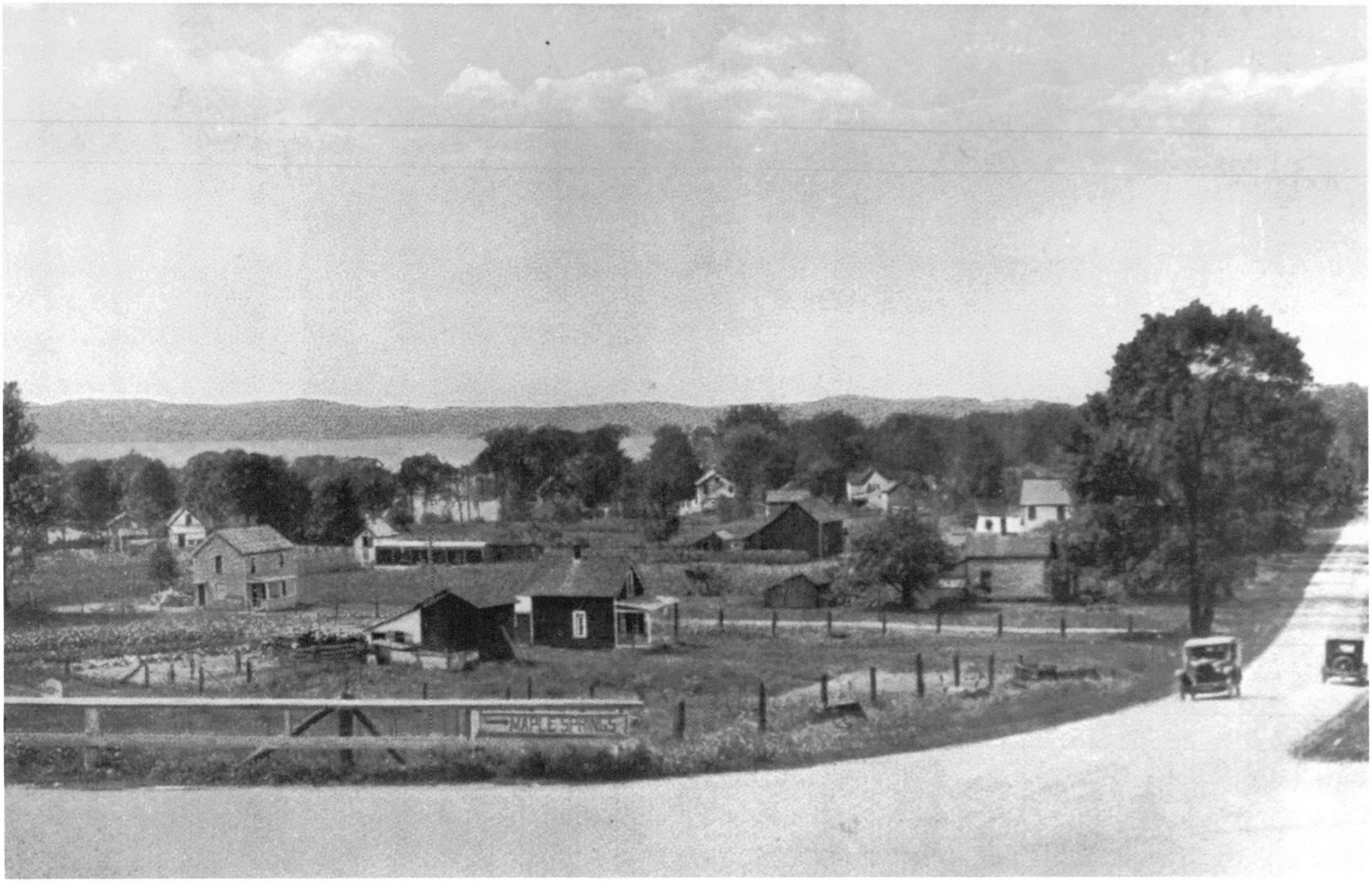

Maple Springs, 1923. The entrance to Maple Springs from State Road (old Route 17). *FHS*

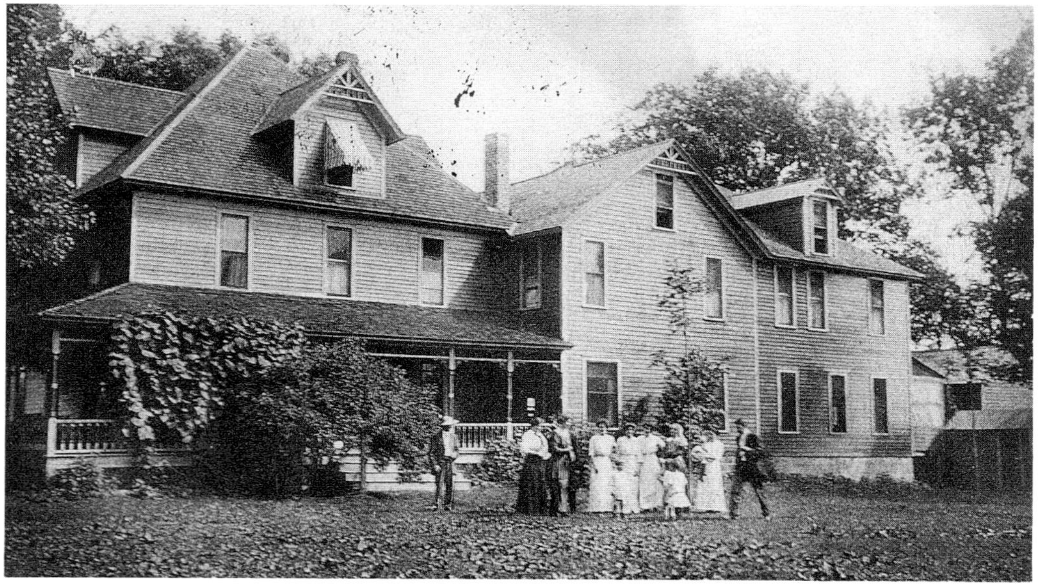

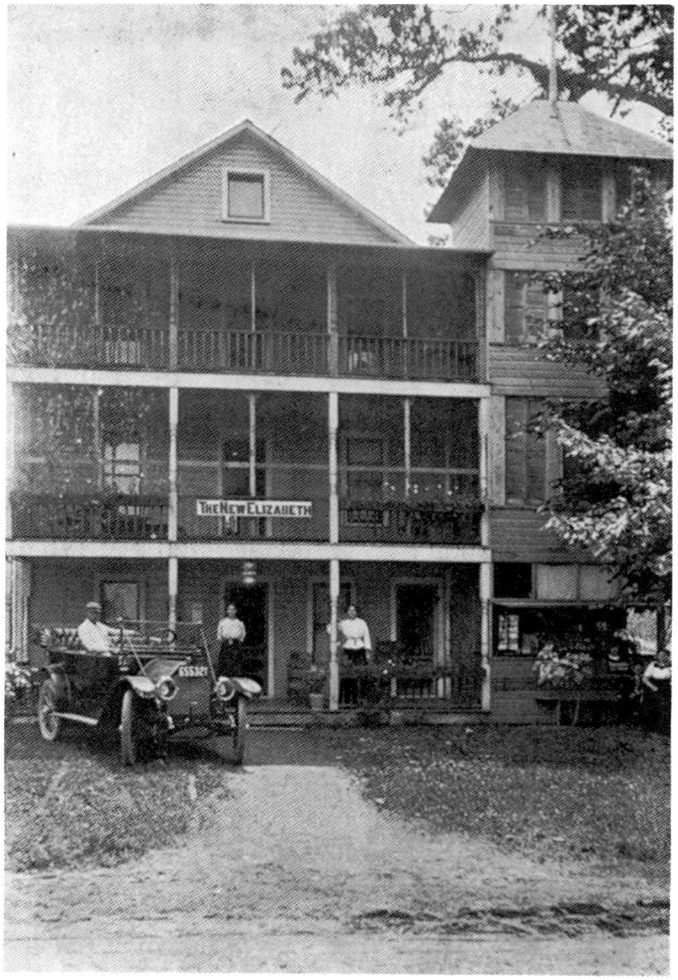

Maple Springs, ca. 1915. A number of boarding houses such as the Campbell Cottage and the New Elizabeth were built around this time. The hotels and boarding establishments provided summer employment and social life for local young people and, as today, pumped money into the local economy. *RL*

Harewood, ca. 1915. Harewood was the Broadhead summer estate. The former Maple Springs Inn was purchased by Miss Flora Broadhead and her sister, Mrs. Mertie Howard, in 1913. They called the property "Harewood." The home remained in the Broadhead family for many years and was finally torn down in the 1980s. *FHS*

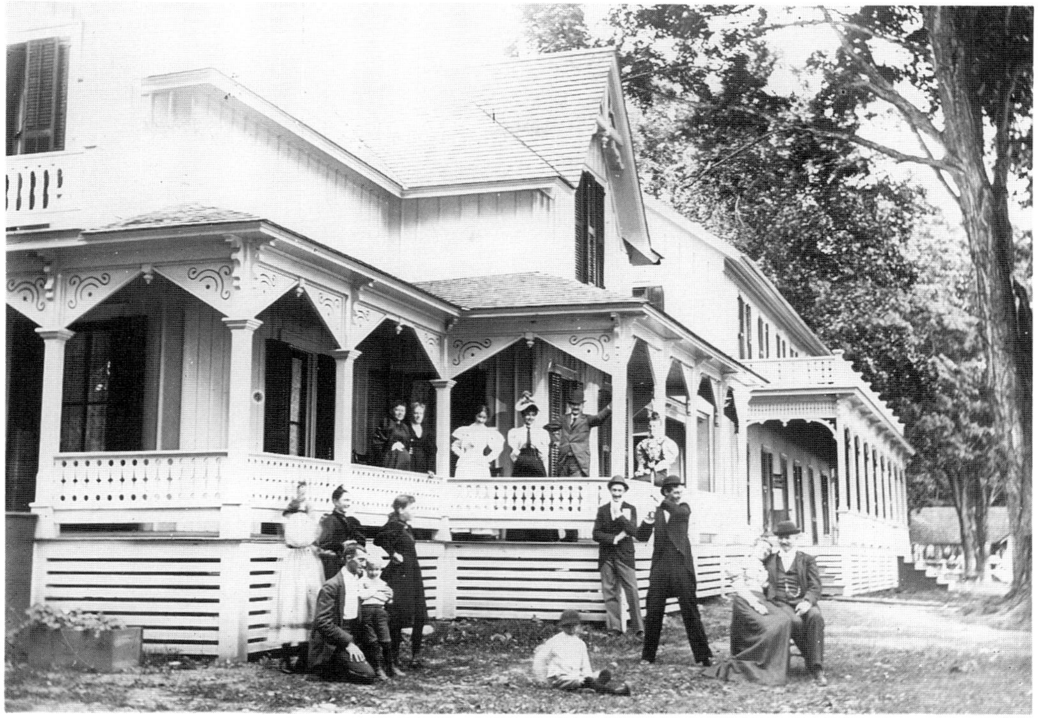

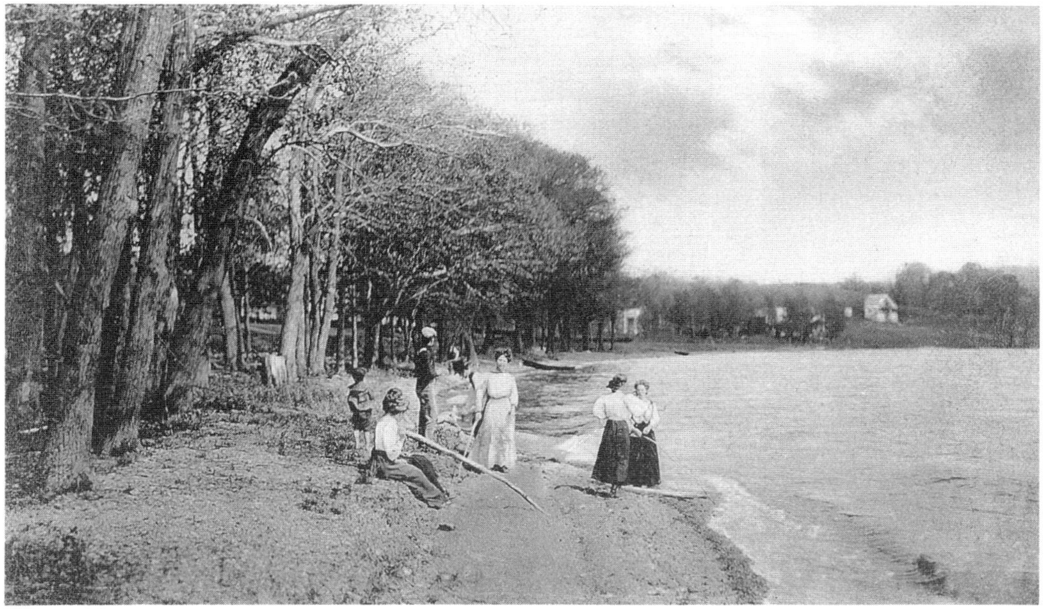

Maple Springs, ca. 1910. The beach at Maple Springs looking down the lake toward Bemus Point. *RL*

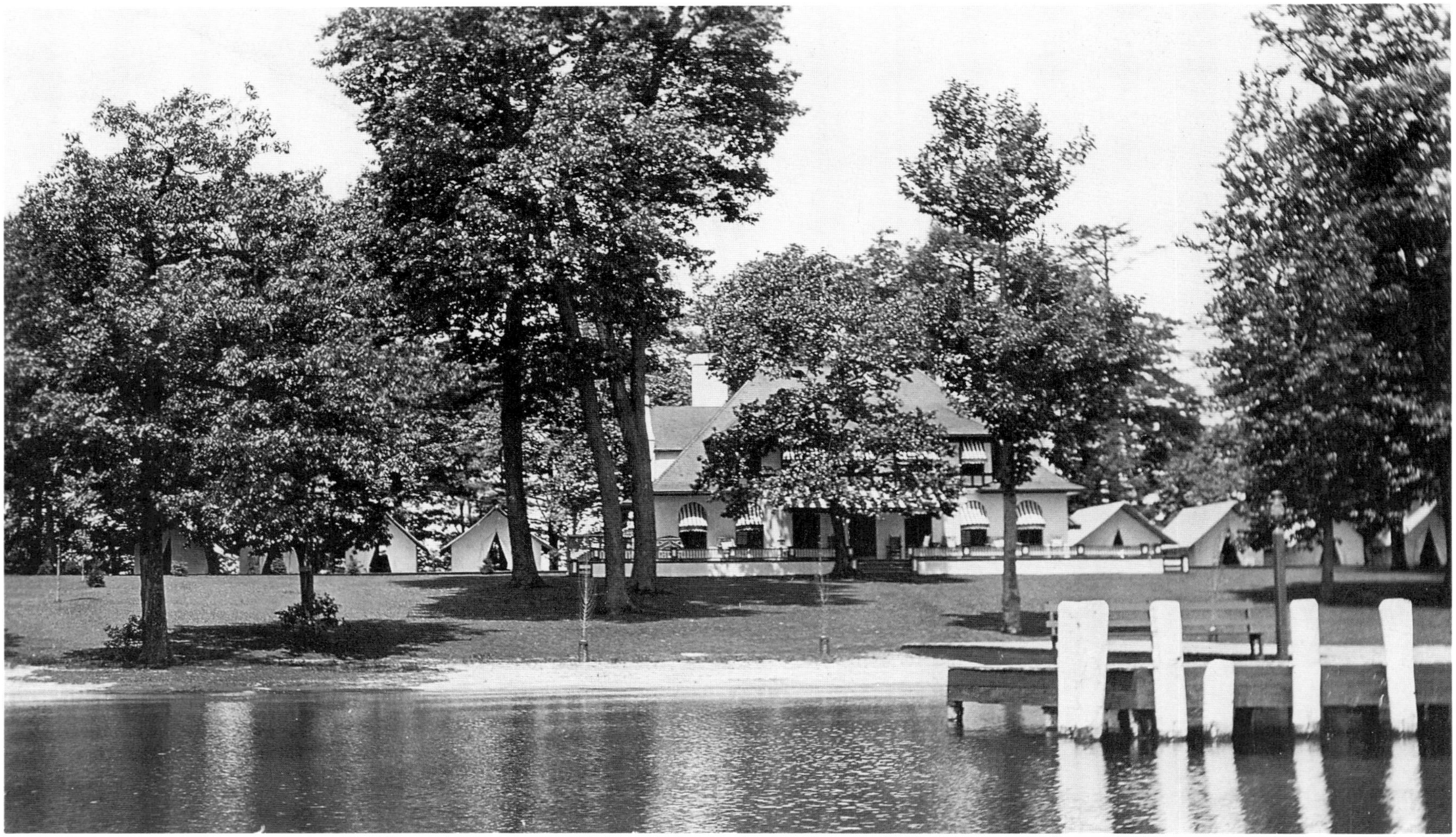

LONG POINT

The name "Long Point" is fitting for this slender peninsula located at the deepest part of Chautauqua Lake between Bemus Point and Maple Springs. Recognized early as the perfect spot for picnic parties, the grounds were cleared for that purpose in 1869 by Perry Barnes, who later built the Maple Springs Inn. He installed a steamboat dock, short because of the lake's depth at the point, and a picnic pavilion. In 1873 Henry Harley, owner of the Chautauqua Lake Navigation Company, purchased several acres at Long Point and built a private residence there. He added attractions such as balloon rides, fireworks, and competitive games. In 1887 Abner Elisha Allen of Jamestown, owner of Allen's Opera House, leased the property for an amusement park and zoological gardens.

Long Point was acquired by Frank Gifford, a Jamestown banker and son-in-law of the late Governor Reuben E. Fenton, in 1887. He resided in the mansion built by Harley and leased the park to the Jamestown, Chautauqua and Lake Erie Railroad. The popularity of the park waned, however, after the opening of Celoron Park. In 1907 the railroad refused to renew its lease. The company had developed Midway by this time and felt that a single picnic park on the east side of the lake was sufficient. In 1908 the property was leased for a short time to Ralph Preston who constructed the beautiful summer home now in ruins there.

After Preston's lease expired, the Giffords continued residence at Long Point until Frank Gifford passed away in 1934. John and Cecile Fenton Gifford Minturn subsequently occupied the house. The Minturns donated the 120-acre estate to the State of New York in 1954.

Long Point, ca. 1910. R.J. Preston's "bungalow" at Long Point. Prior to his residence at Long Point, Mr. Preston leased the enormous Greenhurst Hotel for his private use. *RL*

Long Point, July 4, 1881. For years Long Point was a favorite destination for excursion boats and church and club picnics. The triple-decked *Jamestown*, formerly the *Nettie Fox*, is shown unloading throngs of people for a glorious Fourth of July picnic at the Point. The day ended with fireworks and a moonlight ride. *CCHS*

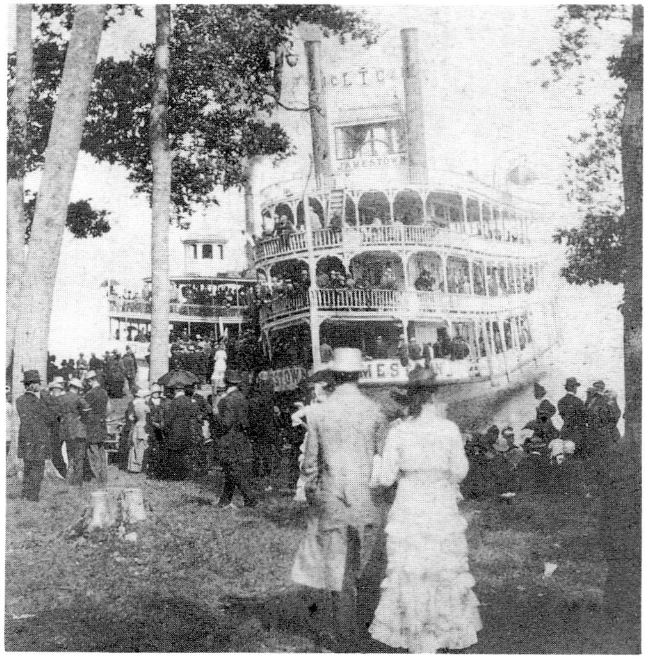

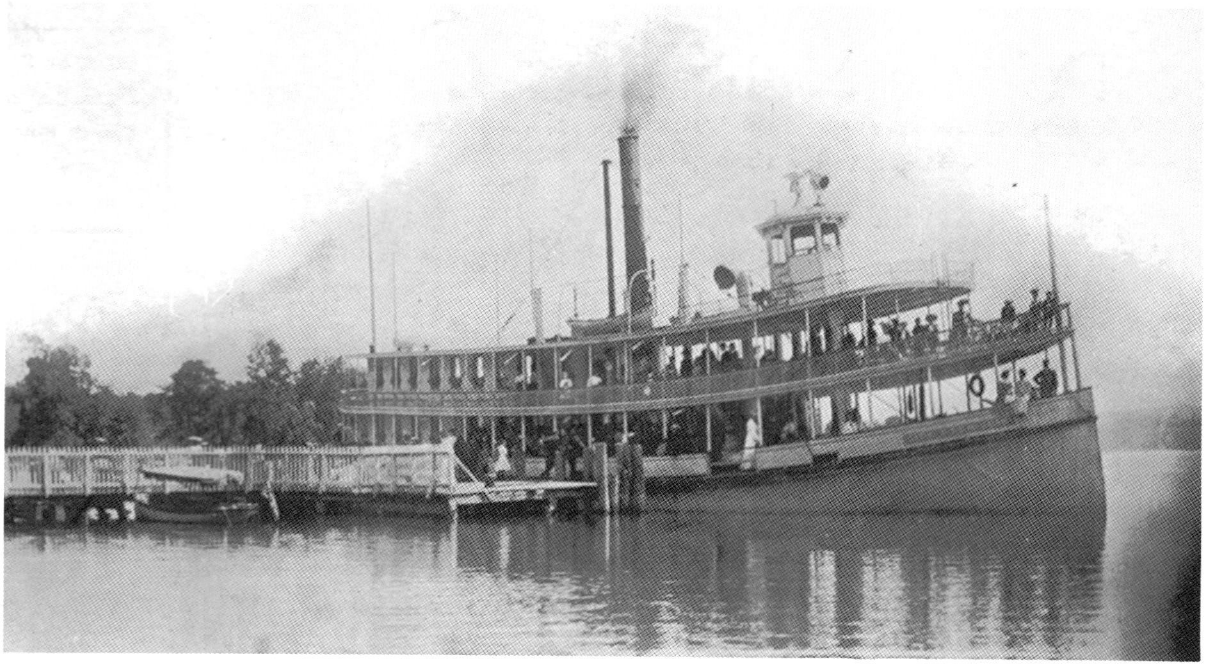

Long Point Dock, ca. 1887. A view of the dock and the steamer *Nightengale*, later the *City of New York*, after Long Point had become an amusement park and zoo. The dock was fenced in for the collection of gate fees. The zoological grounds lasted a single year. *RL*

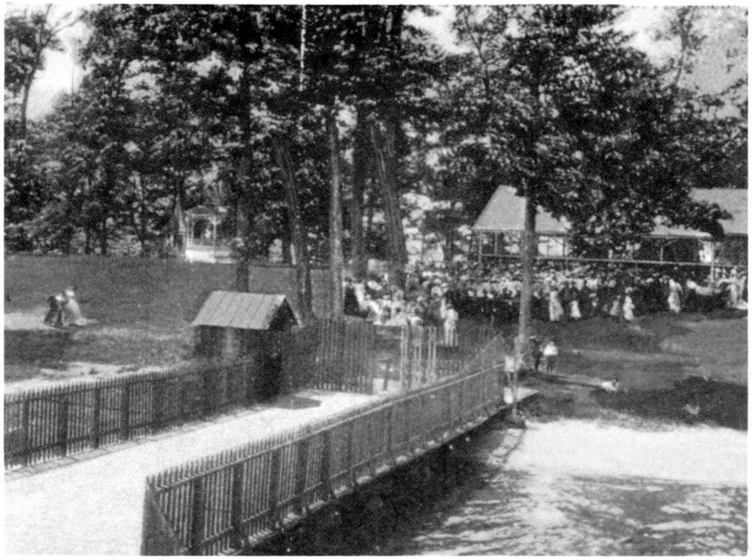

Long Point dock and picnic grove, ca. 1900. Note the sandy beach. *RL*

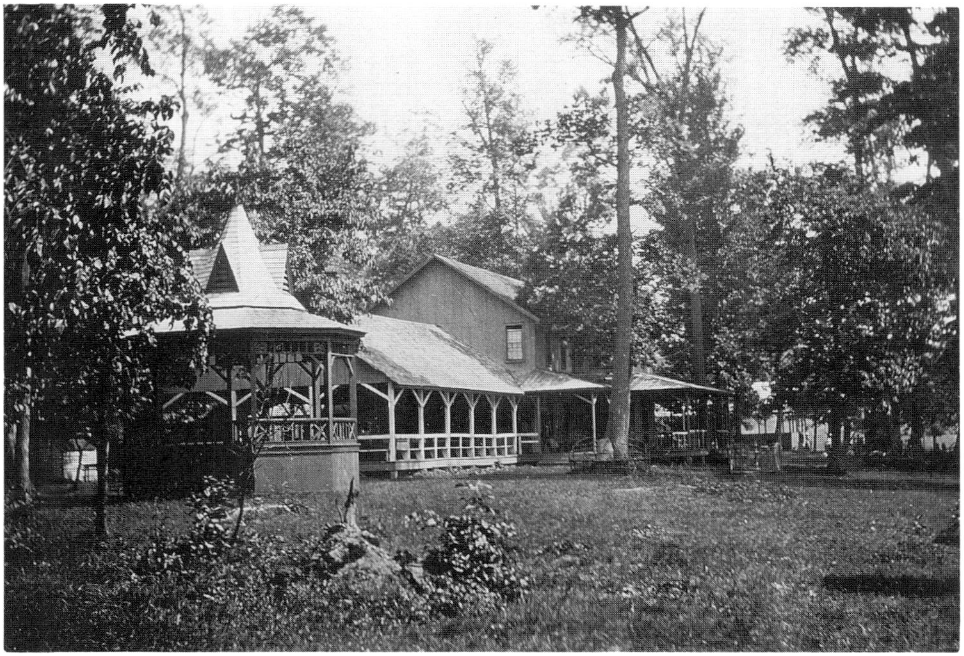

Gazebo and picnic shelter, ca. 1875. Victorian picnickers always faced the challenge of inclement weather. The lake is partially visible behind this building. *CMN*

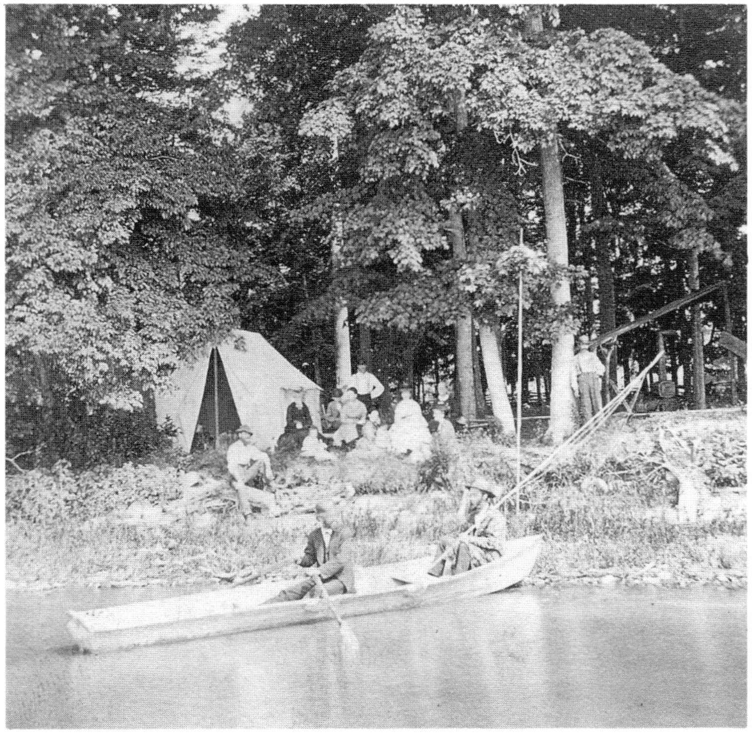

Long Point, ca. 1875. "The Cicerone," a local advertising publication, identifies this stereopticon view as Long Point. Camping was never encouraged at Long Point and would have required the current owner's permission. *CCHS*

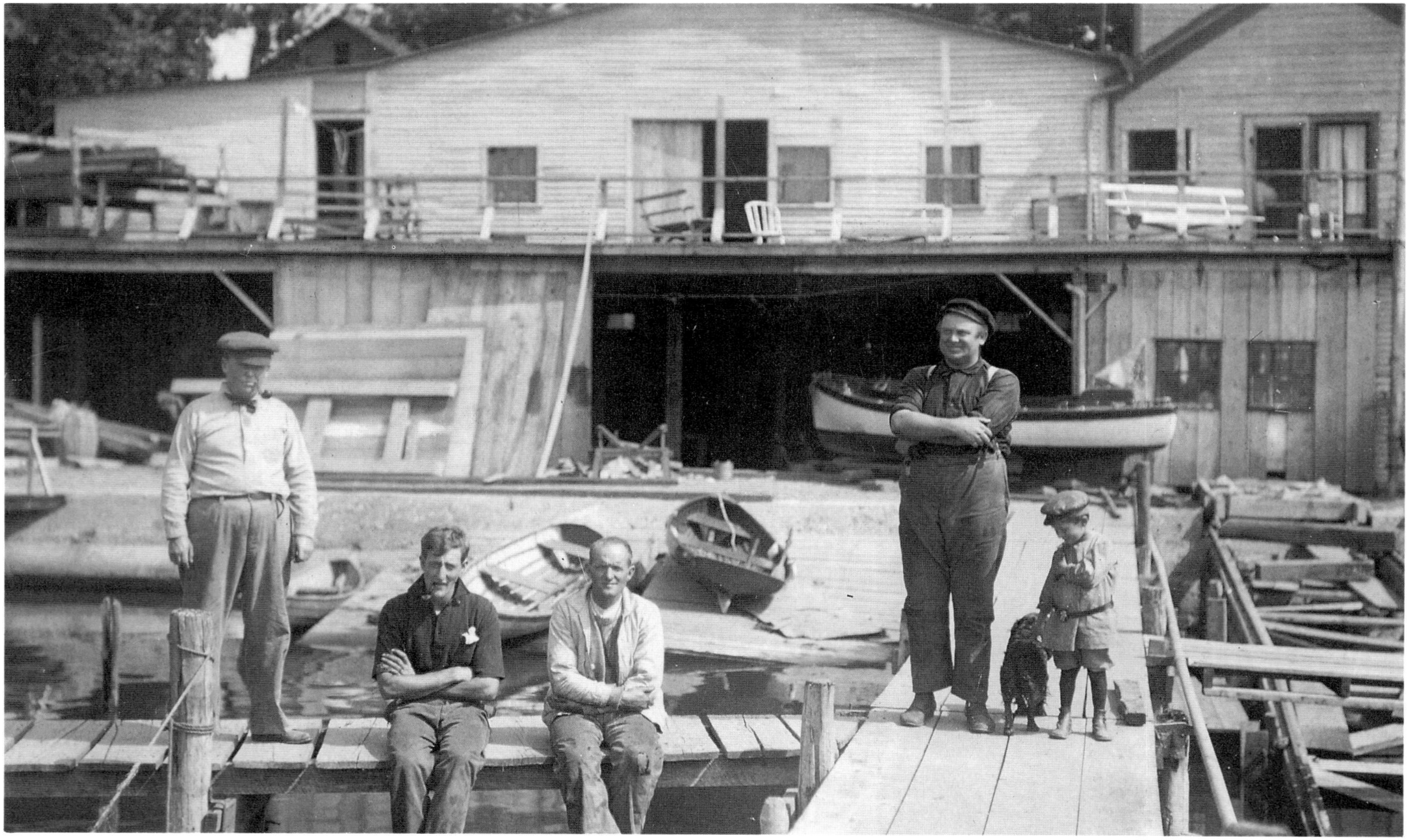

BEMUS POINT

The quiet and dignified Lenhart Hotel is a pleasant reminder of Chautauqua Lake's resort history and the special part the village of Bemus Point played in it. When the Chautauqua Lake House opened in 1871, the village consisted of a single church, a blacksmith shop, harness shop, and perhaps fifteen dwellings. Its convenient location at the narrowest point on the lake, about midway between Jamestown and Mayville, made Bemus Point a natural stopping spot for travelers. The immediate success of the Chautauqua Lake House confirmed the village's potential as a resort area. By the turn of the century, four large hotels, including the Lenhart, faced Bemus Bay along Lakeside Drive. Beautiful scenery, tall trees and a "health-giving breeze" gave the village its reputation as one of the finest and most romantic locations on Chautauqua Lake. The Point was easily reached by steamboat and later by rail, and a ferry across the lake had been in operation as early as 1811. The area was especially popular with fishermen. Bemus Point is named for the Bemus family, whose patriarch, William Bemus, settled along the bay in 1805. William Bemus married Mary Prendergast, sister of James, for whom Jamestown is named. Descendants of William Bemus still reside in Chautauqua County.

Johnson boatyard, ca. 1911. John O. Johnson maintained his boatyard for many years next to the Bemus Point steamer dock. Johnson and his crew were famous for building rowboats. Lawson's and the Italian Fisherman now occupy this site. *RL*

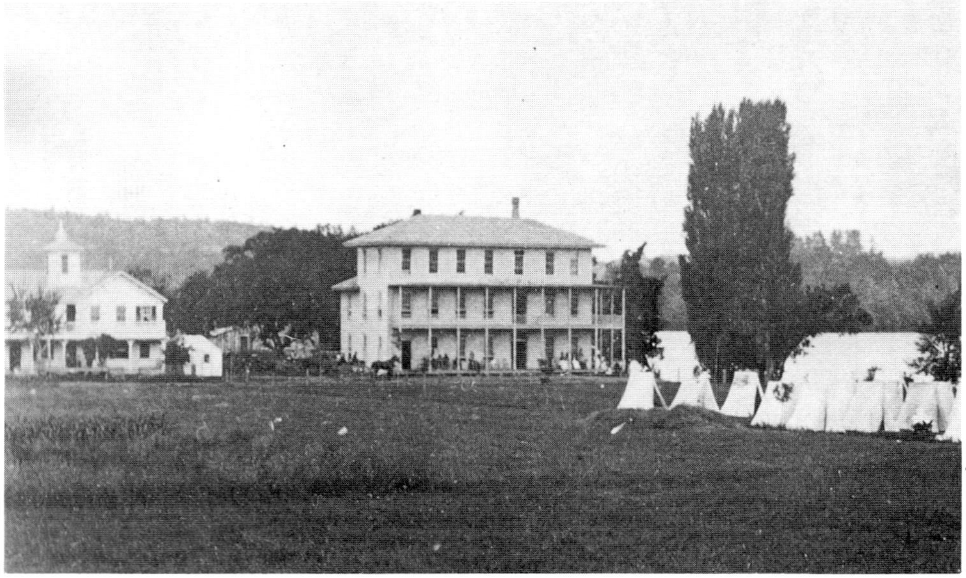

Camp Byron, ca. 1873. Military groups regularly held summer encampments along the banks of Chautauqua Lake. Camp Byron was a group from Titusville, Pennsylvania. The Chautauqua Lake House is in the background. *JE*

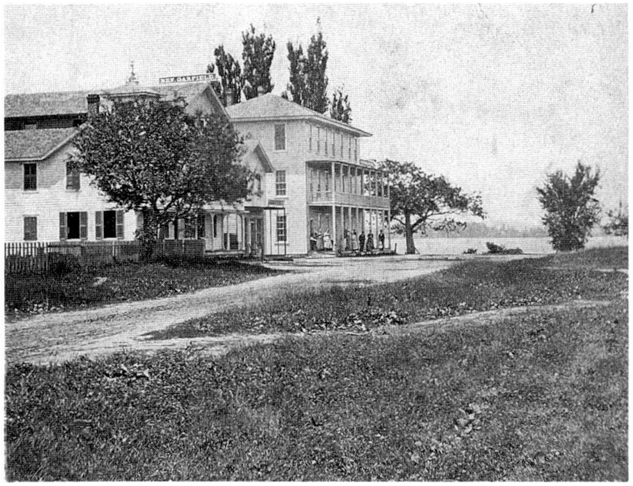

Chautauqua Lake House, ca. 1873. An early view looking toward the lake. The front door opened on Main Street which appears in the photograph as little more than a dirt path. *CCHS*

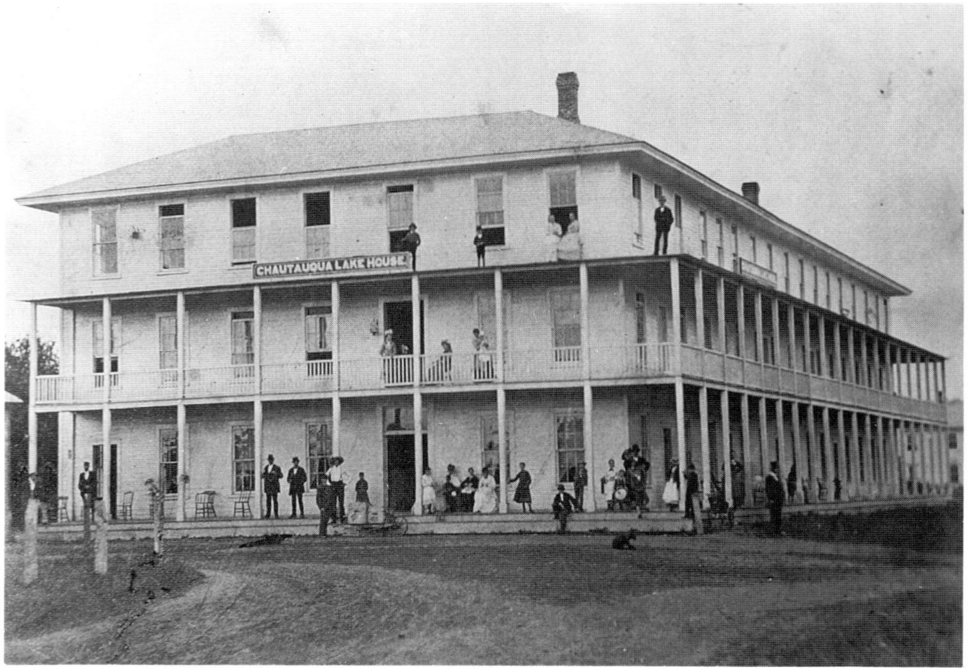

Chautauqua Lake House, ca. 1877. Bemus Point's first hotel opened in June, 1871 with room for 40 guests. "The crown of Bemus Point," its rates were $10.00 per week or $2.00 per day. Under the management of Jack Pickard, the hotel flourished. First-class accommodations and a picturesque view made the Chautauqua House extremely popular among vacationers. Its success encouraged the growth of Bemus Point and the construction of other summer establishments. It was destroyed by fire in 1888. *JE*

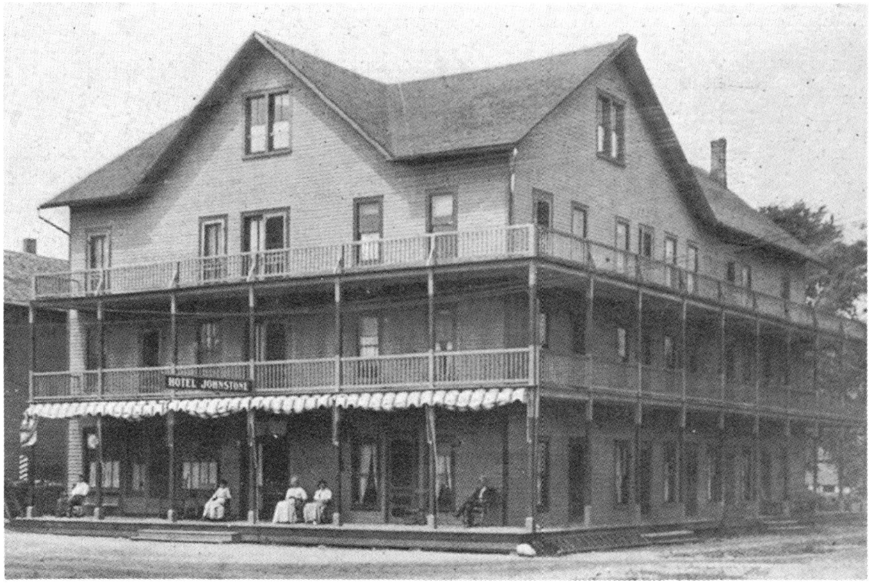

Hotel Johnstone, ca. 1905. Built as the American House in 1880, this popular hotel was known in later years as the Hotel Rappole. It is now the See-Zurh House. As with many of the lake hotels, the top floor was a year-round dance hall and was also used for local theatrical and vaudeville productions. *CCHS*

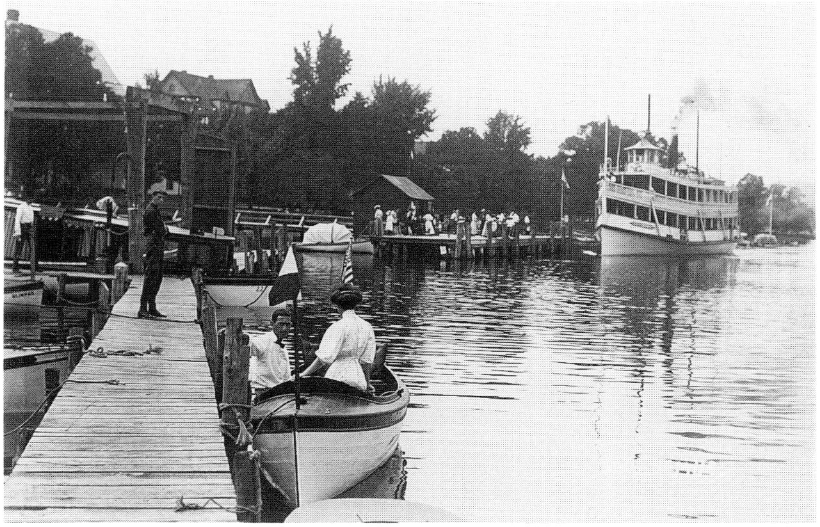

Bemus Point, ca. 1910. A couple leaves Johnson's dock for a romantic boat ride. The *City of Cincinnati* is boarding passengers at the Bemus Point dock. The roof of the Columbian Inn can be seen on the left. *RL*

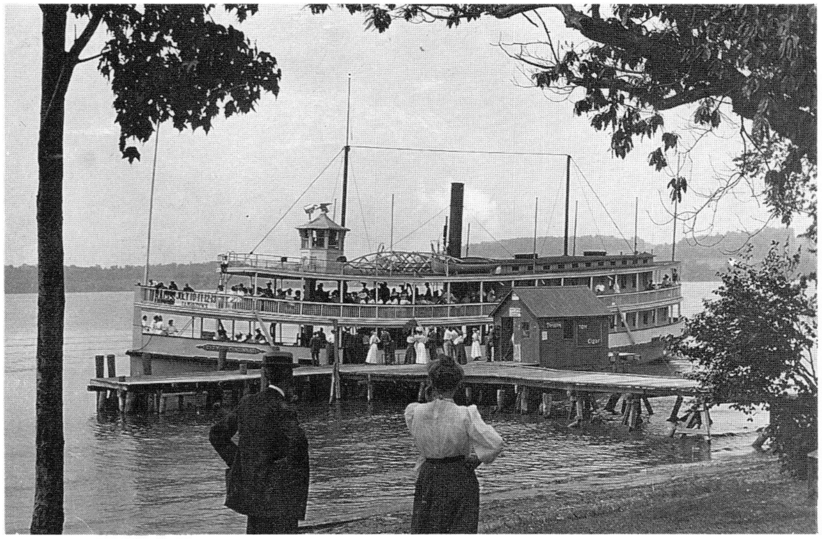

Bemus Point Dock, ca. 1908. The *City of Cincinnati* facing down the lake. The short dock at Bemus Bay belies the lake depth. Steamers followed a narrow channel here to avoid sticking in the mud. *RL*

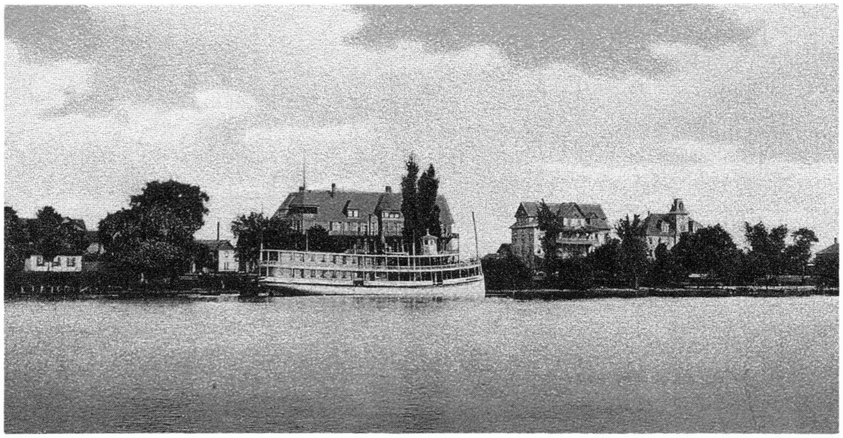

Lakeshore, Bemus Point, ca. 1900. A view from the lake showing the four lakeside hotels. Behind the *City of New York* is the Pickard House and left to right the Columbian Inn, the Browning and the Hotel Lenhart. *RL*

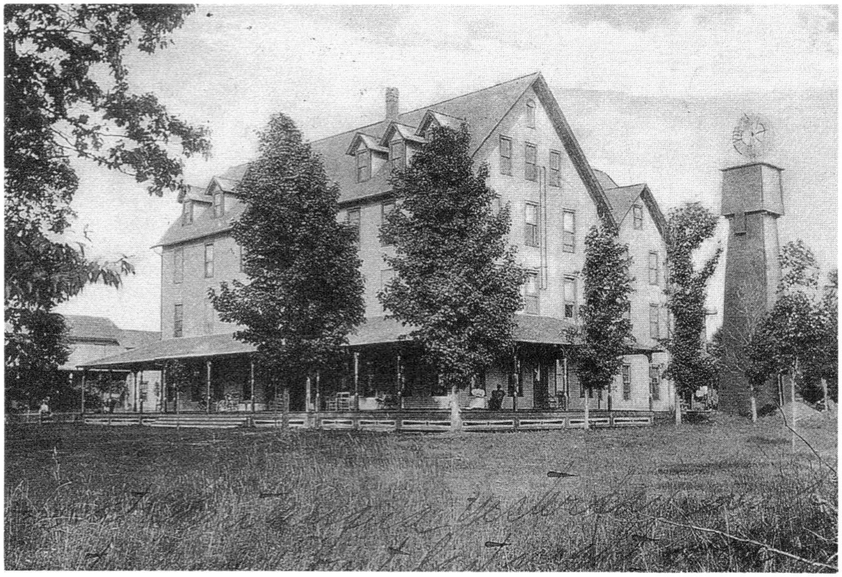

Hotel Lenhart, ca. 1920. Dr. John J. Lenhart opened his first hotel in 1882. After a disastrous fire destroyed the first Lenhart in 1891, a second hotel was built and began operations in 1892. The hotel's porch with its colorful rockers still welcomes summer guests - a remarkable longevity. *RL*

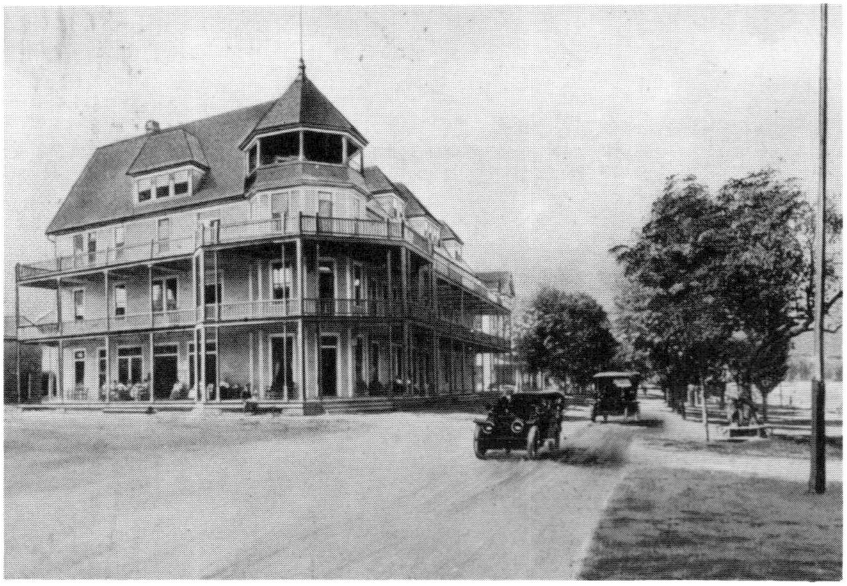

Pickard House, ca. 1915. Built by Jack Pickard in 1889 to replace the burned out Chautauqua Lake House, this "homelike and commodious" hotel had rooms for 150 guests. With an observation tower and three stories of verandahs, it was a most elegant establishment. Its bill of fare was the best that the market and nearby farms could provide. The grand old hotel saw the evolution from kerosene lamps to gas lighting and electricity; from "chambers" to private bathrooms; and from lake steamers to trolley lines and the automobile. The Surf Club is located on the site today. *RL*

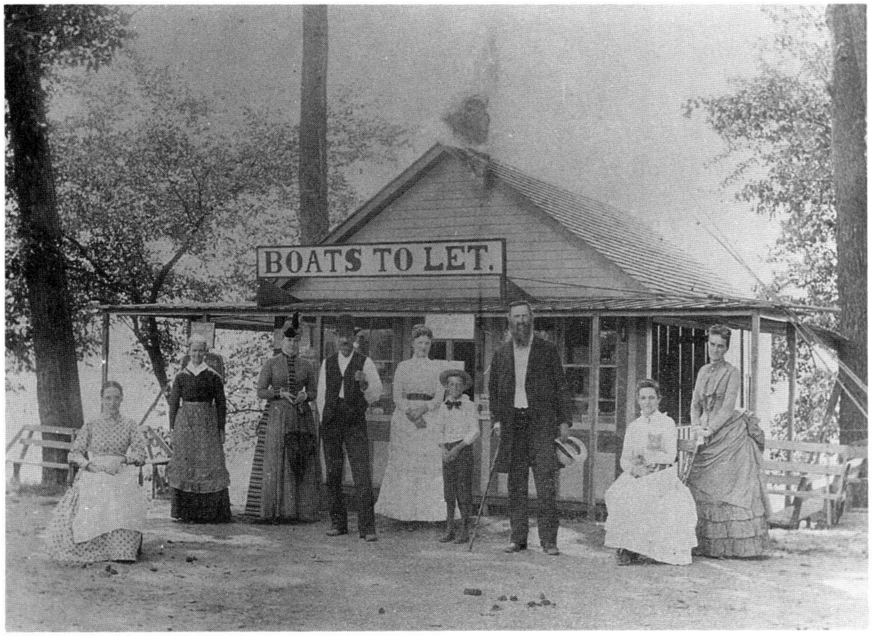

Odin Arnold's Boat Livery, ca. 1890. Rowboats, sailboats and canoes were available at liveries at the various summer colonies around the lake. This livery at the Point stayed in business for many years. As late as 1984, the Norton family was still operating a service near the Hotel Lenhart. The Arnold boat livery was located at the foot of Liberty Street. *JE*

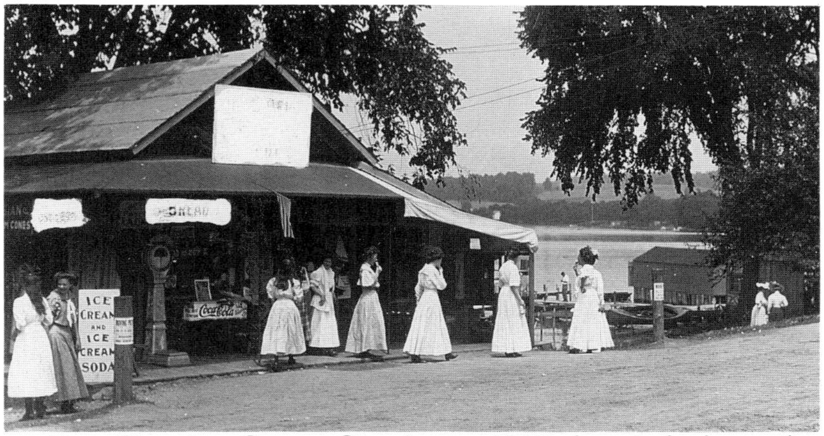

Van Cise Ice Cream Stand, ca. 1910. Located above the steamboat dock in Bemus, this "fast food" emporium did a brisk summer business in post cards, souvenirs, and ice cream. In 1910, ice cream was homemade and had to be eaten right away as there was no way to keep it frozen. Anyone who has seen an old fashioned ice cream maker can appreciate the labor involved. The post card craze was at its height in 1910. The Van Cise stand probably sold stamps to tourists along with the cards. Johnson's boatyard is in the background. *RL*

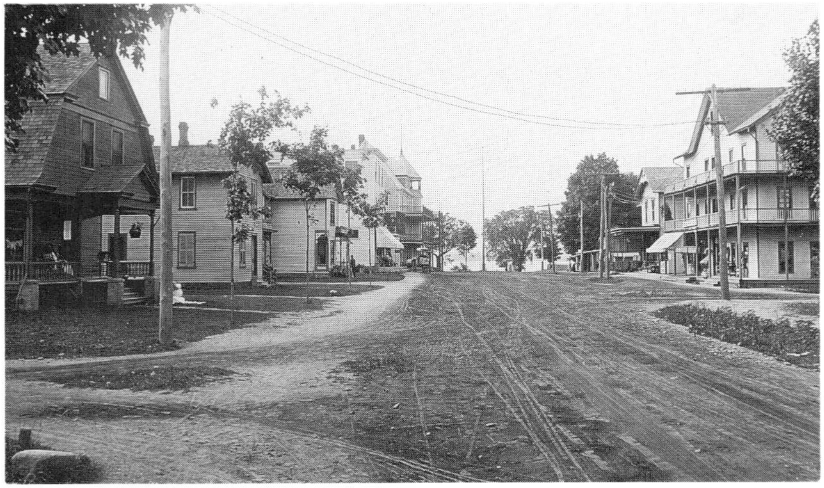

Main Street, ca. 1910. Looking toward the lake. The Hotel Johnstone is on the right. Private homes, Skillman's General Store, and the Pickard House are on the left. *RL*

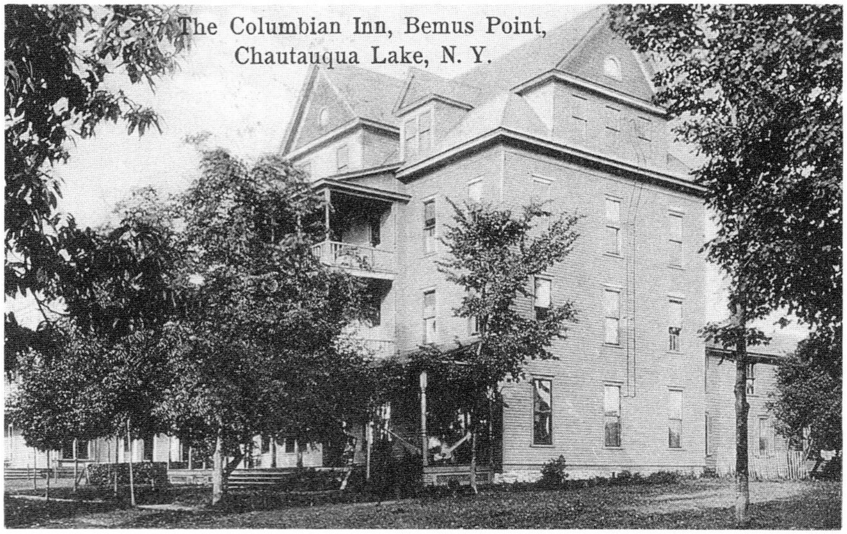

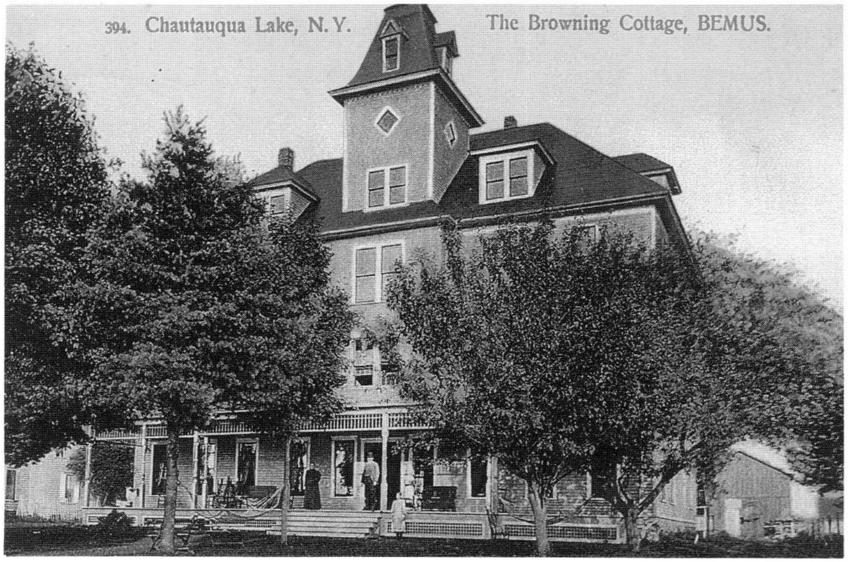

Columbian Inn and the Hotel Browning, ca. 1900. Both of these hotels were opened in 1893. They stood between the Pickard House and the Hotel Lenhart. The Columbian Inn, built by the Rappole family, had accommodations for 100 guests. The hotel had a bar and billiards room and was a popular eating spot. In 1919 the inn was joined to the Pickard House and was operated as the Bemus Point Hotel until 1930.

The Hotel Browning, formerly the Mason House, was built and operated by Mep Mason and his family. It was acquired by Perry Brown in 1900. The hotel remained in operation until it was destroyed by fire in 1941. The four story structure was of brick - a rare feature among the lake hotels. The upkeep of the lake hotels was time-consuming and expensive. Hotel owners only had about twelve weeks to maximize profits. *RL*

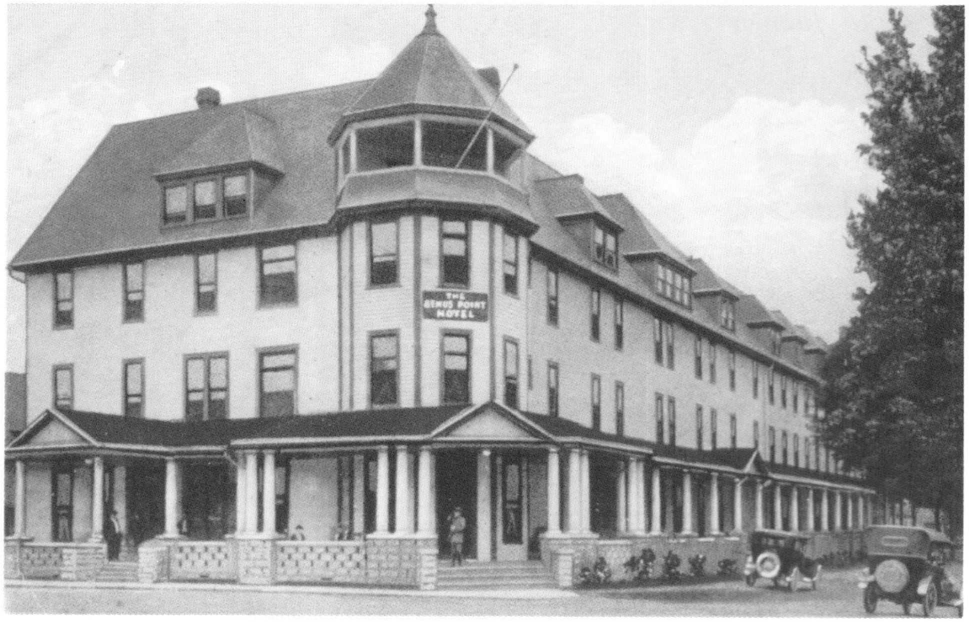

Bemus Point Hotel, ca. 1922. The Pickard House and the Columbian Inn were joined together and renamed the Bemus Point Hotel. The building was demolished in 1930. *CCHS*

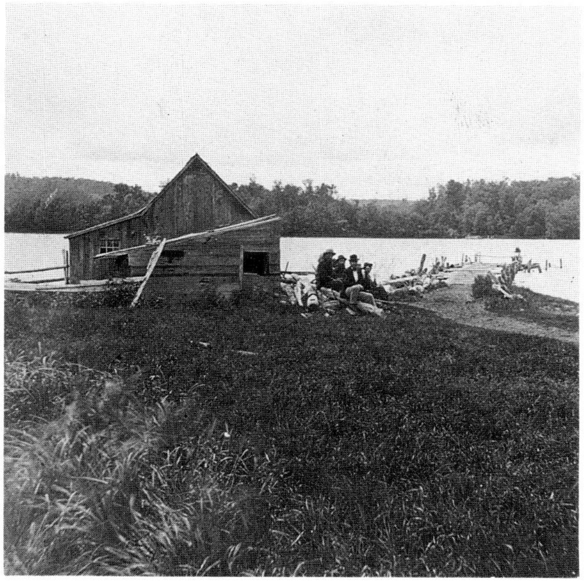

Bemus Point-Stow Ferry, ca. 1873. The early ferries were boarded from docks on either side of the lake. *CCHS*

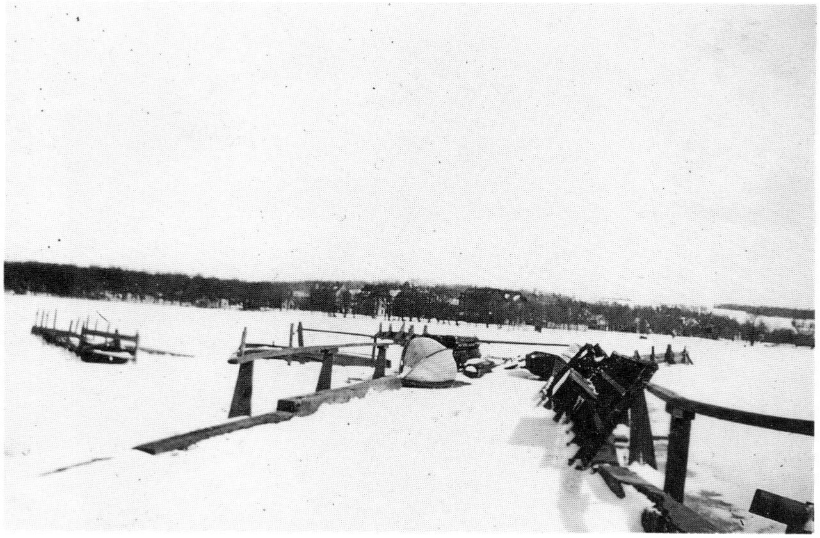

Bemus Point-Stow Ferry, 1916. Obviously, the ferry did not operate in the winter when the lake was frozen. In 1916 a car trip from Bemus Point to Stow would have taken up to three hours. JE

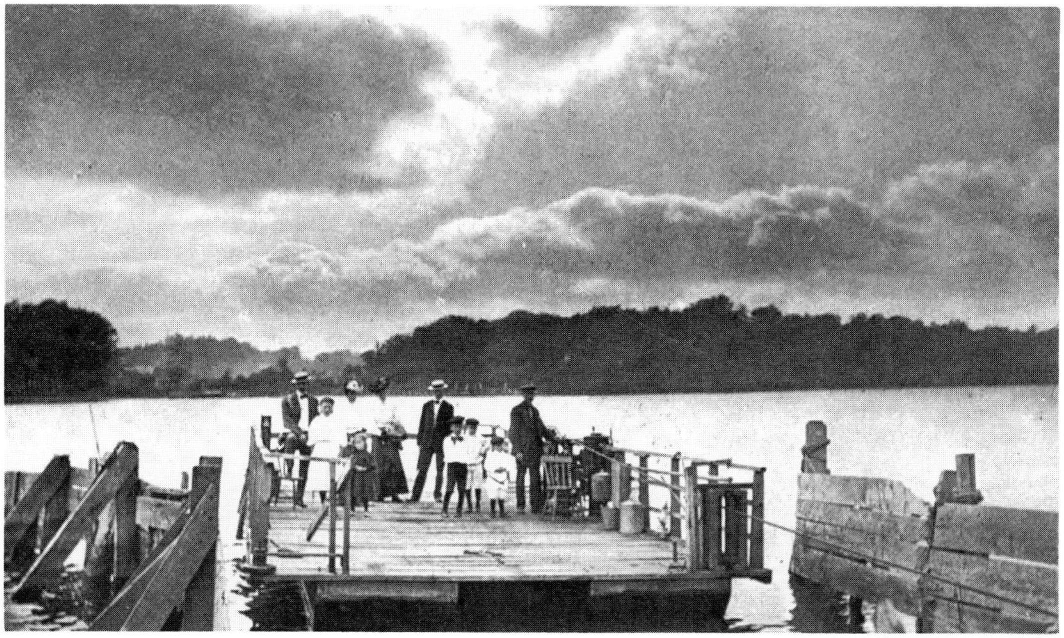

Bemus Point-Stow ferry, ca. 1905. Tom Bemus' first ferry was a simple log raft pulled by hand across the narrows. A steam engine provided power for the version above. The cable line rested on the lake bottom when the ferry was not in operation. *RL*

Bemus Point-Stow ferry, ca. 1905. The *City of Pittsburgh* awaits passage of the ferry. Steamboats had to be extremely wary of the ferry cable. *RW*

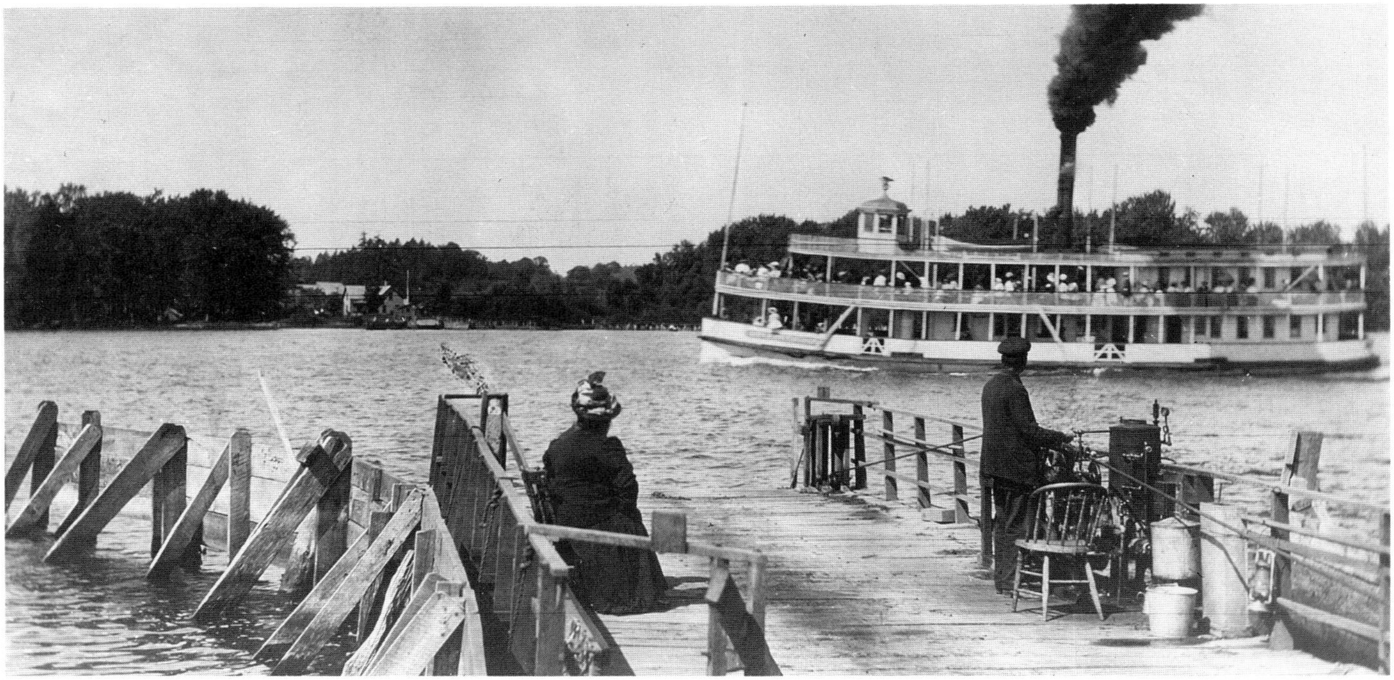

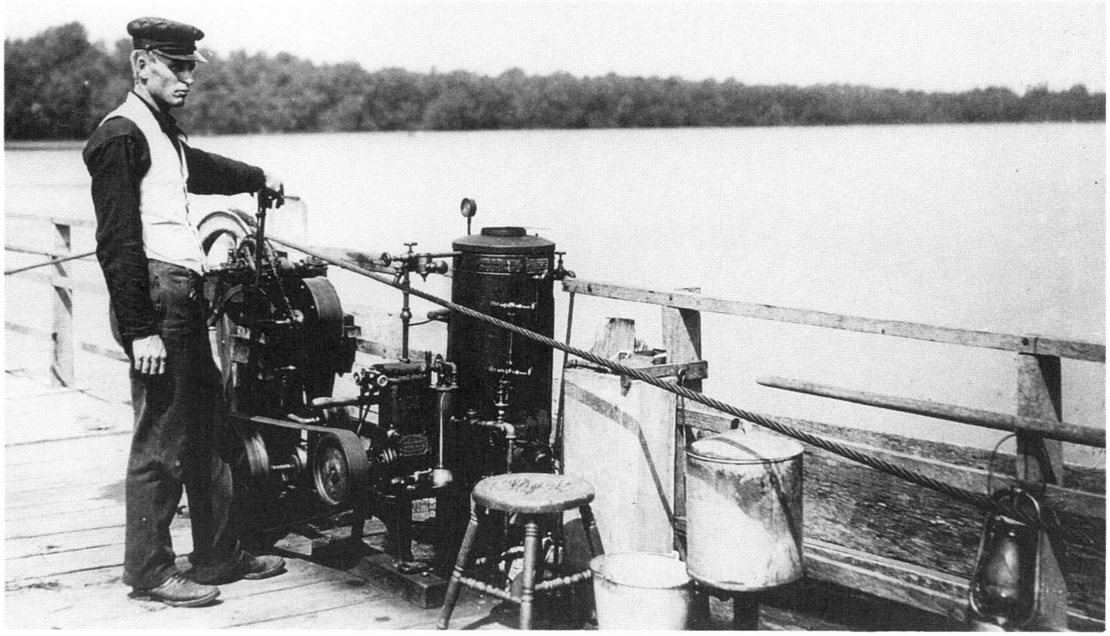

Bemus Point-Stow ferry, ca. 1905. Alton Ball, owner-operator of the Bemus Point-Stow ferry. Alton passed on the operation of the ferry to his son Gerald. His ferry was powered by a steam engine. Note the boiler. A gasoline-driven engine succeeded the steam engine. *FHS*

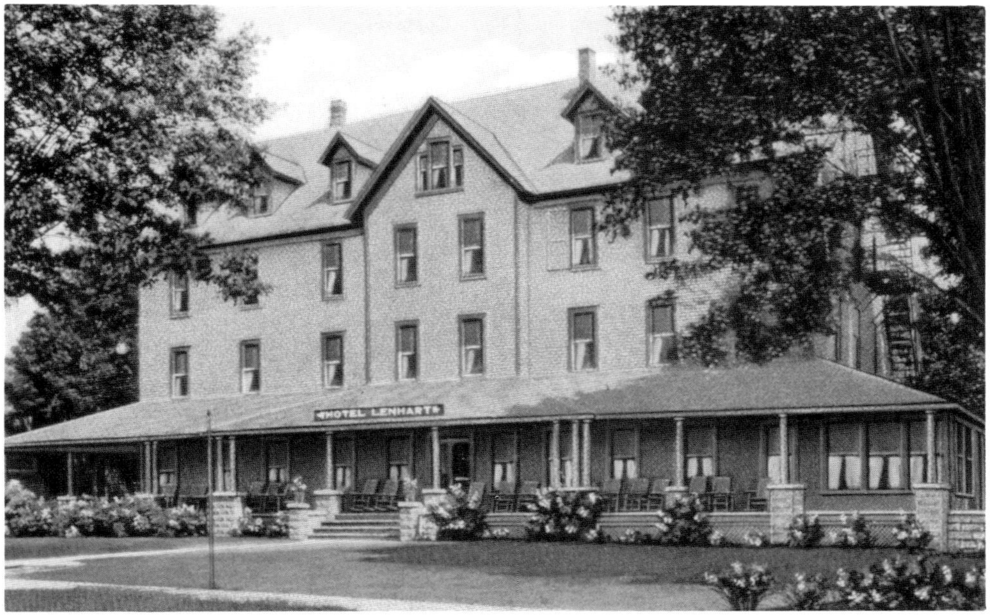

Hotel Lenhart, ca. 1925. One of two surviving nineteenth-century Chautauqua Lake hotels. The Lenhart is operated today by John and George Johnston, grandsons of Dr. Lenhart. *CCHS*

Casino and Village Park, ca. 1930s. The present Casino, situated between the ferry and the village park, was built in 1930. During the Great Depression and the war years, the Casino was the place to be to hear the Big Bands and dance the latest craze. The village park and beach were created in 1926 on land formerly belonging to the owners of the Hotel Lenhart. Still used as a park and swimming area, it is also the site of an annual art show attracting hundreds of visitors each summer. *CCHS*

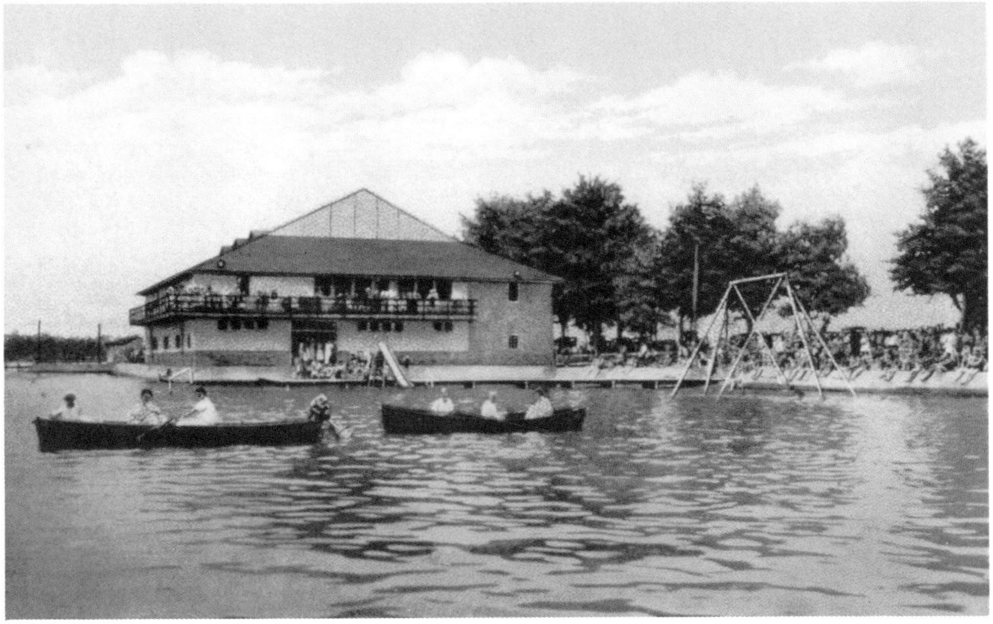

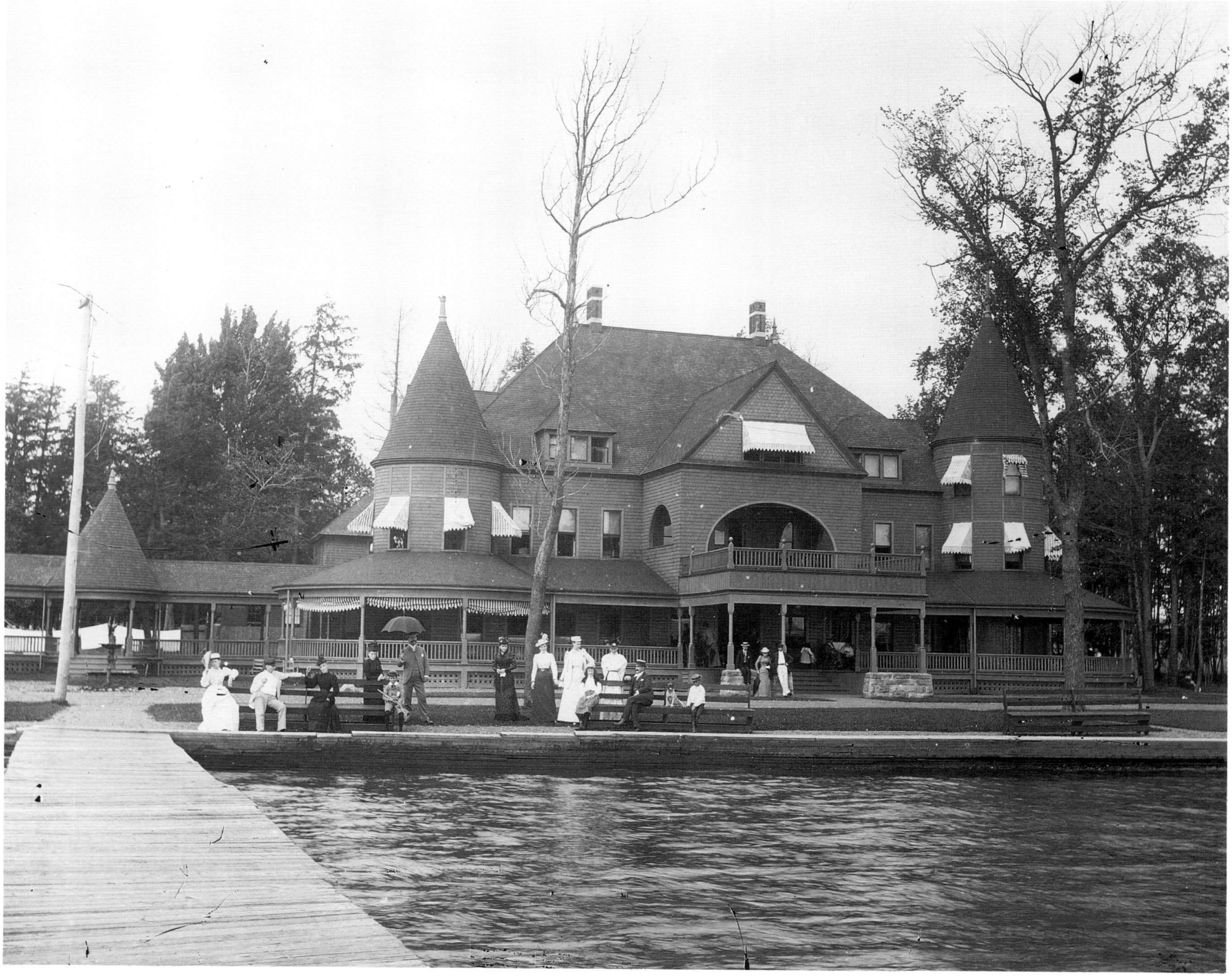

Page 89

LOWER EAST LAKE

BELLEVIEW GRIFFITH'S POINT GREENHURST FLUVANNA

In February, 1805 Jeremiah Griffith left Madison County for Ohio with his wife and six children. While travelling through Batavia, he met by chance two acquaintances who convinced him to go instead to Chautauqua Lake. The family settled at what came to be called Griffith's Point. Jeremiah Griffith's descendants remained, participating in the area's development. Griffith's Point became a favorite spot for fishing, picnics, and sporting events. Its busy hotels, the Lake Shore, and a smaller establishment, the Penfold Hotel, attracted many a summer sojourner, local residents and tourists alike. Joseph Smiley arrived in Chautauqua County in 1810 and settled just above Griffith's Point. The area that became the site of the Belleview Hotel was for a time called Smiley's Point and later Martha's Vineyard. In the late 1870s the area served as grounds for a summer encampment known as Camp Mahoning. Frank Griffith, whose Lake Shore Hotel burned in 1880, built the smaller Belleview a few years later. Griffith's Point is today occupied by the second Sheldon Hall.

Greenhurst was named for Eleazer Green, a prominent Jamestown attorney. In the Spring of 1889, Green, along with C.S. Abbott and A.N. Broadhead, began the development of the Green and Brown tract lying between Fluvanna and Griffith's Point. Building lots and parks were laid out, a state fish hatchery began operations, and a depot for the Chautauqua Lake Railway opened. A year after the guest house opened, it was moved up the lake to make room for the large and extravagant Greenhurst Hotel. The Chadakoin Rowing Club was organized on the Greenhurst grounds in 1889. Local newspapers referred to Greenhurst as the "Newport of the Lake."

Fluvanna was named for Fluvia and Anna, daughters of Nathaniel Fenton and Jacob Fenton. Jacob Fenton and his son, William, operated a pottery in Jamestown. In 1822 they moved the enterprise to Fluvanna to be in closer proximity to the source of clay. Fluvanna became a busy village with a sawmill, gristmill, tannery, blacksmith shop, and light industries including a wagon maker and two shoemakers. The Fluvanna House, built in 1836 when Chautauqua County was still a wilderness, was the first of the lake hotels. Today, the old Fluvanna Road is a residential area and is as pretty and quiet as it was in its early days.

Greenhurst Hotel, ca. 1895. Well-dressed guests await the arrival of a steamboat. The main towers on either side of this "flamboyant" hotel faced the lake and contained "very neat little rooms." The hotel, built in 1890, had facilities for 300 guests. *JE*

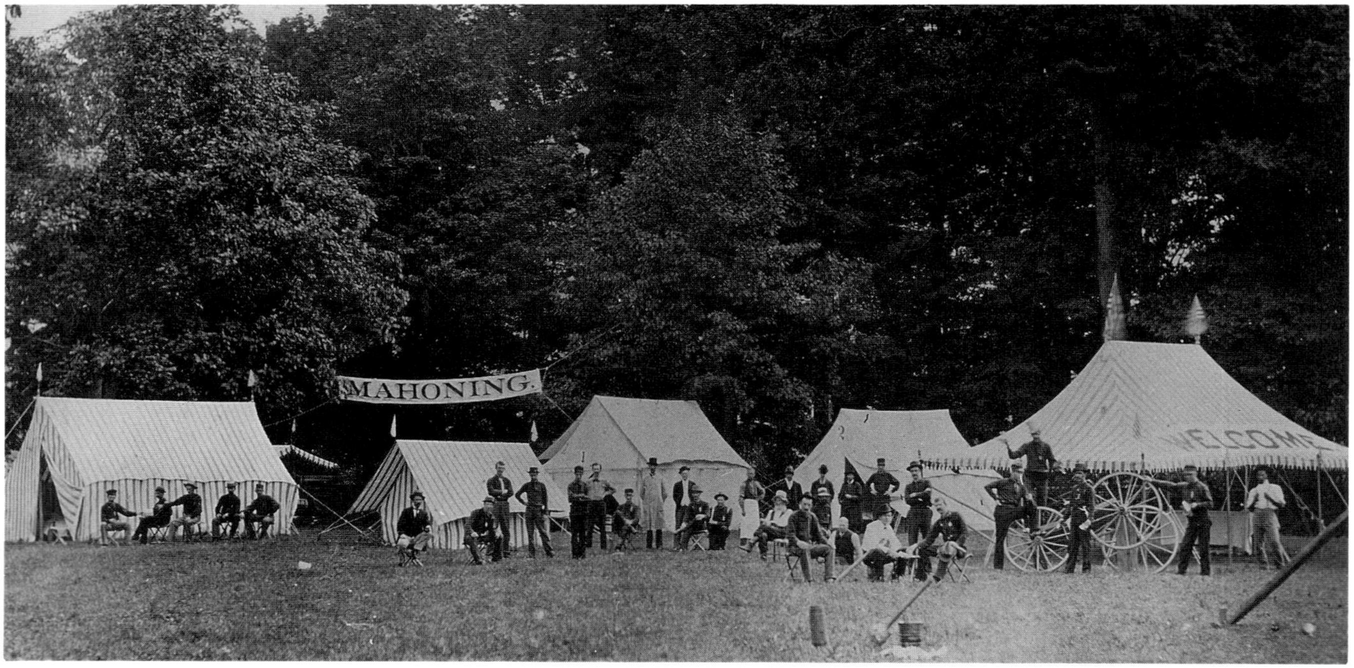

Camp Mahoning, ca. 1879. The site of the future Belleview Hotel was used for several years as the summer encampment of a military group from the Pittsburgh area. The boys probably had a roaring good time during the encampment. The wheeled contraption to the right, known as the "wheel of fortune," was fashioned out of a torn-apart wagon and used for gambling. *CMN*

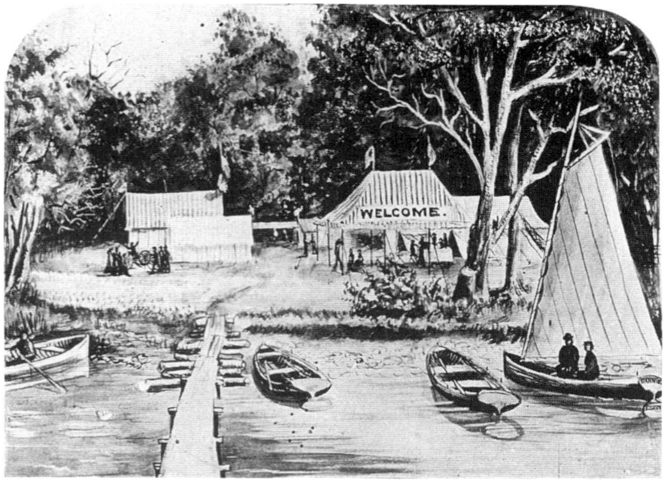

Artist T. J. Nichols' rendering of Camp Mahoning, September 1879. *CMN*

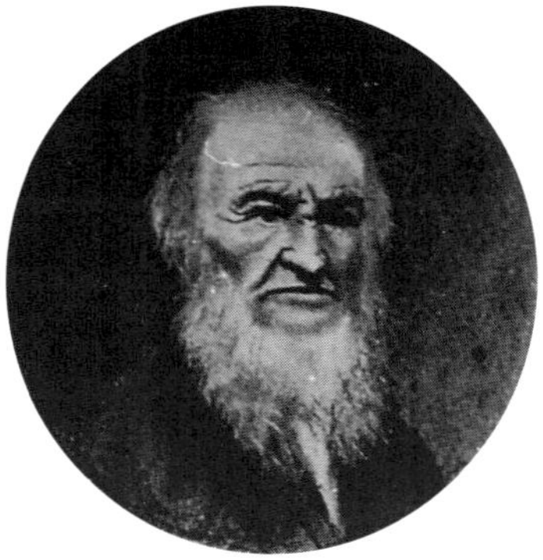

John Smiley, son of Joseph, frequenter at Camp Mahoning. *CMN*

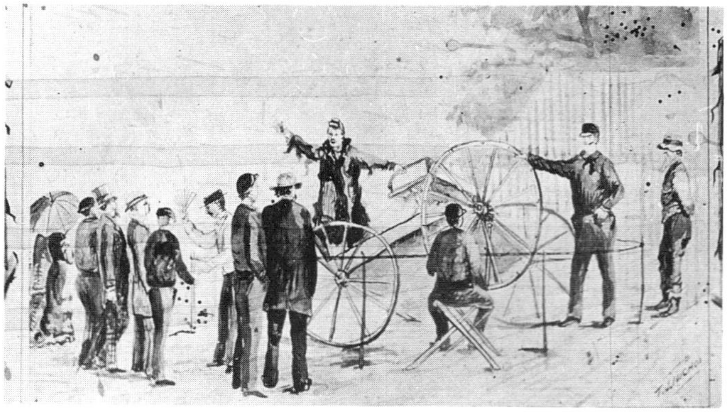

"Let her roll. Let her roll. A hundred can play as well as one." The Wheel of Fortune. *CMN*

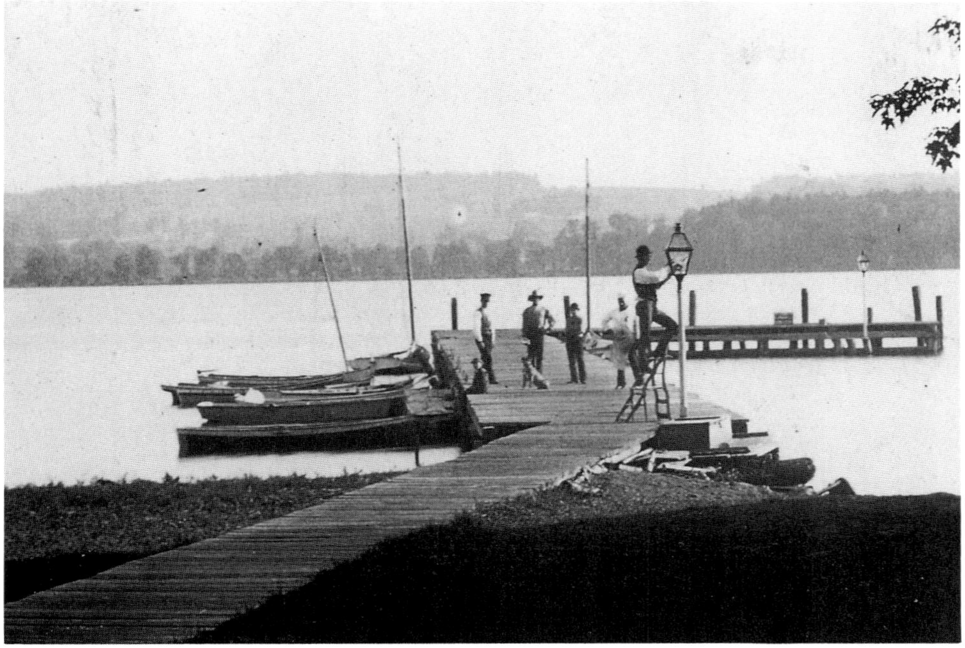

Griffith's Point dock, 1875. Repair or installation of a light fixture at the dock. Lakeview, now Lakewood, is across the water. *CCHS*

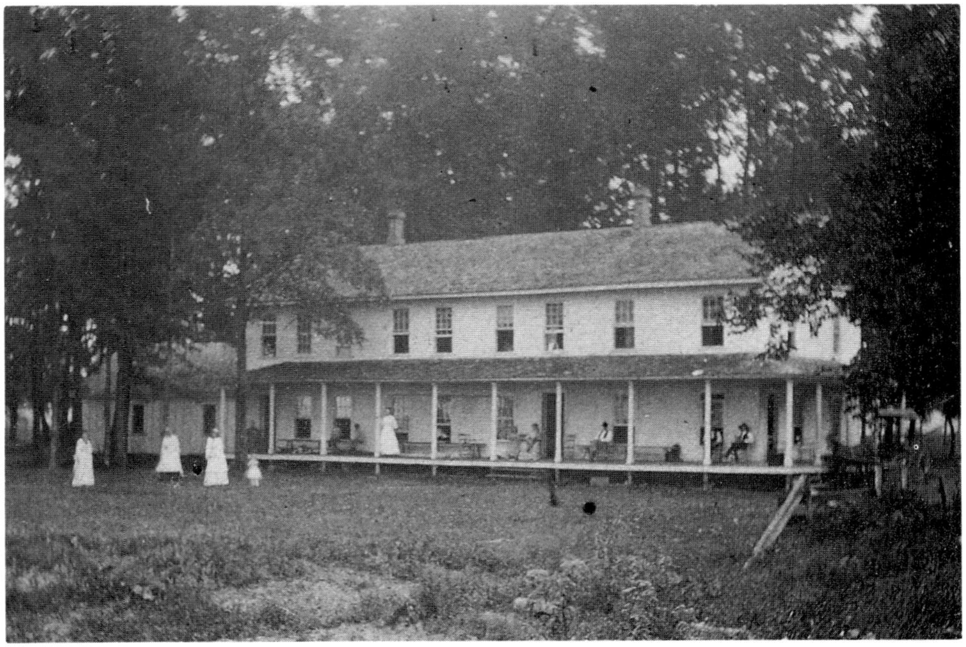

Lake Shore Hotel, ca. 1870. The Lake Shore Hotel, known familiarly as the Griffith's Point Hotel, was completed in 1869 by Jeremiah Griffith's grandson, Frank, and partner Philo Sherwin. The hotel's popularity warranted an expansion after five years which doubled its size. The grounds included a billiards room, dance hall, bowling alley, and laundry. When the addition to the hotel was completed in 1874, this building became the annex. It was attached to the new building at right angles on the lake's upper side. *CCHS*

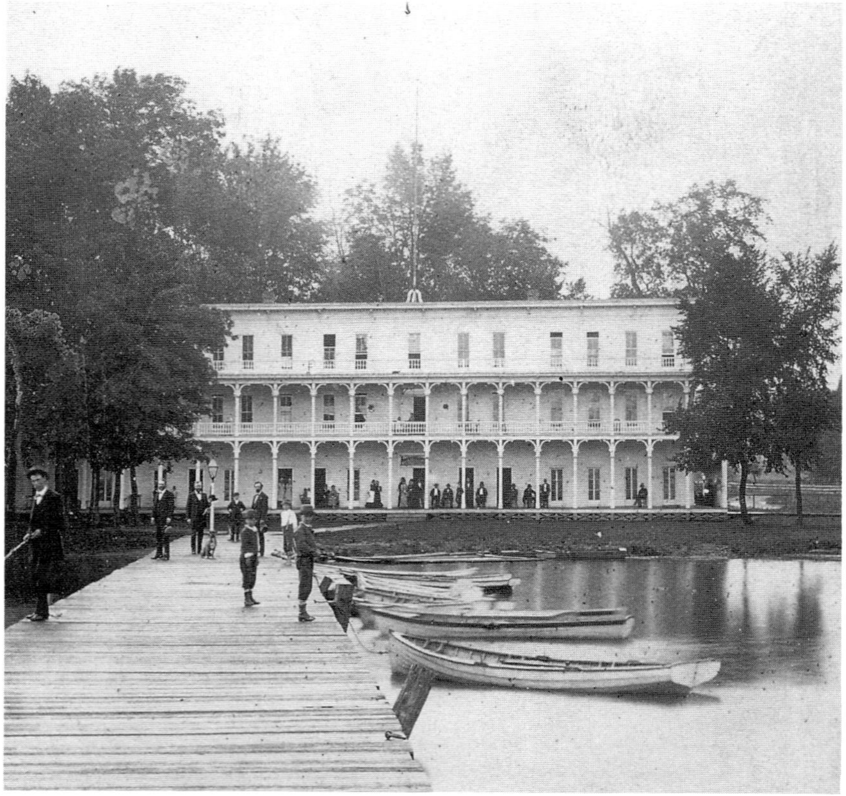

Lake Shore Hotel, ca. 1875. A three-story addition to the hotel, completed in 1874, made the Lake Shore the largest hotel on the lake at that time. Obviously, the hotel was well-patronized. A fleet of rowing, fishing, and sailing boats was available for rent. Griffith's Point was the first regular stop for steamboats out of the boatlanding in Jamestown. The Lake Shore burned to the ground in 1880. *CCHS*

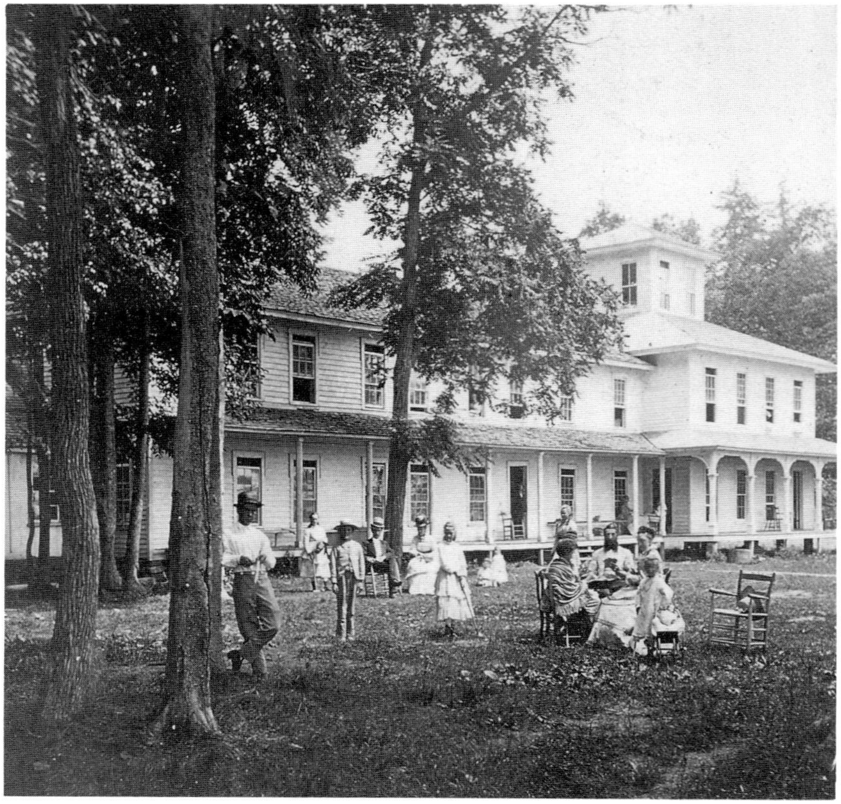

Griffith's Point Hotel, ca. 1876. Victorian era guests lounge in the Lake Shore yard. The party seated in the foreground is playing a game of cards. This photograph was taken from the rear of the hotel on the upper side of the lake. The addition is to the right, the lake beyond. *CCHS*

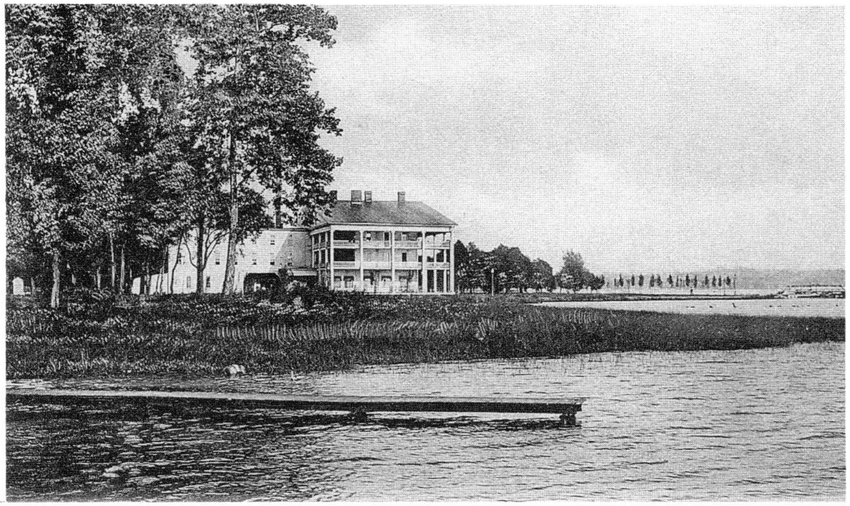

Sheldon Hall, ca. 1910. Sheldon Hall was operated as a hotel under the management of Porter Sheldon's son, Ralph, until 1915. The building was razed in that year, and Ralph Sheldon built a smaller residence for his family away from the water. The second Sheldon Hall remains today a bed and breakfast inn. *RL*

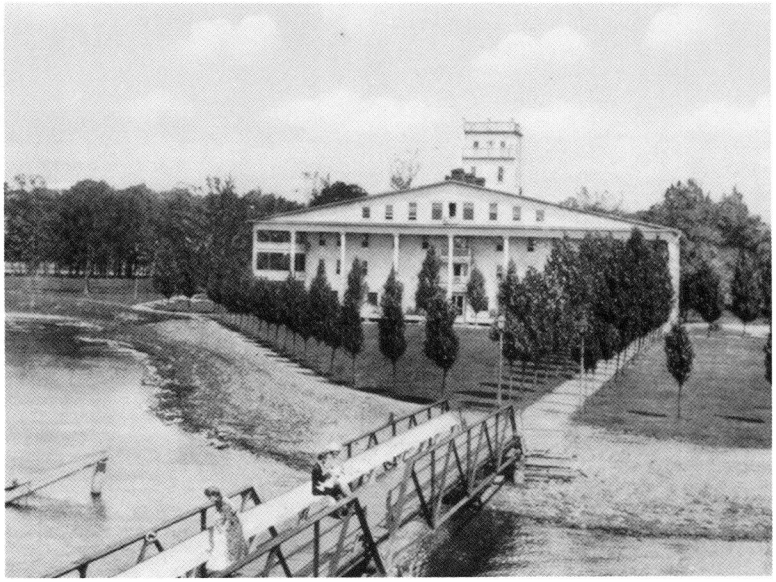

Sheldon Hall, ca. 1910. Porter Sheldon, a wealthy Jamestown attorney, built his magnificent lakeside home and hotel in 1900. The hotel was separated from the lake by a row of poplar trees. The dock was well-constructed, the grounds beautifully manicured, and all appointments first class. Mr. Sheldon had already made his fortune before he invested in a Jamestown firm that manufactured photographic paper. The American Aristotype Company stood just below Mr. Sheldon's Jamestown residence on Prospect Street. Eventually the company was sold to Eastman Kodak. *RL*

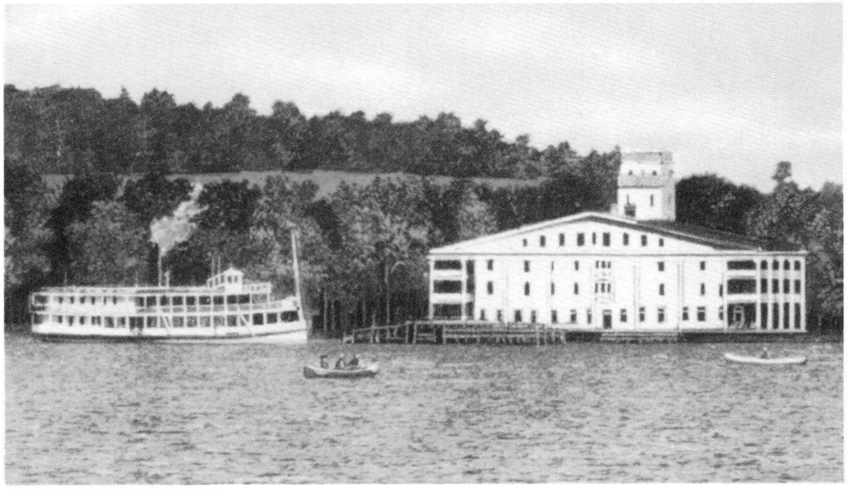

Griffith's Point, ca. 1905. The *City of Pittsburgh* approaches Sheldon Hall. *RL*

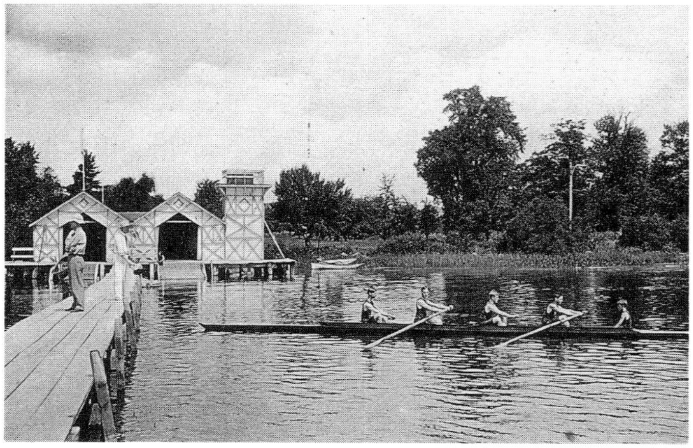

Chadakoin Rowing Club, ca. 1900. Most of the club's members were from prominent area families. The boathouse at Greenhurst featured a tower with a revolving red and white light. The club remained at this location until 1908 when it moved across the lake to Lakewood. *RL*

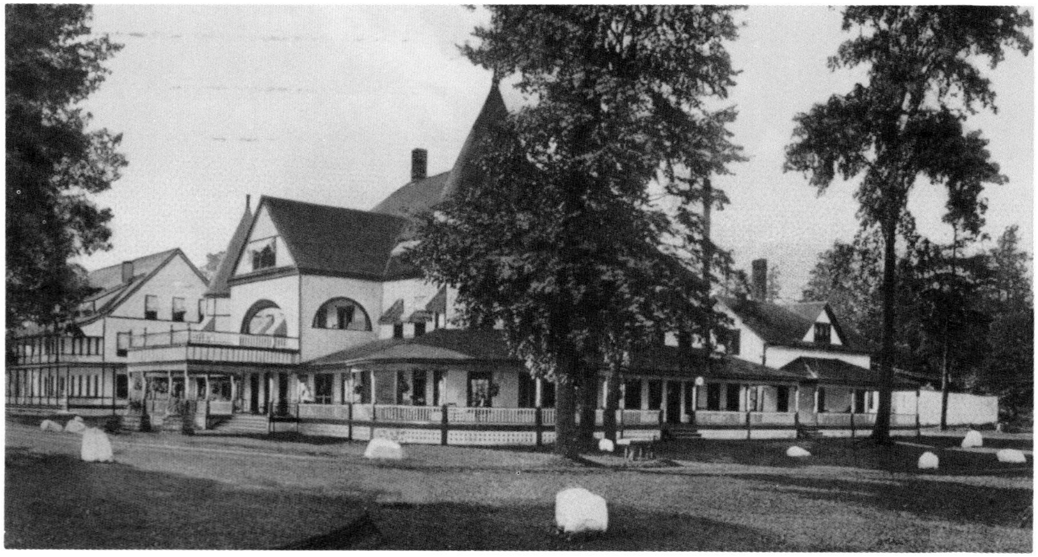

Greenhurst Hotel, ca. 1895. View from the southeast. The original building, a guest house, visible on the left, became the hotel's annex. A covered walkway attached the hotel to the annex. The hotel became the private home of Ralph Preston around 1900. In 1910 it was purchased by George Hurlbert and operated for a few more years as a hotel. The Greenhurst was razed in 1921 by John Prather who had acquired the entire Greenhurst tract. The Annex survived, however, and was operated until 1931 when it was destroyed by fire. *RL*

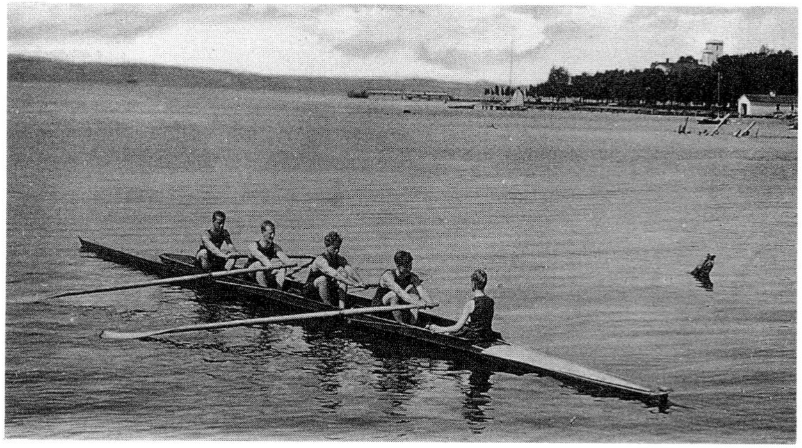

Crew of the Chadakoin Rowing Club. The boathouse in the distance is just below Griffith's Point. *RL*

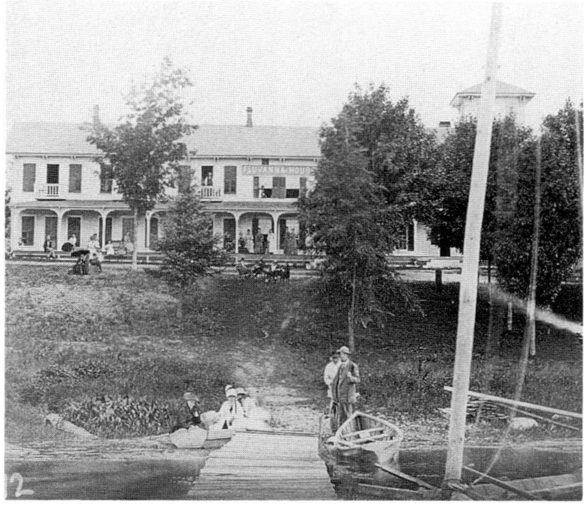

Fluvanna House, ca. 1875. A view from the dock shortly after renovation. The Fluvanna House, built by Samuel Whittemore in 1836, was originally a single-story structure catering to hunters and fishermen. After almost forty years of operation, a second story was added. The hotel was operated under strict temperance guidelines by the Whittemore family until 1888. In the mid 1890s Mahlon C. Martin bought the Fluvanna House and divided it into three sections which he moved to various parts of the farm. These structures became private residences. One remains today. *CCHS*

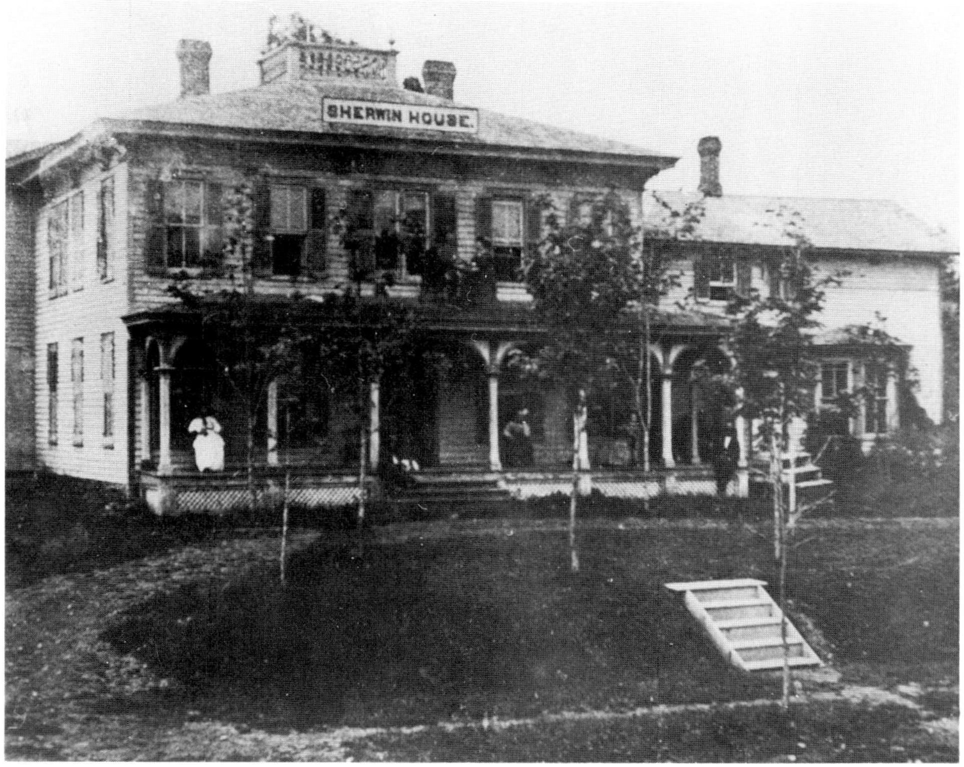

Sherwin House, ca. 1888. Philo Sherwin's hotel, built in 1872, stood just below the Fluvanna House. The hotel achieved great notoriety under the name Hotel Florence in the 1890s after a murder-suicide occurred on its premises. It was called the Bonny Inn when it burned in 1918. *VN*

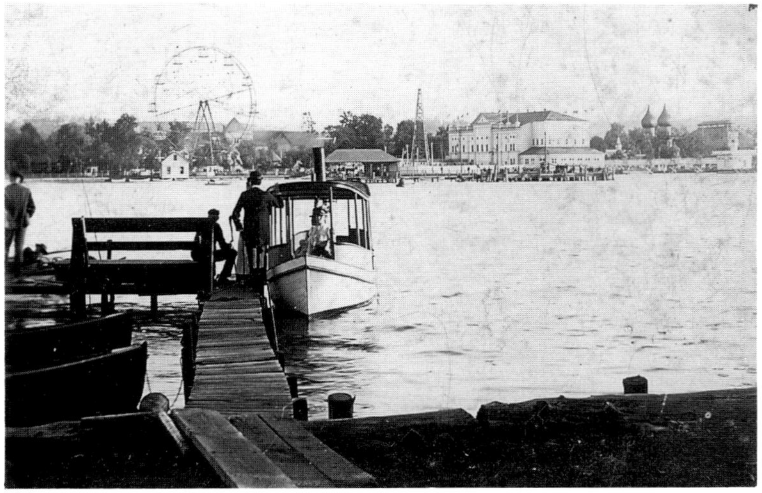

"Celoron from Sooneron," ca. 1900. Celoron Park lay directly across the lake from Fluvanna. The name "Sooneron" was a play on "Celoron." The Burtis Bay area just above Celoron was at this time called "Lateron." *CCHS*

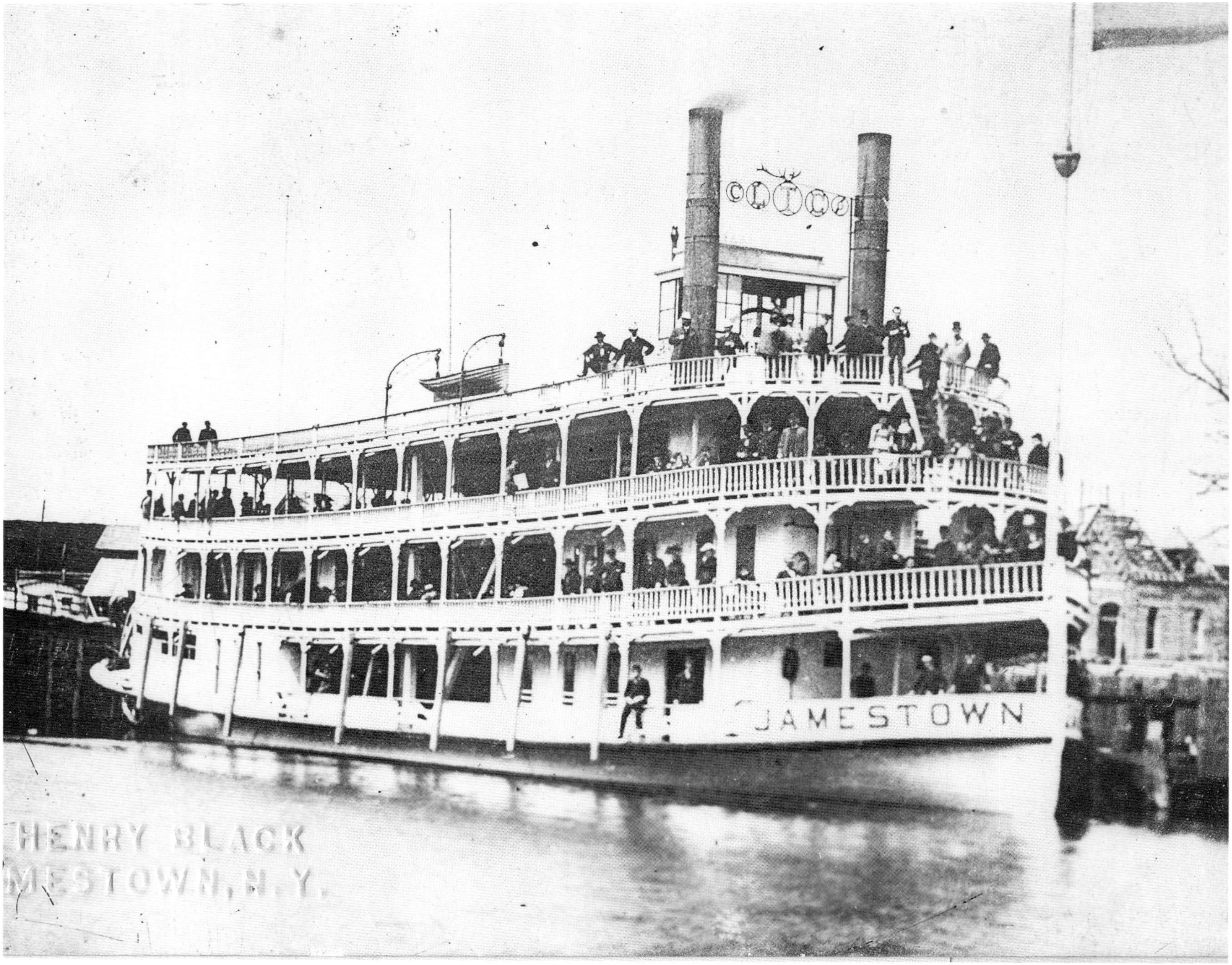
JAMESTOWN
HENRY BLACK
MESTOWN, N.Y.

BOATS

The grace and beauty of Chautauqua Lake's steamboat fleet complemented the physical beauty of the lake and its surroundings. The first steamboat was launched in 1828, a mere twenty-five years after the county's first settlement at Westfield. The boat was called the *Chautauque*. For most of the nineteenth century lake destinations were accessible only by water. By the end of the century, when the lake hosted a thriving summer trade, the fleet had grown out of proportion to the available traffic. Competition for passengers was fierce until the Broadhead family acquired the two major competing lines in 1891. The steamers usually changed names with successive owners. Before the Broadheads' acquisition, many were named for American Indians. The Broadheads named their boats after the major cities from which Chautauqua Lake drew its summer trade. After the arrival of the trains, which were faster and more efficient, steamboats were used largely for excursion or pleasure trips. The last of Chautauqua Lake's great steamboats, the *City of Jamestown*, made its final trip in 1958.

The *Jamestown*, formerly the *Nettie Fox*, ca. 1882. Three separate steamboats carried the name "Jamestown" on Chautauqua Lake. This impressive steamer, the second *Jamestown*, was the first stern wheeler and the largest boat ever to run the lake. After the third deck was added in 1879, she could carry three thousand passengers. "CLTCO" between the smokestacks signifies "Chautauqua Lake Transit Co." The Fairmount Avenue bridge and the boatlanding water pumping station are visible behind the *Jamestown*. *CCHS*

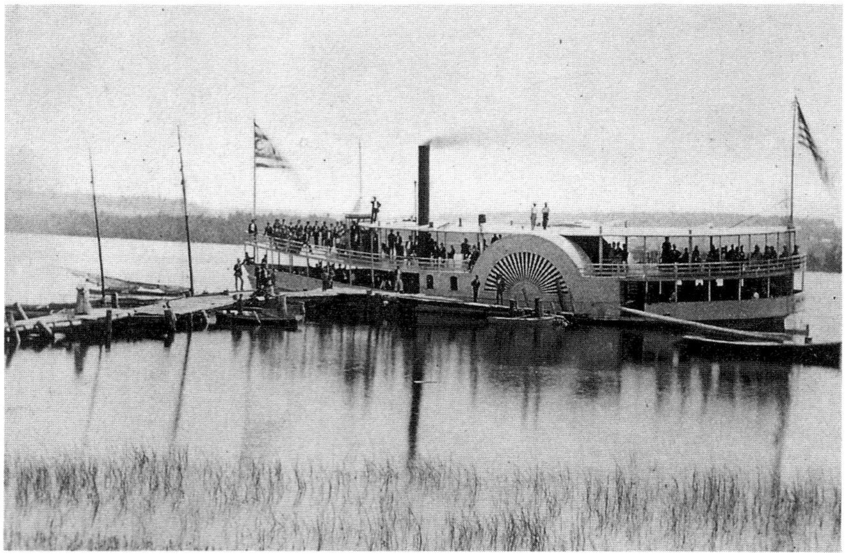

The *Col. Phillips*, ca. 1873. A steropticon view at what looks like the Griffith's Point dock. The *Col. Phillips* had a short life. She was built in 1873, rebuilt and lengthened in 1875, and burned at Mayville in 1876. *CCHS*

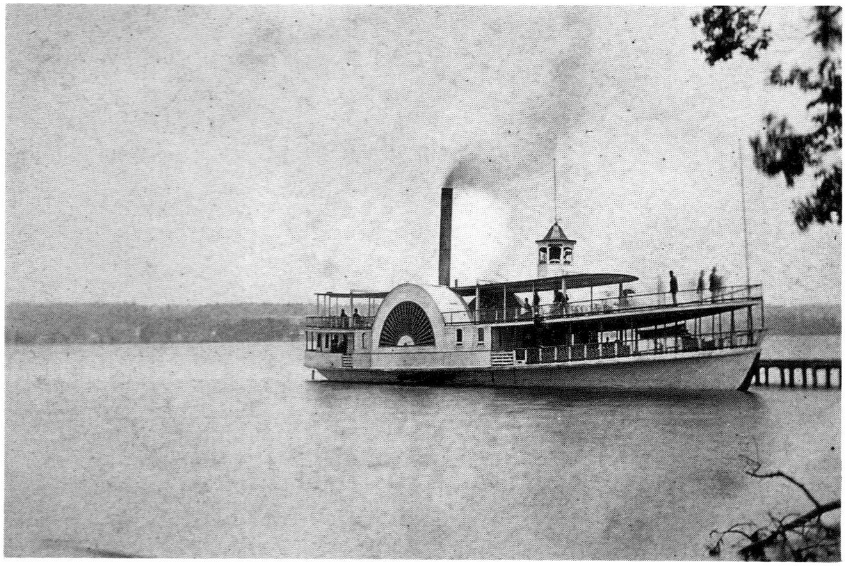

The *Col. Phillips* at Lakeview (Lakewood) landing. ca. 1875. A stereopticon view after she was rebuilt. Note the pilot house on top, the smokestack farther toward the stern. *CCHS*

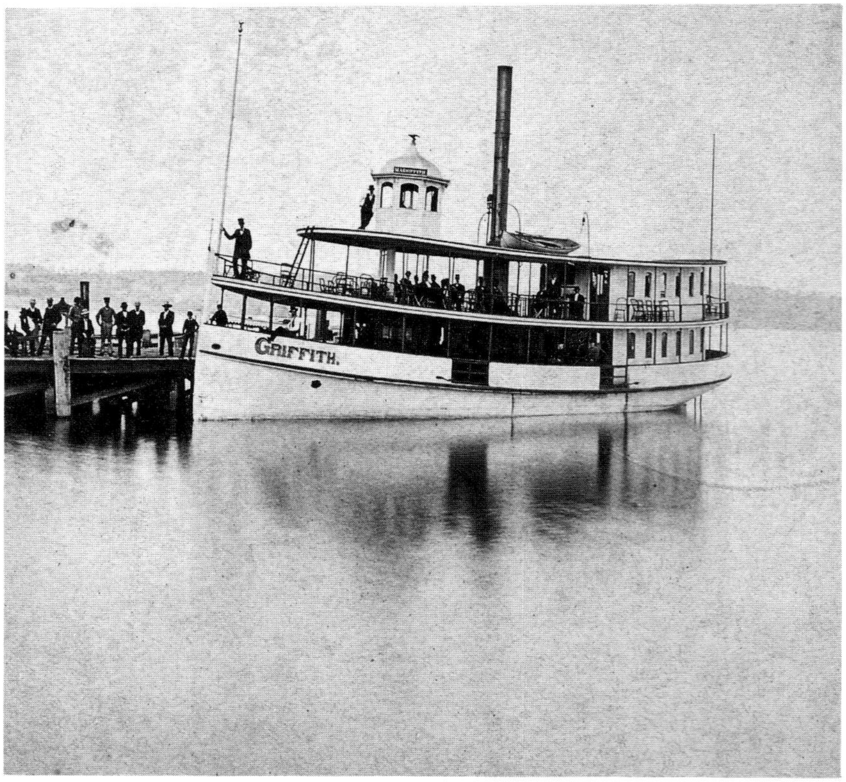

The *Griffith* docked at Mayville, ca. 1875. Originally the *M.A. Griffith*, she was owned by the Griffith family. She later became the *Winona* and after the Broadheads acquired the steamers in 1891, the *City of Erie*. *CCHS*

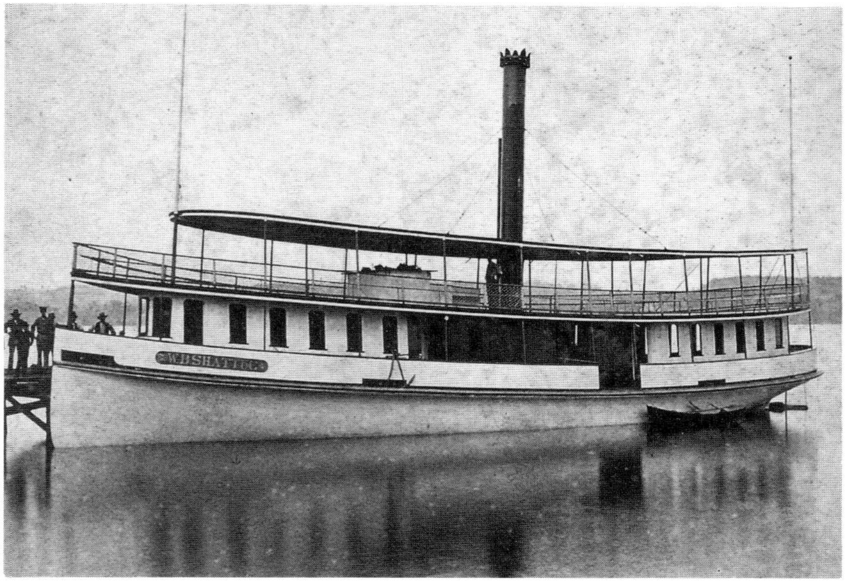

The *W.B. Shattuc*, ca. 1879. The *W.B. Shattuc* was one of several boats financed by railroad men. She became the *Minehaha*, then the *City of Pittsburgh. CCHS*

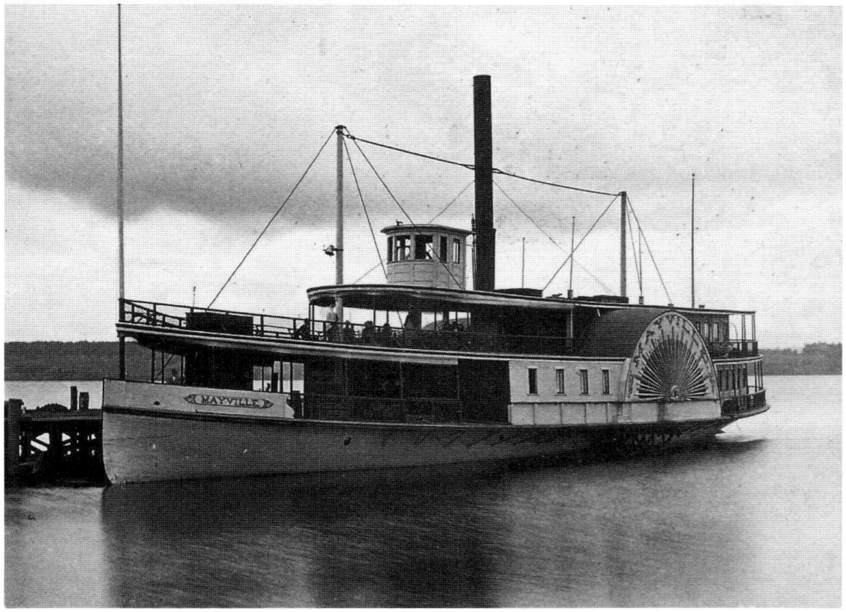

The *Mayville*, ca. 1880. The side wheeler *Mayville* was built in 1876. Although she was well appointed inside, she seemed to soak up water. Posts and superstructure above the deck were an attempt to keep the *Mayville* in proper shape. The *Mayville* was not commissioned after 1885. She was demolished in 1892. *CCHS*

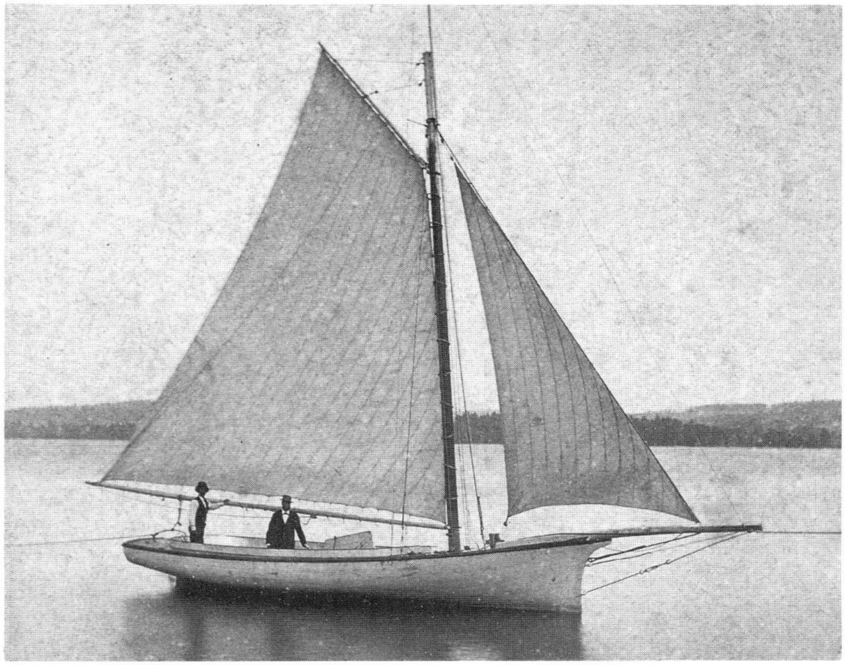

The sailing yacht *Kate Dunham,* ca. 1880. The beautiful lines of a nineteenth-century sailboat. *CCHS*

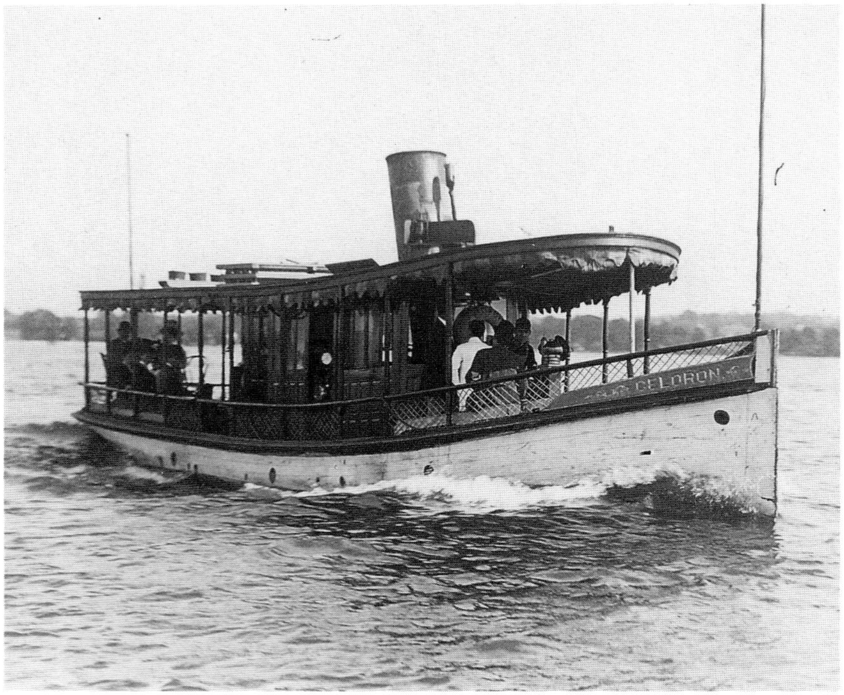

The ferry *Celoron*, ca. 1898. Formerly the *Arabia*, the *Celoron* was one of two identical fifty foot steamers purchased by Almet Broadhead in 1895. This and the *Greenhurst*, formerly the *America*, were part of Chicago's Columbian Exposition fleet used to carry excursion parties out to Lake Michigan. The little steamers ran between Celoron, Greenhurst, and Lakewood. After the 1911 season, they were pulled from the water because of the stiff competition from small gasoline launches. *RL*

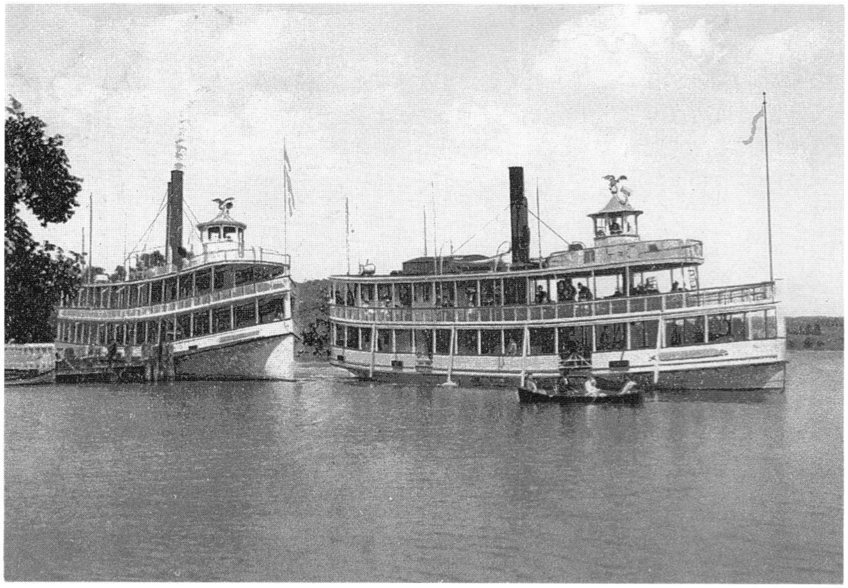

The *City of New York* and the *City of Cleveland*. The City of New York was the picnic boat after the second *Jamestown* was destroyed in 1892. She is shown here tied up at Long Point dock awaiting the return of her excursion party. The short dock at Long Point could not accommodate two large steamers. Passengers from the *City of Cleveland*, on her regular run, had to pass through the *City of New York* to reach the dock. *CCHS*

The *City of Buffalo*, ca. 1900. Her partly steel hull made her one of the steadiest boats on the lake. The flagposts, added by the Broadheads after their purchase, flew Scandinavian flags. She was burned at Celoron in 1929. *RL*

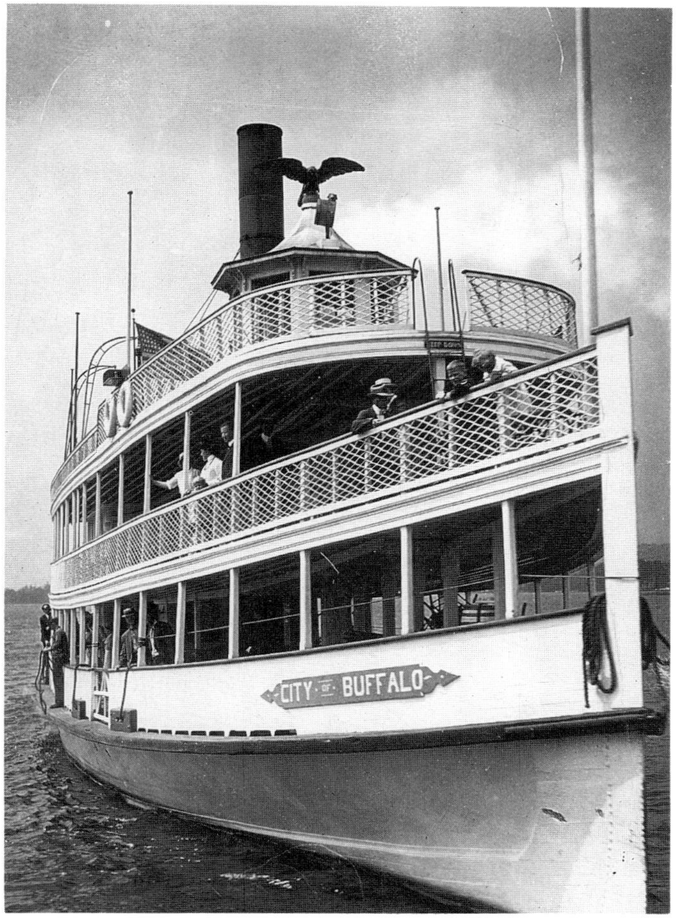

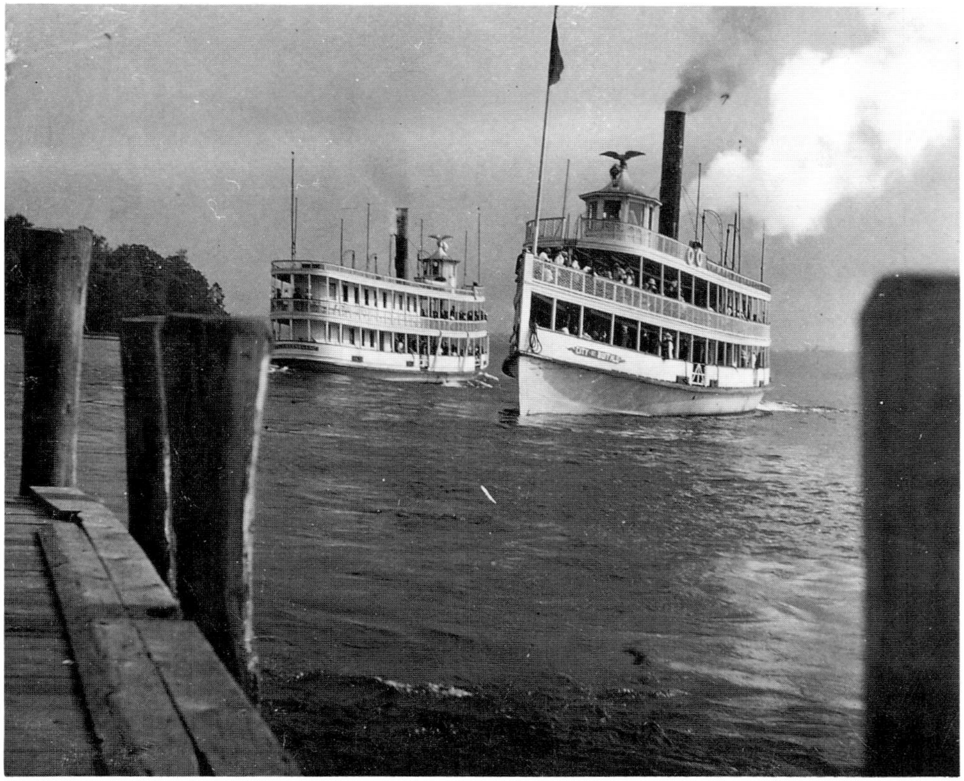

The *City of Buffalo* approaches Midway Park as the *City of Cleveland* departs. Maple Springs is visible to the left. *RL*

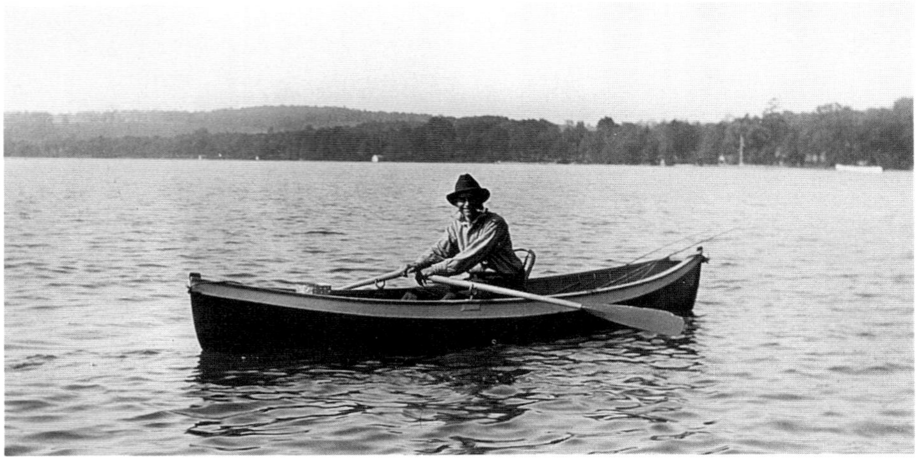

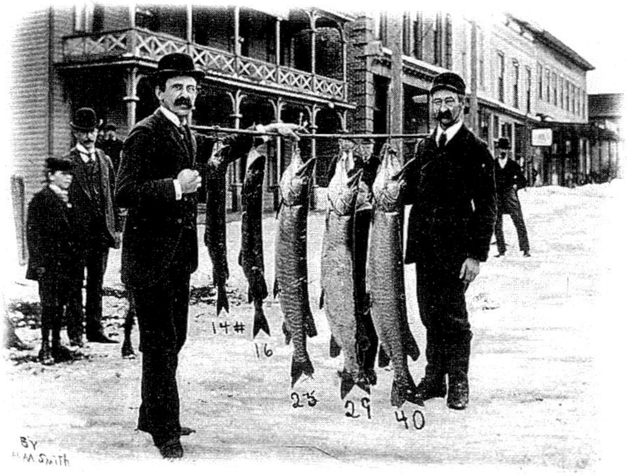
14#
16
23
29
40
BY

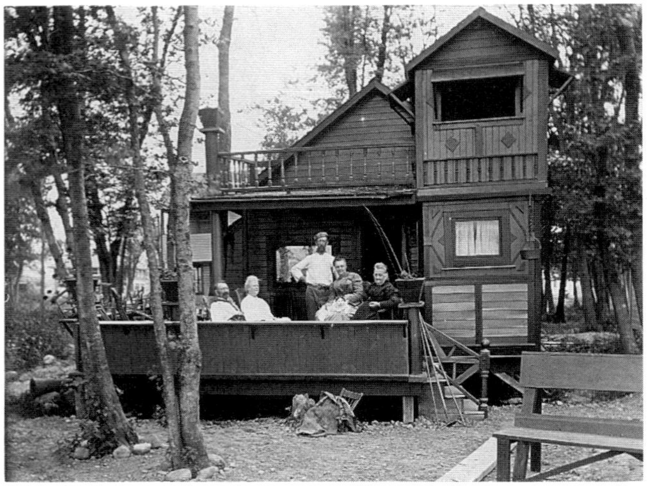

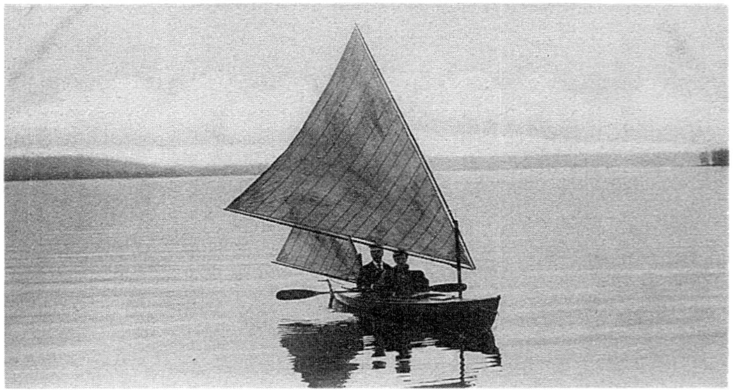